Guaranteed
Annual
Income:
An
Integrated
Approach

GUARANTEED ANNUAL INCOME: AN INTEGRATED APPROACH

Background Papers and Proceedings of
the Nuffield Canadian Seminar
Held at Ste-Adèle, Quebec, April 12-14, 1972
Organized by
The Canadian Council on Social Development

Copyright © 1973 by The Canadian Council on Social Development
Published May 1973 by The Canadian Council on Social Development,
55 Parkdale Avenue, Ottawa K1Y 1E5, Canada

International Standard Book Number 0-88810-000-0
Library of Congress Catalog Card Number 72-96831

Printed in Canada by The Runge Press Limited, Ottawa
Design: Eiko Emori

Price: $6.00

The Canadian Council on Social Development is pleased to present the Background Papers and Proceedings of the Nuffield Canadian Seminar, 1972. *Guaranteed Annual Income: an Integrated Approach* is a contribution to the important and growing debate on a reformed social security system for all.

On behalf of the Council and its Board of Governors, I strongly endorse the thanks, expressed in the Foreword by the seminar co-chairmen, to those who contributed to the success of the project. I would also add our profound gratitude to the co-chairmen themselves, J. Harvey Perry and Gérald Fortin, for the devotion and skill they brought to every phase of their heavy and challenging assignment.

Agnes M. Benidickson
President
The Canadian Council on Social Development

Ottawa
May 1973

Contents

Foreword

The Nuffield Canadian Seminar was established by the British Nuffield Foundation to discuss subjects of current concern and involve individuals from a variety of backgrounds and disciplines, from Canada and other countries. The Canadian Council on Social Development was chosen by the Nuffield Foundation Canadian Policy Committee, whose secretariat is provided by the Association of Universities and Colleges of Canada, to organize the 1972 seminar. The topic submitted by the Council was an integrated approach to guaranteed annual income.

The Council proposed this important subject both because of the general wide interest in it and because its examination is a key part of the work of our Task Force on Social Security, which is engaged in "a comprehensive consideration of policies and programs, both current and desirable, for Canadian social security." The task force has been responsible for planning the seminar through a special sub-committee.*

According to the terms of the Nuffield award for the seminar, about 30 participants were to be selected on the basis of one-half from Canada, a quarter from other British Commonwealth countries and a quarter from the rest of the world. The final number was 33: Canada, 17; United Kingdom, 4; Australia and New Zealand, one each; United States, 4; and one each from France, Israel, Sweden, Switzerland, West Germany and Yugoslavia. In addition, 15 Canadian observers attended. These were mainly members of the Council's task force who were not included in the participants, and representatives of federal and provincial government departments. Observers took part in the small group discussions but not in those of the plenary sessions. The seminar was conducted in French and English and the proceedings are published in both languages.

In selecting participants, the Planning Committee sought strategically placed and knowledgeable people in Canada and in other industrially advanced countries so that the conditions and experience to be discussed would be broadly comparable. The participants were drawn from backgrounds and disciplines such as social welfare, economics, sociology, government, taxation and public finance,

*See the Appendices for the listing of both groups as well as the list of participants and observers.

business and organized labor. They were chosen as experts who would exchange ideas and information and discuss the various approaches to guaranteed income, rather than formulate specific plans and programs.

The general approach of the Planning Committee to the seminar program embodied the assumption that, at least for the foreseeable future, the most desirable form of guaranteed annual income is achieved through full-time employment with adequate earnings or through an adequate and dignified form of income security for unemployables, and that the seminar should examine the implications of the fact that for many people this cannot or does not occur. The subjects of the background papers, commissioned from authors with leading positions in their particular fields, were designed to provide material that would assist in discussion of the actions necessary to correct this situation. The seminar agenda was organized around these topics. Plenary sessions alternated with small group discussions, the highlights of which were reported on the final day.

In this book, the background papers have been placed before the summary of the discussions since the papers were read in advance by those attending the seminar. We asked Reuben C. Baetz, Executive Director of the Canadian Council on Social Development, and a seminar participant, to provide an introduction, from his personal viewpoint, that would help the reader assess the major themes of the wide-ranging, diverse and often contradictory material presented in the papers and the seminar discussions. Since Canada as the host country has a special stake in the results of the seminar, we also asked Mr. Baetz to comment, against the background of the seminar, on guaranteed annual income in the Canadian scene today. We believe, however, that much of what he has to say will be applicable to other countries.

We feel that the seminar, through its background papers and discussions, has made a real contribution to the understanding of a guaranteed income for all, and of the difficulties to be overcome in achieving this challenging goal. The participants' use of this increased knowledge and understanding and the publication of this book will, it is hoped, be of much assistance to Canada and other countries in their search for solutions to social and economic problems.

Finally, we wish to thank, on behalf of the Planning Committee, the Task Force on Social Security and the Canadian Council on Social Development, the many who made the seminar possible. Among these are the Nuffield Foundation itself for its initiative in bringing the seminar into being and its substantial financial grant; The Canada Council which made a grant toward travel expenses of participants; and the Department of the Secretary of State for Canada which assisted with the substantial costs of translation.

The Canadian Council on Social Development bore the major financial burden of the seminar, mainly through the provision of personnel; most sincere thanks are due to staff members who contributed so unsparingly to the planning, organization and operation of the seminar, and to the publications staff, all of whom were heavily involved in the book. In particular, we should like to express our deep gratitude to Patricia Godfrey, the Project Director, whose helpful ideas and unstinting attention to every detail contributed immeasurably both to the success of the seminar and to the book, of which she was editor-in-chief. As co-chairmen, we also want to express to our colleagues on the Planning Committee our appreciation of the large amount of time and thought they devoted to developing the concept and agenda of the seminar.

Last, but not least, we thank those attending the seminar – especially the authors. Without the participants' and observers' generous contribution of time, knowledge and ideas, no seminar could, of course, have been held and no book published.

J. Harvey Perry
Executive Director
The Canadian Bankers'
Association

Gérald Fortin
Director
Centre for Urban
and Regional Research
National Institute for
Scientific Research
University of Quebec

Co-chairmen
Nuffield Canadian Seminar, 1972

The Nuffield Canadian Seminar and After: A Personal View

by Reuben C. Baetz
Executive Director
The Canadian Council on Social Development

When the Planning Committee for the Nuffield Canadian Seminar, 1972, invited me to contribute an opening article for this book, it asked for considerably more than the usual short introduction. The request was to indicate what I see as the principal accomplishments and highlights of the seminar, and then, with the seminar's deliberations in mind, to discuss a guaranteed annual income as it relates to the Canadian scene today and in the near future.

Obviously, what I have to say is based on my own opinions which may or may not be shared by the Planning Committee or by others attending the seminar. My hope is that my statement will provide a useful focus and framework for readers, particularly Canadians, to the wealth of material that follows.

The Seminar: Accomplishments and Themes

The seminar was not intended to produce a detailed blueprint for a program that would achieve the goal of a guaranteed annual income. Rather, it aimed at collecting views and opinions from experts with a variety of backgrounds and disciplines to assist the Canadian Council on Social Development in developing a comprehensive and integrated approach to the subject. It is not surprising, therefore, that no definitive recommendations and conclusions, and only a limited consensus, emerged from the seminar discussions. However, these and the background papers have provided us with something perhaps even more important: the identification of major issues and questions which must inevitably be faced in considering the objective of a guaranteed annual income, and an intensive examination of the advantages and pitfalls and of alternative methods which might be designed to achieve that goal. Through the seminar, we have brought together in this book, for the first time in Canada or indeed anywhere, a wide range of factual knowledge and informed opinion, as well as possible choices in shaping the future of social security and social development measures not only in Canada but also in other countries. Thus, in my view, the seminar accomplished its purpose to a highly satisfactory degree.

Both in the background papers and in the sessions, the discussion ranged from a high philosophic plane to down-to-earth grappling with many of the practical problems inherent in the seminar topic. Some felt that too much time was spent on the high plane, others showed impatience with the extensive attention given to specifics. Yet, through this wide approach, few if any, I think, left the seminar without some enhancement of their knowledge and understanding or change in their view of the total subject. In particular, the seminar's international character, which made possible an exchange of information and views among people from different countries and with different experience, was both interesting and valuable.

It is difficult to make a limited selection for comment from among the many highlights of the seminar. I shall therefore confine myself to three major broad themes that recurred again and again in the seminar discussions: the definition and scope of guaranteed annual income, employment and GAI, and the interdependence of social and economic policies. These themes appear to me to be a significant base from which to assess and apply to the Canadian scene the great variety of more detailed opinions and proposals presented and analyzed in the background papers and seminar sessions.

1 Definition and Scope of the Guaranteed Annual Income

No attempt was made at the seminar to agree on a precise definition of a guaranteed annual income. This lack of agreement led at times to problems in semantics and communication. For some, the term "guaranteed annual income" was used as a concept, a desirable socioeconomic goal or objective; others saw it as being synonymous with one specific method, such as the negative income tax (NIT), employed in achieving that goal. Still others applied the term equally and interchangeably to *either* a specific method *or* a general objective. Nonetheless, there was implicit agreement in the discussions that a GAI, in whatever form, must be adequate to achieve a decent standard of living for all. However, participants identified two differing schools of thought as to how to measure adequacy – or the reverse of the coin, inadequacy and poverty.

The first approach, and the one most often used, is that of attempting to define in absolute terms some level of income necessary for providing a minimum standard of living – that is, providing a subsistence income. Both the Economic Council of Canada and the Special Senate Committee on Poverty have drawn poverty lines expressed in absolute dollar levels. Since these poverty lines are not much in excess of present social assistance levels, persons who define poverty in this manner tend to visualize any approach to a guaranteed annual income as a tidy replacement for the present cumbersome and fragmented income security system. As Nicole Martin's paper demonstrates, measures using this approach may improve the actual income position of the poor, but do not necessarily lift them out of poverty; the basic level of GAI payments may be set well below the poverty line, as indeed it is in most current proposals.

The second school of thought tends to regard poverty more in relative than in absolute terms. Hence the ultimate objective of a GAI is the reduction of the disparities in the current *distribution* of income among the entire population. This view maintains that the present spread of income in Canada and many other countries is not only inequitable but iniquitous, and that until it is narrowed, the lowest quintile of the population will always be in poverty. Tom Philbrook points out in his paper that Canadian folklore includes the assumption that anti-poverty measures in the past have reduced inequality, whereas in fact (as his presentation clearly reveals), this is not the case. For example, there was practically no change in the cash income redistribution pattern in the 15 years from 1954 to 1969.[1] S.M. Miller and Martin Rein also argue that income inequity itself is the cause of poverty, and go on to illustrate why present tax and transfer mechanisms have not effectively altered the existing patterns of income distribution.

A consensus was reached – the major one in the seminar – that whichever approach to defining adequacy of income is followed, no one monolithic income maintenance program can achieve this objective for all. A basic cash payment can only be part of a combination of programs (e.g., social insurance, health, housing and other social services), along with purely economic measures, that would together guarantee an adequate standard of living for all. This supports the approach taken by the Canadian Council on Social Development (formerly the Canadian Welfare Council), in its 1969 statement.[2]

The degree to which a basic cash payment would modify or even replace at least parts of such programs was a matter of much debate in the seminar. Some participants argued strongly that a new or reformed basic cash income payment should be the centrepiece of the total system; others (perhaps the majority) saw it as fulfilling a supplementary or complementary (almost residual) function, at least in the foreseeable future. It was also urged that both a short- and long-term view of reaching a GAI should be kept in mind. It is unrealistic to suppose that deeply entrenched programs could be

1. See Philbrook paper, table 3, p. 90.
2. Canadian Welfare Council, *Social Policies for Canada* (Ottawa, 1969).

easily eliminated; nor, indeed, should their potential in helping to achieve a GAI be ignored.

2 Employment and a Guaranteed Annual Income

The relationship of employment to a GAI (including the effect on incentive to work) was, as one might have anticipated, a major and recurring theme in the seminar. Would a GAI result in large numbers of employable people opting for a life of idleness at a minimum level of income? Should those who are capable of working but who refuse to do so be eligible for a GAI? These questions received a good deal of attention – indeed, some participants thought far too much. While some felt that an adequate income guarantee would reduce incentive, others pointed out that a good income security scheme would have more effective built-in monetary incentives to work than do most of the present public assistance programs. Still others thought that a disproportionate weight was given, on very little evidence, to the need for work incentives, since most people want to work if they can. Moreover, it would be difficult to tell how real the problems of incentive are until we provide adequate opportunities for all for *meaningful* work. The target of full employment opportunities of any kind has not, in North America at least, been reached in recent years, and seems unattainable in the foreseeable future.

A number of participants agreed with Miller and Rein that virtual full employment is necessary before an adequate guaranteed annual income can be reached because of the prohibitive costs of an adequate cash income security measure if many employable people have no earnings for long periods of time. However, the majority view appeared to be that, while full employment would certainly make the implementation of an adequate income security scheme more politically acceptable and economically feasible, full employment is not a prerequisite to a GAI. It was also recognized that an adequate income cannot be guaranteed even through the employment of all persons able to work, since the legal minimum wage level does not take family responsibilities into account; in any case, the minimum wage is often inadequate, and loopholes or exclusions in the legislation force many persons to work for less than minimum wages. The working poor are the largest group in Canada requiring an increased income to give them an adequate standard of living.

David Smith's thoughtful paper prompted much discussion on the extent to which government should and could be involved in creating employment through the traditional monetary and fiscal methods of job stimulation. There was also considerable interest in and support for Melville Ulmer's thesis that government must be the chief job creator for workers who lack market power and are the first to be displaced when recession or automation reduces employment in the private sector. Many felt this type of government intervention could deal more effectively with the problem caused by the need for a trade-off between inflation and unemployment than do present monetary and fiscal measures.

The need for new concepts of work was stressed. The Canadian Local Initiatives Program and Opportunities for Youth received a good deal of attention for creating employment possibilities that are socially useful to the community but not traditionally considered productive work. These programs aroused great interest among participants from other countries.

3 The Interdependence of Social and Economic Policies

The importance of the interdependent relationship between social and economic policies in any consideration of a GAI was stressed throughout the seminar. This is the main thrust of the Miller/Rein paper. Social policies cannot be relegated to a residual position and serve as a corrective to basic economic policies; if they do, they become "economic policies for the poor," and too often become poor policies and programs. It was emphasized that the integration of tax policy and the tax system with social policies is particularly necessary. For too long, taxation on the one hand and income security on the other have operated in isolation as two distinct and parallel systems, with resulting inequities and anomalies. As well, social policies should be integrated with policies on public expenditures. What are the socioeconomic priorities and appropriate balance (short- and long-term) in the use of tax money – for example, for building hospitals or roads, providing public housing or stimulating private housing construction, supporting regional development or encouraging oil and mineral exploration? The question of *what* goods and services are included in the assessment of a country's gross national product (as distinct from GNP level and growth) was also raised, since it was felt that this can affect the estimate of resources, and therefore the redistribution process.

Some participants called for a reduction of inequality – not only in income but also in social relationships – which would change the social stratification as well as the economic institutional structures of our society. Others supported the socioeconomic systems of countries such as Canada and felt such systems could be adapted to meet desirable objectives. However, all recognized the political constraints (such as public attitudes to taxation and redistribution, and vested economic and other interests) that stand in the way of change.

18

The Canadian Scene

It is clear that the seminar papers and discussions confirmed the hypothesis of the seminar planners that the subject of a GAI must be approached in an integrated and comprehensive manner. It is also clear that such an approach should involve not only an examination of the various income security schemes but also consideration of other social programs, employment, and monetary and fiscal policies, including the tax system. In view of the continuing poverty for many, the measures in these areas have obviously failed so far to guarantee an adequate income for all Canadians, in spite of an impressive array of socially directed programs.

1 Canada's Inventory of Social Security Measures
It may be useful at this stage to remind or inform readers about the major features of our current approaches to income security and certain other relevant measures.

a *Income Security*
There are many variations in income security programs but essentially only five basic concepts:[3] social insurance, demogrants, social dividends, social assistance and negative income tax. (Among the various federal and provincial programs in Canada in 1972, examples of all but the social dividend technique could be found.)

In *social insurance* the rights of individuals to benefits are linked with previous contributions or earnings covered under the program. The words "social" and "insurance" are both important. There is an insurance element in that risks are permitted to be pooled and a relationship exists between benefits and previous earnings. The insurance is "social" in that it is publicly administered and includes internal subsidies, either from some of the participants or from public funds, both of which distinguish it from private insurance. Also, because of the internal subsidies, the schemes are not completely actuarial. Principal examples of social insurance programs in Canada are the federally operated unemployment insurance, the Canada and Quebec pension plans, and provincially operated workmen's compensation schemes.

Under the technique of *demogrants,* flat-rate benefits are paid to a population group; the payments may be varied by age or family size and may be taxed. Payments are, in theory at least, based on the presumed need of the group to be covered by the particular benefit. Residence is the only other qualifying condition. The two

---

3. See paper by J.I. Clark, Appendix, pp. 274–275; and Canada, Department of National Health and Welfare, *Income Security for Canadians* (Ottawa, 1970), p. 19.

examples of this technique in Canada at present are the federal programs of family and youth allowances (*not* taxed) and old age security for persons age 65 and over (taxed).

The *social dividend* is the application of the demogrant approach to the entire population; the payment is always subject to recovery, in part or entirely, through taxation.

The *social assistance* technique depends on establishing eligibility by testing the need or means of a person or family. Social assistance may include the provision of health and welfare services as well as cash assistance payments. The needs test is an assessment of individual and family budgetary requirements as well as available resources in order to determine that person's or family's scale of benefits. The means test involves an investigation of income and assets; since assistance by this test is provided only up to a predetermined level, no account is taken of budgetary need. Under both types of assistance, eligibility is limited by the level of assets. The federal Canada Assistance Plan forms the framework of federal sharing of the costs of provincially operated social assistance programs.

The *negative income tax* involves paying benefits to families and individuals whose incomes fall below prescribed income levels. These levels could either be the income tax exemption level or some other minimum income standard. The benefit payments are calculated to fill all or part of the gap between actual income and the minimum income standard, or to cover the unused tax exemptions to which a non-taxpayer would be entitled if he paid tax. To determine eligibility for and the amount of the benefit, an income test is applied prior to a person's receiving the benefit. (This contrasts with the social dividend and some forms of demogrant where a benefit is paid out in advance and a test is subsequently applied through the income tax machinery.) The negative income tax approach is applied in the federal guaranteed income supplement for the aged.

b *Taxation*

Operating parallel to the income security programs and presumed by many to be supplementing the redistributive effects of these programs are the various forms of taxation that make up the tax system – for example, the personal income and sales tax applied by the federal and provincial governments, and the property taxes imposed by municipal authorities.

c *Employment*

A third dimension of our social security system falls under the general heading of manpower and employment. This includes job placement, adult retraining programs, worker relocation, regional economic expansion, and federal and provincial minimum wage laws – all measures designed to maintain and increase the workers' earnings in the traditional market. There are also more recent innovations in creating work opportunities not restricted to the market economy, such as the federal Local Initiatives Program and Opportunities for Youth.

d *The Social Services*
The social services have a crucial role in any integrated and comprehensive approach to a GAI, as Nicolas Zay's paper shows. For example, he quotes estimates to show that the provision of public housing and universal health services can raise the actual standard of living by 20–30 and 7–9 per cent respectively. This would obviously have a major effect on the cash income component of a GAI. Among other programs that must be considered in attempting to reach an adequate standard of living for all are those for education and housing and for the "personal" social welfare services such as day care and homemaker services.

2 Essential Criteria in Achieving a Guaranteed Income
Even the above brief inventory of current programs and systems indicates the complexity and multi-faceted nature of an integrated approach to a GAI in Canada. Hence, for me to attempt now to give precise and definitive answers to how effectively all these programs contribute to or fail to provide an adequate GAI, and what specific reform is required, would be foolhardy as well as tedious. Perhaps the most useful contribution I can make is to discuss what I believe to be six essential criteria or principles for all social programs – criteria which therefore should be applied in any country to any program or series of programs designed to guarantee an adequate income for all. My view that these criteria have universal, not just Canadian applicability was strengthened by the number of times they were referred to either explicitly or implicitly during the seminar by people from different countries.

In my view, the criteria to be applied (not in the order of priority) either to programs individually or collectively should be:
a. Do the programs lend themselves to efficient administration?
b. Will they provide most help to those who need it most?
c. Are they equitable (fair to all concerned)?
d. Do they enhance human dignity and a spirit of community?
e. Are they economically feasible?
f. Are they politically acceptable?

a *Do the Programs Lend Themselves to Efficient Administration?*
The belief that a guaranteed income could be simply, efficiently and economically reached through a single monolithic, automated,

super income plan replacing the plethora of current fragmented and disjointed schemes is the main attraction for many of its advocates. However, important as the criterion of efficient administration may be, I share the view of most seminar participants that we must abandon any such simplistic approach and that a combination of programs pursued in an integrated fashion will be required. This does not mean that in developing a more integrated approach a good deal of jurisdictional overlapping resulting from the incremental or patchwork development of the programs, as well as cumbersome bureaucratic machinery, cannot be replaced. Following are two examples.

(1) *Income security for the aged*
The current income maintenance programs in Canada designed to provide income security for the aged are a good example of an incremental, fragmented approach to meet a common need which surely could be streamlined and integrated. With the establishment in 1967 of the guaranteed income supplement (GIS) for the aged, Canada accepted the goal of a guaranteed income for the aged. Hence, the question could be asked why it is necessary to continue to employ four different concepts of income maintenance measures for the aged, each with its own separate administration: the flat-rate old age security (demogrant); the wage-related contributory Canada and Quebec pension plans (social insurance); the GIS (negative income tax); and the needs-tested, Canada Assistance Plan (social assistance). Early consideration might well be given to some, if not complete, integration of these programs that could make for more efficient and economical administration without lessening effectiveness.

(2) *Social assistance*
The present social assistance programs operated by the provinces under the Canada Assistance Plan provide a further example of cumbersome and inefficient administration based on methods of giving financial assistance which are becoming increasingly outdated. These weaknesses are well documented in "A Developmental Approach to Public Assistance," a report prepared in 1971 by a federal task force, and in *Poverty in Canada,* the 1971 report of the Special Senate Committee on Poverty. Because of the administrative inefficiencies, and for other reasons which will be discussed later, different approaches to providing a mass cash benefits program have been proposed, such as the social dividend or a negative income tax. For example, advocates of a negative income tax point out that simple application forms and declarations of income could be processed by computer with benefits established and remitted quickly and accurately. It is felt that the computer could

largely replace the time-consuming and costly staff process of examining the individual circumstance of each applicant for assistance, though it was recognized at the seminar that no computer can completely substitute for the caseworker. It could not, for example, take account of individual emergency and special needs which call for direct staff assessment.

> *The criterion of administrative efficiency should continue to be rigorously applied to every individual program. Moreover, the same criterion should be applied to any total "package" of programs aimed at providing a GAI to ensure that the various components do not overlap but supplement and complement one another in achieving the desired goal. However, the application of this criterion should be viewed in proper perspective, keeping in mind that an integrated approach to GAI must meet the unique and personal as well as the common needs of people.*

b *Will the Programs Provide Most Help to Those Who Need It Most?*
A common question posed by a tax wary and tax weary public is why poverty in Canada persists in spite of the billions spent on social security measures and a supposedly progressive taxation system. Even a cursory review of these programs and measures indicates that at least one reason for continued inadequate income for some 20 to 30 per cent of our population is the failure of the various measures, either intentionally or inadvertently, to meet the crucial criterion of helping most those who need it most.

(1) *Social assistance*
Our public assistance programs, designed exclusively to meet the income needs of the poor, do help most those who need it most – provided they are eligible for assistance. But the role of social assistance in helping to meet this criterion in Canada breaks down on the question of eligibility. Far too many people who most need help are excluded from the program, either by definition or because of low ceilings on assistance. For example, although under the Canada Assistance Plan the federal government will share costs of approved welfare expenditures for the needy or those about to be in need (including the working poor), provinces, with one or two exceptions, tend not to assist the working poor; although they need help, they are arbitrarily excluded simply because they work. Moreover, since federal funds under CAP are shared equally with the provinces, the poorer provinces, even with federal-provincial equalization grants, cannot take full advantage of the federally shared funds, although these provinces have the highest percentage of poor people and the fewest resources. Consequently, many of those in real

need do not receive adequate assistance. An income-tested program financed by federal revenue (for example, a negative income tax scheme, with an adequate guaranteed floor as a right and sliding scales of allowances based purely on an income test and disregarding arbitrary eligibility regulations based on the *reasons* for low income) could better contribute to helping those who need it most.

(2) *Unemployment insurance*

Our unemployment insurance scheme, even though now one of the most generous in the world, cannot by its very nature effectively help the unemployed who need it most because it is a wage-related program. Persons with highest earnings receive highest benefits; conversely, those with lowest wages receive least. Moreover, wages are not related to presumed, let alone actual, need (such as those arising from family responsibilities); unemployment insurance benefits reflect this fact, even though internal subsidies direct a somewhat greater proportion of funds to lower than to higher earners, and there is a slight increase in benefit for a recipient with one or more dependents and very low previous earnings. It was not suggested in the seminar (nor is it in most current proposals) that there is no place in a GAI for a wage-related program for temporarily unemployed regular members of the labor force, although questions have been raised about its appropriateness for people with short-term employment records. In countries with unemployment insurance plans (such as Canada) the social acceptability of the program cannot readily be challenged. However, unemployment insurance is no substitute for a basic income-tested program that is required to help those that most need help.

(3) *Family allowances*

Canada's family and youth allowances programs were not primarily designed as anti-poverty measures or to give most help to those who need it most: they were intended to give some help to *all* families with dependent children. Indeed, since our flat-rate and universal family allowances are not taxable, the higher net benefits accrue to those with highest incomes. It was estimated in 1971 that, in actual cash, only 24 per cent of the family and youth allowance benefits went to families with incomes less than $5,000 a year. A reformed family allowances program could be a more effective instrument than it now is for diverting more of the funds to the lower-income group. For example, as suggested by the Canadian Council on Social Development, the allowances could be raised and taxed either under regular or special rates, and the tax exemptions for children and youth be reduced or eliminated.

(4) *Tax system*[4]

Any integrated approach to a GAI requires a progressive tax system designed to help most those who need it most. Canadians generally take for granted that because of the apparently progressive nature of the provincial and federal personal income tax we have such an approach. However, a closer examination of the overall tax system indicates that we have by and large a proportional system. For example, a study[5] for Canada's Royal Commission on Taxation concluded that, in 1961, people paid out approximately one-third of their income in one or other form of taxation, regardless of their income level. The exception here is for persons with an income of under $2,000 a year (including those receiving transfer payments) who paid more than half their income in taxes. This study indicated that many taxes are regressive, especially property taxes and federal and provincial sales taxes. Not only has the taxation system failed to redistribute income from upper- to lower-income groups, but the lower group itself pays an overwhelming amount of its income in taxes.

The use of exemptions in our personal income tax is regressive because the exemptions are deducted from taxable income; therefore, the higher that income the greater the benefit.[6] The proposal to eliminate or at least reduce the income tax exemption for children, and at the same time increasing but taxing family allowances, is an excellent example of using the tax system to help most those who need it most. Another device is the substitution of tax credits for exemptions, as proposed by Canada's Royal Commission on Taxation in 1966 to replace some exemptions. Tax credits are flat-rate reductions of actual personal income tax to be paid; they remain constant whatever the amount of the tax and thus benefit the lower-income taxpayer more, on a proportionate basis. They could benefit lower-income groups still more if they were used not only to reduce income tax but also to provide payment from the treasury where the tax credit exceeds the amount of tax due; payments would rise as incomes descend and a non-taxpayer would receive in cash the full amount of the tax credit. A way of using

---

4. For the remainder of this section, dealing with the second criterion, I am much indebted to material prepared for our Task Force on Social Security by David P. Ross of the Council staff, on which I have drawn heavily.
5. W. Irwin Gillespie, *The Incidence of Taxes and Public Expenditures in the Canadian Economy*, Royal Commission on Taxation, Studies No. 2 (Ottawa: Queen's Printer, 1966).
6. For instance, a person who has no taxable income before tax exemptions for children are applied gets no advantage from these exemptions; at a 17 per cent income tax rate, the advantage amounts to 17 per cent of the exemption; at a 47 per cent tax rate, the benefit is equivalent to 47 per cent of the exemption.

this method as part of an approach to GAI was proposed by the British chancellor of the exchequer in his 1972 budget speech and embodied in a government green paper for public discussion.[7] In 1970, the government of Ontario proposed a system of property and sales tax credits, and both Ontario and Manitoba instituted a property tax credit system for the 1972 tax year, using the federal government's income tax collection machinery. Alberta is also moving in this direction. However, generally in Canada, much more can and should be done to develop a more progressive tax system.

(5) *Employment services*

A closer study of our employment services also indicates in a disconcerting number of ways how those who need most help seem to get the least. In the job placement service of the Department of Manpower and Immigration, manpower centres are oriented more to the employer than to the person seeking work. Even more pertinent is the fact that persons who are more difficult to place seem to receive the least help.

Experience with the adult retraining program of the Adult Occupational Training Act, 1967, indicates that since there is considerable competition for the number of training positions available, manpower officials tend to select the cream of the crop – people who have fairly good employment and educational backgrounds and who are judged likely to succeed in training. The training act generally only allows for 52 weeks of basic educational upgrading. However, since about one half of the heads of families living in poverty have no schooling, or have elementary schooling only, it is extremely difficult (if not impossible) for them to qualify for a vocational training school. Hence, the system is basically stacked against those who need it most.

(6) *Regional economic expansion*

It is still too early to assess accurately whether and to what extent the regional expansion program under the Regional Incentives Act of 1969 has helped most those who need it most. A look at regional unemployment and per capita income data suggests that the various incentive programs have so far not been overly successful in helping people with inadequate incomes. Probably one reason is that the program basically provides capital allowances, and so does not encourage labor intensive production processes. Another shortcoming of the incentive approach is that there is no obligation on the recipient firm to train or hire labor from the region in which

---

7. Martin Rein describes this proposal in his paper, page 207. He refers to it as "a comprehensive negative income tax system, with some benefits integrated into the tax system."

it is located. Consequently, there is a tendency to advertise nationally, at least for the more skilled jobs.

(7) *Minimum wages*

Legislation to establish adequate minimum wages could be one major device for guaranteeing an adequate income for the working poor. However, the current minimum wage range[8] in Canada is still so low that it cannot provide an adequate income for working heads of families. Even the British Columbia rate of $2 an hour provides an individual who works 40 hours a week with an annual salary of slightly less than $4,200 which, with normal payroll deductions and taxation, is barely enough to keep an individual and one dependent from living in poverty. All other prevailing rates would keep an individual and a dependent in poverty unless there is some form of income supplement. While there is a great deal of debate on whether minimum wages do more overall good than harm, there is little question that as anti-poverty devices the prevailing rates do little to guarantee an adequate income, especially for families with dependent children.

(8) *Work opportunity programs*

Surprisingly enough, work opportunity programs, specifically the federal Local Initiatives Program and Opportunities for Youth, have also not helped most those who need it most. Information obtained in 1972 showed that only 25 per cent of people involved in LIP projects had been on welfare, and 23 per cent had been drawing unemployment insurance. What about the income groups from which the other 52 per cent were drawn? Obviously more needs to be done to ensure that the most vulnerable people and those in greatest need can benefit under work opportunity programs. This in no way detracts from the valuable function of LIP and OFY: giving people the opportunity for meaningful work of their own design. These short-term projects have the obvious disadvantage of providing only temporary help. This suggests that as long as the private market economy cannot absorb all the employable manpower, meaningful work opportunities of longer duration and continuity should be devised.

(9) *Education*

The extent to which our education services have failed to provide greatest help to those who need it most has been documented in

---

8. In 1972, minimum wages in Canada ranged from $1.10 an hour for women in Prince Edward Island to $2 an hour for men and women in British Columbia.

numerous studies and surveys. Children in poor regions and poor sections of cities are likely to receive an inferior education rather than the better one required to compensate for their disadvantaged situation. There are a number of reasons for this, including the manner in which education services are financed. For example, in Canada, federal cost-sharing for formal education applies only to post-secondary institutions. This means that, except for grants in relation to the development of bilingualism in French and English, the provinces do not receive any direct federal aid for other schooling within the regular education system. Since children from poor families are under-represented at universities, federal subsidies go primarily to children of the middle and upper classes. In my view, constitutional limitations notwithstanding, ways should be explored to apply federal funds to increasing the overall quality of primary and secondary education to the greater benefit of the poor.

(10) *Health*

Many of the health problems of the poor are directly associated with their low incomes and their inability to provide themselves with even the basic human needs, including proper diets. They find themselves caught in the vicious cycle of poverty, poor health, dependency and more poverty. A study of children from poor families in Montreal revealed that 34 per cent suffered from malnutrition and 31 per cent from retarded growth.[9] Canada has had a hospital insurance scheme since 1957 and, with the introduction of the federal Medical Care Act in 1966, another long step forward was taken in assuring better health for all income groups. However, although our expenditures on health care are now proportionately high compared to those of many countries, most help is still not available to those who need it most. Free health care for people "on welfare" is provided in all provinces; however, only about half include certain essential but expensive services such as dental care and the provision of drugs and eyeglasses. These exclusions from the basic public scheme for health care also apply to the rest of the population. Also, in six provinces, people not on welfare must pay individual or family premiums. (An exception is the elderly who are exempted from the payments in three of these provinces.) Since most of the premiums are flat rate, their effect is regressive, constituting a relatively heavier burden on the budgets of lower-income people such as the working poor and many pensioners. Deterrent

---

9. The Corporation of Professional Social Workers of the Province of Quebec, Brief presented to the Special Senate Committee on Poverty, Third Session, No. 4 (October 22, 1970), p. 37; as reprinted in Canada, Parliament, Senate, Special Committee on Poverty, *Poverty in Canada* (Ottawa: Information Canada, 1971), p. 124.

or user fees, in spite of any arguments in their favor, tend to deter the poor rather than the middle- or upper-income groups, and hence can lead to inadequate health services.

(11) *Housing*

In the field of housing, the federal government intervenes in a substantial manner through the authority of the National Housing Act. In the past, however, most Central Mortgage and Housing Corporation (CMHC) activity has been in guaranteeing and supplying mortgage funds. This has produced lower interest rates for those who have the money to make down payments and can assume mortgages. The poor lack the savings to make conventional down payments, and consequently they have not been able to avail themselves proportionately of the CMHC benefits. CMHC has become more active in providing public housing and funding non-profit housing corporations, but the amount of funding is considered inadequate for even the backlog of people in desperate need of housing. Moreover, the rents in public housing projects are automatically adjusted to a rise in income so that up to 25 per cent of the increased income is taken away in higher rent payments. Increases in social assistance benefits frequently lead to increases in rents even in housing controlled by public authorities. It is well known that when public benefits to low-income families living in private housing increase, their rents tend to increase as well.

(12) *Legal aid*

In 1970 John Turner, then the federal minister of justice, stated: *We must understand that, whereas the law for most of us is a source of rights, for the poor the law appears always to be taking something away. That we have to change. Those of us who have been given the temporary custody of our laws by the people must ensure that those laws and our courts treat all equally – rich and poor alike.*[10]

Unfortunately we have not yet translated this valid principle into practice. The form of some laws, as well as the difficulty of gaining access to legal assistance, has meant that many poor people are hampered in escaping from poverty. Although seven provinces now have comprehensive legal aid systems, the type and coverage varies. One of several shortcomings of most legal aid plans is that they provide assistance for remedial but not preventive action; a survey of the Ontario system showed that 90 per cent of the certificates granted for legal aid were for litigation, while only 2.6 per

---

10. John N. Turner, "Justice for the Poor," *Canadian Journal of Corrections,* XII, 1 (January, 1970), p. 10.

cent were for legal advice. All too often poor people unable to afford legal advice are trapped into unfair but binding contracts.

> *There is obviously still much to be done by way of effectively applying to our income security, social services and taxation systems the principle of helping most those who need it most. Unless and until we are committed to the application of this criterion on all fronts in approaching the goal of a guaranteed annual income in an integrated and comprehensive fashion, the objective will remain as elusive as quicksilver.*

c *Are the Programs Equitable (Fair to All Concerned)?*
Equity is defined in the Oxford Dictionary as "fairness; recourse to principles of justice to correct or supplement law." More strikingly, a seminar participant described equity as providing equal help to equals and unequal help to unequals – the latter to be exercised in accordance with the principle of helping most those who need it most. Both these kinds of equity can be achieved either *horizontally* (between people with the same income but varied family responsibilities) or *vertically* (between people with different incomes and either the same or varied needs).

(1) *The working poor*
Probably the most apparent and widespread example of inequity arises from the general practice of not providing to the working poor the cash assistance and certain free or subsidized social services available to those on public assistance. This "all or nothing" approach results in many of the working poor existing at a standard of living lower even than that of persons with similar needs who receive public help. This inequitable situation creates dissatisfaction and alienation, and all too often a "welfare backlash" and a determination to reduce the benefits of the family on social assistance. It is remarkable that, in spite of much talk about assisting the working poor and the obvious inequity of not doing so, Canada seems so far to have been almost entirely unable to augment their income through supplements. Indeed, as indicated earlier, we continue to impose income, sales and property taxes on the working poor at inequitable rates.

(2) *"Taxation" of benefits*
Arbitrary and unfair definitions of eligibility and sharp cutoff points, instead of the gradual reduction or tapering of benefits, frequently lead to inequities. The whole subject of reducing benefits ("taxing" them) for any additional income, earned or otherwise acquired, is beset with a series of hazards. A common one is

the "notch" problem when only a few additional dollars earned may put the beneficiary into an income bracket that reduces benefits out of all proportion to the additional income and may result in a net loss of income.

The current common procedure (with minor exceptions) of reducing social assistance benefits by $1 for every dollar earned, is also increasingly recognized as unfair to employable people. In spite of the frequent argument that allowing welfare beneficiaries to retain some of their earnings is merely indirectly subsidizing uneconomic and low paying enterprises, the practice of 100 per cent "taxation" requires revision for employables not only for the sake of equity but also, in the view of many, to provide some monetary incentive to work.

(3)   *Work incentives*

While monetary work incentives can be considered a desirable feature of a comprehensive income security scheme designed to provide a guaranteed annual income, they can also lead to inequities if proper safeguards are not established.[11] Work incentives can be grossly unfair if appropriate gainful employment opportunities are not available or if the beneficiary is incorrectly judged to be employable; determination of who is really employable and who is not is far too often made on the basis of subjective judgment rather than reality.

The dangers of building a monetary work incentive feature into, for example, a negative income tax scheme, are exacerbated by the nature of the NIT approach. As J.I. Clark states in his paper, a NIT program has three variables, any two of which automatically determine the third. These variables are:

The income guarantee, the payment which a person or family would receive if he had no other income.

The implicit tax rate, the rate at which the basic guaranteed income payment is reduced as income from other sources rises.

The break-even level of income, or the level of income at which the income guarantee is reduced to zero.[12]

This mathematical straightjacket can lead to inequities. For example, in Canada, the Special Senate Committee on Poverty wished to provide a monetary incentive to work by reducing allowances by 70 per cent for any earnings, but at the same time did not wish to

---

11.   Monetary considerations are not, of course, the only incentive or disincentive to work. For example, a strong incentive is the work ethic in our society and the stigma it casts on employables who are unemployed even through no fault of their own; lack of satisfaction in one's job can be a disincentive to work.

12.   See J.I. Clark, appendix, p. 274.

extend any financial assistance to anyone whose total income went beyond any given poverty line. Having thus established two of the variables, the committee was forced to set the third variable, namely the guaranteed income floor, at 30 per cent below the poverty line. Unfortunately, for unemployables covered under the scheme, monetary incentives to work are meaningless, and guaranteeing their income floor at 30 per cent below the poverty line would merely provide "guaranteed poverty" at that level. Thus, ironically, the scheme would produce an inequitable effect on the most vulnerable members of our society – the unemployables. Participants at the seminar recognized these dangers, and there seemed to be a consensus that it would be inequitable to apply the same income floor to employables and unemployables alike. It was suggested that the floor for unemployable persons should be set at least at a poverty line that provided an adequate minimum income.[13]

> *Equity requires that sound socioeconomic programs must be designed to safeguard and enhance the opportunities and well-being of all members of a nation. Nevertheless, an equitable approach to a GAI also requires that we give special consideration to the most vulnerable groups in our society.*

d *Do the Programs Enhance Human Dignity and a Spirit of Community?*

For some, this twofold and interrelated criterion is a pious platitude. Yet if, even in the process of establishing a GAI, we create stigmas and destroy human dignity and self-respect, the result is likely to be a dependent, helpless and thus degraded person. Not only will we have caused human misery; we will also have created a social and economic liability.

Urban and technological society has so far tended to diminish, dehumanize and alienate individuals. It can shatter and fragment the sense of community and fraternity, and work against the goal of social development, discussed by Gérald Fortin in his comments concluding the seminar. Therefore, it is especially important in this milieu that programs designed to guarantee an annual income should develop the spirit of interdependence and strengthen and support the individual as well as integrate him into the community, rather than cause or assist his disintegration. As the Council's 1969 statement declares:

The objective of social policy is human well-being. This has two aspects. On the one hand, the individual must be guaranteed the

---

13. Two floors would be similar to the two-stage approach recommended in the *Report* of the Quebec (Province) Commission of Inquiry on Health and Social Welfare, Vol. V (Quebec: Official Publisher, 1971).

freedom and opportunity to carry responsibility, so far as he is able, for meeting his own needs and aspirations. On the other, the achievement of human well-being, especially under today's conditions, is as much a social as an individual responsibility. Only through collective planning and action can the conditions be established that will enable all people to realize their potential and contribute creatively to society.[14]

In too many of our programs we fail to apply the criterion of enhancing human dignity and the spirit of community. This may be illustrated using examples from the fields of income security and employment.

(1) *Income security*

There is much evidence to suggest that the present social assistance program is too much imbued with at best an unhealthy paternalistic attitude and at worst a punitive one. Present social assistance programs tend to set apart from the mainstream of society those who require public help. Grants are issued with an obvious reluctance, especially to those considered (in Victorian parlance) to be the "undeserving poor." The system reflects a widespread, if largely irrational, public feeling that large numbers of people prefer to exist at a bare level of social assistance rather than to work.

Although the Canada Assistance Plan and the counterpart provincial legislation imply a right to assistance, actual practice all too often does not treat social assistance benefits as a right but as a degrading handout. The hesitancy with which provincial governments have introduced effective appeal procedures is further evidence of this lack of public conviction about the right to assistance.[15] An appeal is meaningless, after all, if there is no right established in the first place.

Such attitudes and practices are, of course, most destructive of human dignity and of the spirit of community. These problems of stigma and of establishing rights, as well as administrative problems, led a large proportion of the seminar participants to reject social assistance as a main avenue for income security in a GAI program. It was generally assumed, of course, that public cash payments should be subject to an income test (for example, even family allowances should be taxed). However, it was generally agreed that eligibility should be squarely based on a *right* that is applied under clear conditions and regulations, with a minimum of subjective and often judgmental involvement in the decisions.

Obviously a demogrant or social dividend (a flat rate universal

14. Canadian Welfare Council, *Social Policies for Canada*, p. 2.
15. Canadian Council on Social Development, *Appeal Procedures under the Canada Assistance Plan* (Ottawa, 1972).

payment made to a group or to all) would best fulfil these conditions. The income test is applied by recouping some or all of the benefit through the regular taxation system at normal income tax rates or at special rates. Since the payment is made as a right to all involved, there is obviously no stigma attached. Nor would there be a stigma in taking back money from those who do not need it; nobody has ever been denigrated by paying income tax! Through a taxed flat-rate benefit, the goal of "selectivity within universality" can be achieved without loss of human dignity. It was recognized that such a benefit would involve financial problems through the large advance outlay of funds, even if a good deal were recouped through payroll deductions on a monthly basis. This could, in effect, represent an interest-free loan (until it could be reclaimed in taxes) to those not eligible for all or part of the payment. There would also be the usual problem of tax evasion or avoidance (leakage). There was, therefore, considerable support in the seminar for the NIT program as being the more feasible scheme since – although the determination of eligibility is more individualized (special declarations being required) – its determination of benefit *prior* to payment could be more accurate and economical. However, it was suggested that there might be room for both techniques in the desirable mix of an integrated GAI.

(2) *Employment*
Obviously much more needs to be done to enhance rather than undermine the dignity of the individual by providing him with cash assistance through income security schemes. It is also argued that there is particular danger that, in our work-oriented society, cash assistance extended to employables, no matter how objectively provided, may demean individuals and destroy their self-respect. There is at least some theoretical recognition that technology is increasingly threatening our conventional work opportunities and that, as well, people have a right to refuse mind-numbing routine tasks. But the work ethic – that market-directed employment of any kind is more worthy than idleness or socially-directed work – is still a predominant characteristic of western society and likely to continue to be so in the foreseeable future. Thus, the concept of unemployment for employables (even when enforced by lack of jobs), with an income guaranteed, still raises questions and eyebrows. This is especially true for youth and the middle aged; enforced idleness at age 65 can be rationalized as retirement and is therefore more acceptable to society, even though not to those individuals concerned who might rather be gainfully employed.

Recognition of this danger and the fact that it is aggravated, in North America at least, by an almost chronic high rate of unemployment, led the seminar to consider the question of more publicly created socially useful work opportunities. Obviously the major source of employment will continue to be the market economy. However, Melville Ulmer and others provided some convincing arguments that in our present situation it is unrealistic to expect the private market economy to offer satisfactory employment to all employables. Canada, of all the industrialized nations in the world, is perhaps least likely to be able to do so in the near future.

Between now and 1980 it is anticipated that more than 2.5 million people in Canada will be applying for jobs.[16] This represents a 30 per cent increase, or a compound annual growth rate of 2.4 per cent, compared to projected annual increases in the same period of 1.4 per cent a year for the United States, 0.5 per cent for Sweden, and 0.4 per cent for Japan. The Ninth Annual Review of The Economic Council of Canada, 1972, projected an annual growth of 2.8 per cent in the labor force up to 1980 (slightly less than in the 1960s) and an average growth of opportunities for employment in the market economy of 3.1 per cent annually.[17] While this forecasts a decline in our unemployment rate, it nevertheless leaves a rate of about 4 per cent unemployed. There is real danger, in view of current and recent experience, that this level may be accepted as tolerable. Should we not rather consider, for the next decade at least and perhaps permanently, ongoing non-market employment opportunities, based on the LIP and OFY concepts and Dr. Ulmer's proposals, as one part of any comprehensive program to achieve a GAI for all in Canada?

> *In summary, the dignity of the individual and the sense of community would be enhanced by including in an integrated approach to guaranteed annual income not only a basic annual transfer payment (or payments) made objectively as a right, but also "guaranteed" employment opportunities and, as discussed in an earlier section, a more progressive tax system.*

e *Are the Programs Economically Feasible?*
Assuming that the goal of an adequate GAI for all is socially desirable, it must also be accepted by a country as being economically feasible. This complex problem could not be solved at the seminar for any one country, nor can I attempt to do so here for Canada. At best, I can try to provide, through a few observations and additional questions, some direction in finding the answer for the foreseeable future.

---

16. Sylvia Ostry, Statistics Canada, in a report to a Conference Board of Canada meeting, Montreal, October, 1972.
17. Economic Council of Canada, *The Years to 1980,* Ninth Annual Review (Ottawa: Information Canada, 1972), p. 36.

(1) *Economic growth*

The first question is: What is meant by *economically feasible?* Presumably any scheme that was perceived as unduly diverting too much capital from other sectors of the economy or (as mentioned in the seminar) causing the emigration of highly "productive" members, would not be considered economically feasible. The second major problem lies in the objective of an adequate GAI. If the level of adequacy set is some fairly low poverty line, agreement on economic feasibility might soon be reached but poverty would continue and the goal of a GAI become meaningless. In essence, decisions on both these points are political ones. However, what are some of the economic considerations that must be kept in mind?

Economic projections made in the Ninth Annual Review of The Economic Council of Canada provide us with reason for some optimism about our economic ability to move toward a GAI. It states:

At current rates of taxation, government revenues are projected to increase strongly in the Canadian economy as it moves to a high employment level. If spending were to be determined solely by the requirements of existing programs, revenues would soon considerably exceed expenditures, creating undesirable fiscal drag, and it would not be possible to sustain high rates of growth in output and employment. . . . Transfer payments to the personal sector from the various levels of government accounted for 23 per cent of government expenditures in 1970. (Such payments include old age pensions, veterans' pensions and allowances, family and youth allowances, unemployment insurance benefits, workmen's compensation benefits, adult occupation training payments, assistance payments, grants to benevolent associations, scholarships and research grants, and grants to universities.) . . . To offset projected growth in government revenue, transfer payments would, we assume here, be increased somewhat more rapidly, allowing some margin for the introduction of new programs or the expansion of present ones. On this basis we have projected an increase of 9.6 per cent per year in transfer payments over the course of the decade to nearly $18 billion (current dollars) compared with $6.8 billion in 1970.[18]

These figures indicate that it will be economically possible to expand and improve our social security programs and expenditures

---

18. Economic Council of Canada, *The Years to 1980*, pp. 33–34. One of the causes for "undesirable fiscal drag" may perhaps arise from Canada's changing demographic pattern. For the last 20 years our unusually high birthrate has placed tremendous demands on the economy (notably for education) to help dependent children and young families. As this demand declines with the reduced birthrate, which is projected to continue in the foreseeable future, funds required for these purposes will be reduced, and the savings could be directed to such objectives as providing a GAI.

up to that point in time, even without raising taxes. We could provide an adequate income for all unemployables now dependent on public financial aid without prohibitive additional expenditures. But what about the working poor? To bring their incomes up to adequate standards will obviously add considerably to the costs – not only through increased transfers but also because of lost revenue through relief from taxation. Transfer payments and tax relief must both be involved; it would create a cruel illusion to simply increase transfers to the working poor with one hand and take the additional revenue away with the other through regressive taxation.

(2) *Recoverable costs*

In estimating *net* costs we should not forget to include all recoveries. For example, the allowances will be partially recouped through taxes (on the extra goods and services which the poor will be able to purchase) such as sales taxes and indirect taxes, even if these were made less regressive. We must also consider savings in the hidden costs of keeping so many Canadians in poverty. The Fifth Annual Review of the Economic Council[19] referred to these costs as "lost output" and "diverted output." The lost output is that wealth which the employable poor would have created had their production potential been more developed and effectively used through better education, adult retraining, relocation, etc. The costs of "diverted output" are those expenditures required, for example, to treat sickness which might not have occurred had the poor lived in decent housing, had proper diets and preventive medical attention. They also include costs of palliative public welfare payments, rehabilitating slums, and maintaining law and order and correctional services to cope with poverty-inspired delinquency, juvenile or adult. Then there are the uncountable costs. What is the cost of a shattered sense of community and people of one nation divided into hostile camps? What is the cost of human suffering, diminution and frustration?

(3) *Source of funds*

In trying to determine whether an adequate GAI is economically feasible in Canada, we should not delude ourselves about costs. Certainly any good plan will cost additional money. Some of the funds could come, as we have seen from the Economic Council's projections, from our growing gross national product. Some could come from elimination or reduction of administrative and operational costs of our present income security programs. But some of

---

19. Economic Council of Canada, *The Challenge of Growth and Change,* Fifth Annual Review (Ottawa: Queen's Printer, 1968), p. 105.

the funds would undoubtedly have to come from the pockets of the "haves" via income redistribution methods.

f *Are the Programs Politically Acceptable?*
In a democracy, political acceptability is the ultimate criterion for policies and programs. Decisions that will lead to a GAI for all can only be made in Canada by political leaders at the two senior levels of government. However, although leaders must lead and not merely follow, their actions and decisions must eventually be sanctioned, explicitly or implicitly, by a large section of the population.

Whether a GAI as a clearly stated national objective will ever become politically acceptable in Canada will depend largely on the extent to which the integrated approach to the goal can be shown to pass muster with the five preceding criteria. If Canadians are convinced that the various measures required to achieve the goal are equitable, economically feasible, well organized, and designed to help most those who need it most, they are unlikely to reject the goal of a GAI. However, there are a number of major political difficulties in the way of reaching and implementing a GAI in Canada.

(1) *Federal-provincial relations*
In our federal system, where social policies are largely the responsibility of the provinces, and economic and fiscal policies are primarily under the jurisdiction of the federal government, the establishment of a GAI as a clearly stated national policy or goal is most complex. This is especially so if, as the seminar emphasized and I have reiterated, the goal of a GAI can be only achieved through the development of integrated social and economic policies. The fact that the present parameters of the social and economic fields are so hazy adds to the difficulty of determining the limits of federal and provincial responsibilities. It would seem imperative, therefore, that Canadians urge and assist their provincial and federal leaders to press on in a spirit of cooperation, not competition, with a restatement of respective responsibilities and roles in the social and economic fields.

(2) *Scheduling implementation*
Another major difficulty will be to schedule the full implementation of an integrated approach to a GAI, since obviously not all the required measures in the fields of income security, social services and fiscal measures can be introduced at the same time. For example, Canadians, having just gone through a long period of soul-searching and so-called tax reform, are not likely to be prepared to do so

again in the immediate future. Yet, further reform of the tax system is required if the goal of a guaranteed annual income is to be vigorously pursued. What will most likely be required, as the seminar participants recognized, is a staged or programmed implementation leading to a specific long-term target. For example, if a new basic cash income program as a matter of right is to be established as the centrepiece in achieving the goal of a GAI (as I personally believe it should), consideration could be given to moving forward still further in the steps we have already taken in providing a GAI for the aged by extending it to, say, families with dependent children, and gradually to all. However, this kind of schedule assumes comprehensive planning and a clearly stated time objective which would almost certainly be set beyond the normal four-year life span of our federal and provincial governments. (For example, in my view, we should set now a target date of 1980, but governments would find such an advance commitment difficult, perhaps presumptuous.) There will have to be sufficient political accommodation (presumably among political parties and the federal and provincial governments) that will make it possible to move forward in a planned and systematic fashion. In reaching any specific long-term goal there will also be a need for non-government involvement not only to help set targets for content and timing, but also to interpret to the Canadian public the aims and the problems involved.

(3) *Public attitudes*

Finally, the most crucial question in considering political feasibility is that of public attitudes, particularly towards poverty. Although a shocking 20 to 30 per cent of Canada's population is living in poverty, the poor are still a minority of the population. They are becoming more vocal, but they still wield little political clout. Acceptance of the goal of a GAI will depend on the attitude of the majority of Canadians. The appeal to them must rest not only on such moral and philosophical considerations as human rights, the dignity of every Canadian and a commitment to the sense of fraternity and interdependence. It must also be based on an assurance that such a program would not damage the country as a whole, nor adversely affect the better-off people unduly.

For example, there appears to be a widespread and deeply-rooted fear that a GAI would reduce incentive to work. Whether or not this fear is justified (it is hoped that current U.S. experiments and those being planned in Canada will throw light on this point), it is undoubtedly at present a major political obstacle to the acceptance of a GAI. The fear can be reduced through the use of built-in monetary incentives to work in new or reformed income security measures for employables, plus measures for "guaranteed" employment; the latter will have to be accompanied by the creation of a better public understanding of the changing concept of employment and its effect on the work ethic.

Canadians who are better off financially naturally fear an adverse personal effect from redistribution of income, but such redistribution is inevitable if an adequate GAI is to be achieved. Although there is considerable debate about the desirability of continued economic growth *per se,* people must be reminded again and again that the Canadian economy is, in fact, growing. For example, it is projected that, in current dollars, our gross national product will more than double by 1980 to $180 billion from the $84 billion achieved in 1970. Even with continued inflation, this would make it possible for everybody to receive more income; thus, better redistribution of income can be achieved without reducing the standard of living for the "haves." In fact, their standard of living can continue to grow, but at a somewhat lesser rate than it now does and lesser than the rate at which the income of the "have-nots" will grow in the future.

If anything like an adequate GAI is to be achieved, most Canadians will have to be convinced that increased transfer payments, as suggested by the Economic Council, is a better use of Canada's financial resources than measures such as tax cuts which would chiefly serve to improve the lead position of higher-income groups. This is indeed the crux of the political problem related to GAI in Canada. I would suggest that the development of a happier and more equitable community should appeal not only to the heart but also to enlightened self-interest.

The major lesson of the seminar was, in my view, that we cannot achieve the goal of an adequate guaranteed income at one fell swoop or through one measure alone. However, the recognition that we shall not achieve the goal simply and easily should not lead us into the trap of doing nothing at all until we can attain everything. Furthermore, as Professor Miller noted in the seminar discussions, "in the modest recognition of what cannot be accomplished lies the possibility of beginning to talk constructively." It is in this spirit that Canada and other countries should consider accepting an integrated approach to a guaranteed income as an attainable goal and move forward to implement it as quickly as possible. In my view, refusal to accept this goal is tantamount to admitting that Canada's economic system cannot produce enough wealth to ensure an adequate standard of living for all, or conceding that the concept of equitable distribution of wealth has no place in our scale of values.

Background
Papers
for
the
Nuffield
Canadian
Seminar

Guaranteed
Annual
Income:
An
Integrated
Approach

Why a Guaranteed Annual Income?

by Israel Katz
Director General,
National Insurance Institute, Jerusalem, Israel

It seems that, with the exception of certain primitive societies, man has always lived at a level of scarcity. Some select groups, or elites, have been able to take for themselves more material goods than others, in spite of a relatively low level of material productivity. The existence of most groups, however, has often been threatened. It has been a law of God, nature or the economy that this should be so. Inequality in the command of income has usually been viewed as a "natural inequality" which Jean-Jacques Rousseau distinguished from "moral or political inequality" arising out of the conventions of human society. He defined "moral or political inequality" as consisting of:

the different privileges which some men enjoy to the prejudice of others; such as that of being more rich, more honored, more powerful or even in a position to exact obedience.[1]

Guaranteed income is about moral and political inequality. Essentially, it relates to a guaranteed condition for existence and thus allows for a degree of freedom to act, think and feel. Consequently, it enables more independence or self-dependence. Its absence threatens one's existence and survival and limits freedom.

The threat of starvation against those unwilling to accept demands imposed on them may limit man's freedom not less than the use of force against dissenters by their rulers. And though the right to live and to have food, shelter, medical care, housing and education, etc., is a belief deeply rooted in humanist traditions, in reality it has been a right that was, and is, often restricted to those who some consider to be socially "useful." A guaranteed income would help remove such a restriction. Guaranteed income in its truest form implies, or should imply, that man has, indeed, a right to live. The recognition of this right in actual fact would establish a degree of true freedom as a reality rather than a slogan.

Erich Fromm suggests that guaranteed income reflects a shift from a psychology of scarcity to one of abundance and, as such, it is among the most important steps in human development. A psychology of scarcity generates anxiety, envy and egotism, while a

---

1. Jean-Jacques Rousseau, *A Dissertation on the Origin and Foundation of Inequality among Mankind.*

psychology of abundance produces initiative, faith in life and solidarity.[2]

Fromm's interpretation of a guaranteed income may be too optimistic. His concept of guaranteed income as reflected by its name may be erroneous in the light of contemporary analyses of guaranteed income programs and policy proposals. A guaranteed income is income maintenance by right, usually set out in legislation. Its adequacy for the individual or for particular beneficiaries, and/or its aggregate program adequacy (in terms of its effectiveness as a redistributive or anti-poverty program), does not necessarily reflect a shift from a psychology of scarcity to one of abundance. Moreover, the political and administrative mechanism by which guaranteed cash transfers are brought about may, or may not, produce initiative, faith in life, and solidarity. The concept of a guaranteed income tends, therefore, to hide more than it proclaims. Nevertheless, increasing affluence and rising aspirations and expectations amid poverty, frustration, discrimination and pollution, seem to have a deep and pervasive influence in many of our countries, and increasing support is developing for some type of a guaranteed annual income.

A minimum income, education and good health – which in the past were considered privileges and responsibilities of the individual – are gradually being considered as his rights, usually to be guaranteed by law and secured by the community for his protection and well-being as well as for its own.

In Israel, for example, the interest in a guaranteed income is increasing. Programs of income security have become a matter of wider public concern and involvement. It appears that the main reason for this development is not the recognition that the existing income maintenance system has "failed" as a social institution. It is more the realization that income distribution is not what it was supposed to be in a country committed to the integration of heterogeneous ethnic and socioeconomic groups. And the income maintenance system is believed to be a major instrument for distribution and redistribution of cash. As such, it also brings about, to an extent, the distribution over time of other resources, such as education, housing and other facets of the "good life," in a "better society" than that from which many of us have come. Social security schemes or social insurance are still considered basic instruments for income security and receive wide political backing. Moreover, such schemes are still viewed as developing and in need of ongoing expansion, modification and improvement since they can never completely solve all income security problems.

Old age and survivors' insurance, maternity and family insur-

2. Erich Fromm, "Psychology of a Guaranteed Income," in *The Guaranteed Income: Next Step in Economic Evolution?*, ed. by Robert Theobald (New York: Doubleday, 1966).

ance, work injury and disability insurance, as well as unemployment insurance, are all still relatively new, and reflect achievements to be reinforced in scope and depth by extending the coverage to additional groups, raising the level of benefits in proportion to the rising standard of living, and improving program administration. It is mainly in this sense that the guaranteed income is understood.

There is, and should be, however, a sense of uneasiness about the present state of income security in Israel. There are groups of people and needs that are not covered or are inadequately covered, and the most developed countries are again offering new economic and social inventions that are simple and efficient, such as a guaranteed income in various forms of negative income taxation, which will abolish other forms of income maintenance.

What Kind of a Guaranteed Income?

Today, and for us, more relevant than the question of "why a guaranteed income?" is the issue of "what kind of a guaranteed income?" or "who gets what, when, how?"[3] And, not less important: "what route to social reform will bring about required improvements in income security?"

All income guarantees have their costs. Social development has its cost. There is increasing awareness of the social price to be paid for negative externalities of social instruments. Often these effects may be less recognized than the cost of the environmental and ecological disutilities of economic development and the production of the gross national product.

More hidden than air pollution may be the "social service pollution" created by welfare instruments. The risks and dangers that may be created by guaranteed income measures which divide rather than unify groups in a society are of grave concern in Israel. If division were reinforced and nurtured not only by the "market" or economic policy but also by social policies, Israel's society would be easily divided along lines of origin and ethnicity.

It seems that the essence of the problem of many individuals, families, groups, and regions in the country is that they are, or are apt to become, excluded from the larger "good society" because they do not have the resources, including income, that are needed to sustain an "average" life. Our main concern, therefore, is, or should be, how to develop over time a strategy of greater income equalization in the specific political and social context of Israel. Consequently, the cardinal test of any guaranteed income with its benefits and costs, is its conduciveness to bring about income equalization within the broader context of the distribution of resources,

---

3. H. D. Lasswell, *Politics: Who Gets What, When, How* (Cleveland: World Publishing Company, 1958).

both material and non-material, in the community.

Discussions of income maintenance alternatives, social security, negative income taxes and other cash transfer programs continue: *. . . either in the form of a catalogue of different proposals . . . or short-sighted polemics about the superiority of some one method.*[4]

They relate usually to different targets: the "welfare poor," all low-income groups including the "working poor," and the inequities of income distribution. It is clear that any form of, or approach to, guaranteed income can only be developed or assessed in the light of its explicit objectives. Criteria for assessing its adequacy, stigma effects, horizontal and vertical efficiency, work incentive effects, program cost (both recognized and unrecognized) and political support must be examined with regard to its aim.[5] In the world of social policy and, especially, in that of the social policy maker, the analysis of the dilemmas, which are inherent both in *every form* of guaranteed income and in the socioeconomic context in which policy is being made, is of crucial importance.

But of still greater importance and policy relevance are the questions about objectives and goals which are easily obscured. In particular, the discussion of a guaranteed income leads rapidly to a discussion of technologies of various alternatives that tempt policy makers and administrators. Issues, which S. M. Miller refers to as social policy dichotomies,[6] or "oscillating principles," such as fundamentalism and incrementalism, or universality and selectivity, are being resolved at, and for, the given moment irrespective of value objectives.

Thus, the consideration of an increase in selectivity in income security, removed from an infrastructure of universalism, may indeed lead to increased expenditures on the poor. However, these may not necessarily be on a continuing basis and/or may not take into account significant externalities. Such external consequences of increased selectivity affect the poor, the community and the quality of life. If the guaranteed income is to cope with poverty, defined as relative deprivation, it must address itself not only to the very poor but also to existing and emerging gaps and to the distribution of resources in all meaningful dimensions of modern life. Moreover, it must then use more effectively existing institutions and systems that have provided, are providing, and will continue to distribute resources to those who are not poor. This is a critical demand because it implies change and not a status quo of existing schemes of social, fiscal and occupational welfare; it also implies

4. T. R. Marmor, *Income Maintenance Alternatives: Concepts, Criteria and Program Comparisons* (Madison: Institute for Research on Poverty, University of Wisconsin, 1969).

5. Marmor, *Income Maintenance Alternatives: Concepts, Criteria and Program Comparisons.*

6. S. M. Miller, "Rough Notes on Social Policy" (1964).

possible changes in the direction economic developments must take to increase their contribution to social welfare.

In Israel, it seems that more effective and challenging policy debates about reforms in income maintenance for an adequate and effective guaranteed income are not being initiated for the poor (and certainly not by the poor) but for the sake of the not-so-poor who carry a heavy burden of a nation at war, and who feel relatively deprived although they are above the poverty line as determined by the level of public assistance allowances. Among them are many of the aged, one-parent families, disabled and working poor, and large families. In our situation, the fuller realization of an income guarantee seems to require greater progressiveness in social security; a more comprehensive integration of all forms of taxation with benefits, including relief of tax burdens to offset the regressiveness of taxes for social insurance and personal consumption; and covering additional groups in social security programs to achieve greater "selectivity" in and "positive" discrimination for the poorer sections in the community within our universal schemes.

A reform in the family allowances section of the Family Insurance Program, effective in 1972, considerably increased family allowances and made them taxable. The reform diminished the size of the population in need of public assistance by 50 per cent. The low-wage population in need of wage supplements, which are considered by many working poor as a public assistance dole, will also be decreased significantly by the reform and through introduction of a new program of disability insurance in 1973. (So far, in Israel, where many are concerned about the country's relatively low birthrate, family allowances do not seem to act as incentives to increase family size.)

We believe that if the guaranteed income is to focus on a restricted concept of poverty only – that is, on those with incomes below a poverty line, the "minority poverty," and on "filling" the poverty gap of individuals and families whose income falls short of the "non-poverty standard" – it would essentially not differ from some of the existing programs for the poor. As suggested by Eveline Burns:

Programs that deal only with "the poor" run the danger, not only of being poor programs, but also of polarizing society into two groups, the poor and the non-poor, the one receiving benefits and the other footing the bill. There is growing evidence of a rising resentment on the part of those just above the poverty line that everything is being done for the poor while they are neglected. A program that perpetuates this polarization is inefficient.[7]

7. E. M. Burns, "Welfare Reform and Income Security Policies," a paper presented at the National Conference on Social Welfare, Chicago (June, 1970).

The Guaranteed Income and Other Dimensions of Well-Being

The guaranteed income in its various forms should reduce the negative consequences of lack of income on the well-being of people in the market economy of an acquisitive society. (Even in such cooperative economies as that of the kibbutz, income and income equivalents are guaranteed.) This should not obscure or mask the fact that income is but one of many dimensions and aspects of well-being. Following Richard Titmuss' concern about "the command over resources over time," S. M. Miller and Pamela Roby point to six dimensions of well-being: income, assets, services, education and social mobility, political participation and power, status and self-respect.[8]

Dimensions such as family relations, work and working conditions (including opportunities for work satisfaction), leisure time and leisure time pursuits – or the "right to give" or to be involved in gift relationships[9] – and the opportunity to enter into social contracts are also dimensions or aspects of well-being. Such dimensions could and should be more specifically explored for our better understanding and for more effective intervention to bring about the well-being of the individual, family and community.

Income is not the only dimension of well-being, but it appears to be a central one. It is correctly being argued that improvement of one dimension of well-being does not necessarily insure improvement in other dimensions. However, various externalities of income deprivation are often dysfunctional with regard to well-being in other dimensions. There seem to be some significant relationships among such dimensions of well-being. No doubt more research on the nature and interdependence of these relationships may lead to conclusions about strategies and instruments required for more effective and efficient intervention to diminish deprivation and its behavioral, social, economic and political consequences. Such findings and conclusions would also deepen our understanding and sophistication about the kind of guaranteed income required (for its greatest multiplying effects) to achieve more comprehensive well-being and welfare. Be that as it may, there are indications that justify a guaranteed income approach if it is to relate to relative deprivation or inequality in the command over resources over time.

If we compare benefits and costs of transfer payments and include in such comparison the notion of externalities as, for example, how to increase the willingness of the population to "transfer" income and other resources, many good programs of social

8. S. M. Miller and Pamela Roby, *The Future of Inequality* (New York: Basic Books, 1970).

9. Richard M. Titmuss, *The Gift Relationship, From Human Blood to Social Policy* (London: George Allen and Unwin Limited, 1970).

policy may not be considered as costly as they seem. Thus, transfers come to be viewed as crucial investments, rather than consumption.

The relationship, or links, between a guaranteed income (as a strategy of income equalization) and other dimensions of the distribution of resources must increasingly be recognized. For example, as standards of, and expectations for the use of education rise, so do the demands on the required resources, including income, of the individual and family. The same seems to be true in connection with improvement in housing and better use of more sophisticated social utilities and other services.

In summary, the guaranteed annual income, if it is to contribute meaningfully to comprehensive well-being, must relate to externalities and their multiple effects. If it remains a program for the poor, it will have the major characteristics of traditional public assistance. If it takes the form of the negative income tax or a similar arrangement, it would divide the community between those who receive the benefit and those who pay for it. Moreover, it would hinder and prevent any significant redistribution of other resources such as services-in-kind, opportunities for participation and true integration in the community. It would do so both for the "giver" or provider of the service – that is, the non-poor – and the receiver of services, who would be unable to use them effectively even if and when they are offered.

What is needed, then, is a program (or, essentially, a cluster or combination of programs) benefiting everyone rather than emphasizing elements that divide people and the community they live in. To quote Richard Titmuss:

It is the explicit or implicit institutionalization of separateness, whether categorized in terms of income, class, race, color or religion, rather than the recognition of similarities between people and their needs which causes much of the world's suffering.[10]

---

10. Titmuss, *The Gift Relationship, From Human Blood to Social Policy*, p. 238.

Public Policies for Creating Gainful Employment

by David C. Smith
Professor and Head, Department of Economics,
Queen's University, Kingston, Ontario

Full employment and an equitable distribution of income are usually high on the list of appropriate goals of public policy. The goals are conceptually distinct since the former refers to maintaining adequate employment opportunities for persons seeking employment and the latter refers to a distribution of incomes in the society in relative amounts that satisfy prevailing notions of equity. They are generally advanced more as vague, abstract concepts of what a good society should have than as operational targets for public policy. But the agenda of this seminar indicates the possibility of important areas of overlap between the goals or, more specifically, between the creation of adequate employment opportunities and the guarantee of a minimum annual income.

An annual income to sustain a minimum standard of satisfaction of economic wants can arise from three sources.

(1) The returns to human capital which encompass payments to individuals for their effort, abilities, education, training and particular sources of bargaining strength in the market.

(2) The returns to non-human wealth which include interest, dividends, rent and capital gains on assets.

(3) The transfer of income, principally through government taxation and expenditure policies, from some members of society to other members.

Measures to increase employment, to use the existing labor force or stock of human capital more fully, do not necessarily reduce inequalities in the distribution of labor incomes and do not affect directly the incomes of people outside the labor force. Moreover, work does not ensure an adequate standard of living; a recent Canadian report on poverty estimated that the working poor represent more than 50 per cent of the poor.[1] But employment policies, like all other economic policies, cannot be divorced from their direct and indirect effects on the distribution of incomes.

Full employment policies could make a contribution to raising minimum standards of living in several ways.

---

1. Canada, Parliament, Senate, Special Committee on Poverty, *Poverty in Canada* (Ottawa: Information Canada, 1971), p. 170.

(1) To the extent that unemployment indicates a significant gap between the actual output and income of the economy and the potential output and income which could be achieved with a fuller utilization of the labor force, average incomes and the level of income available for redistribution to the poor will be affected by employment policies. The general problem of maintaining high employment levels with a reasonable degree of price stability becomes relevant.

(2) If higher employment levels benefit low-income groups more than other income groups, the distribution of incomes will become more equal. The effects of general employment conditions on income distribution thus need to be estimated.

(3) Employment policies can differ depending on the extent to which they are directed at improving specifically employment opportunities of low-income groups. Labor market policies have embodied the objective of improved distributional equity as well as the objectives of a lower unemployment rate and greater economic efficiency and growth.

Stabilization at Full Employment

Under-utilization of the labor force imposes social and financial hardships on those directly affected and reduces the general levels of income and output in the society. The experience of the 1930s demonstrated, in an unnecessarily dramatic fashion, the importance of appropriate national monetary and fiscal policies and the high degree of economic interdependence among nations. Governments have since assumed greater responsibility for maintaining full employment, and the management of general levels of demand for labor has been better understood. Despite these changes, national employment problems continue to dominate debate on national economic policies.

Reasons for the persistence of unemployment as a national issue are numerous. Disagreements continue on how low the unemployment rate should be in order to satisfy a full employment goal. Interest has increased in disaggregating the full employment goal and in setting separate targets to deal with areas where unemployment rates differ according to duration, region and demographic features of the labor force. Evidence of inflation at high employment levels – and sometimes at not such high employment levels – has frequently led governments into the painful strategy of curbing inflation through deflationary monetary and fiscal policies that increase unemployment.

A full employment goal is generally presented in terms of a maximum unemployment rate or of a desirable range within which the unemployment rate should fall. Governments have been reluctant to adopt a fixed, precise figure. A low figure which is not achieved

Average Annual Unemployment Rates in Six Western Countries, 1959-1970

	Unemployment rates as published	Unemployment rates as adjusted to U.S. concepts
Canada	5.3%	5.3%
France	1.5	2.4
Britain	2.0	3.0
Italy	3.3	3.8
United States	4.8	4.8
West Germany	1.1	0.7

Sources: A. F. Neef and R. A. Holland, "Comparative Unemployment Rates 1964–66," *Monthly Labor Review*, XC (April, 1967), pp. 18–20; C. Sorrentino, "Unemployment in the U.S. and Seven Foreign Countries," *Monthly Labor Review*, XCIII (September, 1970), pp. 12–33; "Notes on Statistics of Manpower Costs and Unemployment in Major Industrial Countries," *National Institute Economic Review*, LVI (May, 1971), pp. 66–9.

becomes a source of political embarrassment; a higher figure can be used as evidence of the heartless nature of the administration. Statistical and economic reasons also weaken the case for a fixed, precise figure.

Methods of measuring unemployment differ among countries and have differed over time within countries. Much work has gone into improving the methods and into adjustments that make possible at least rough comparisons of unemployment rates among countries. For example, in the accompanying table the average annual unemployment rates in the period 1959–1970 are given for six Western countries. The figures in the first column are those published by the national authorities; the figures in the second column are estimates, made at the United States Bureau of Labor Statistics, to adjust the published national rates to rates that would be more comparable to the concepts of unemployment used in United States measures.

The data give an approximate indication of recent persistent differences in national unemployment rates among countries. They have an economic and social significance only when one probes into differences in the functioning of labor markets, in income maintenance for the unemployed, in the industrial structure of countries and in the full employment policies among countries. Underlying differences in the characteristics of national labor markets mean that the appropriate full employment goal is not a fixed international constant. Moreover, data are limited on other measures of the underutilization of the labor force. An unemployment rate does not include those who have become discouraged from actively seeking employment; it does not capture the distinction between voluntary and involuntary part-time activity.

Crude as a national unemployment rate is as a measure of the utilization rate of labor, it has nevertheless become the key indicator for gauging the success of employment policies. Public concern over the appropriate level for this indicator appears strongly related to its recent levels and movements rather than a conception of some fixed, absolute level. In the mid-1950s in Canada, when unemployment rates in the earlier postwar period had averaged below 3 per cent, unemployment rates of 4 to 5 per cent were regarded as a failure of employment policies. At the beginning of the 1960s and the beginning of the 1970s when unemployment rates have been 6 to 7 per cent, unemployment rates of 4 to 5 per cent have sometimes been regarded as an appropriate range for a full employment goal.

These shifts in the rate of unemployment in the economy are frequently ascribed to fundamental changes in the operation of labor markets. Reasons advanced for the longer-term shifts in the natural or normal rate of unemployment differ. It has been argued that increased state support for the unemployed and dependents of the unemployed have made the costs of being unemployed less severe and increased the incentive to look longer for suitable alternative employment. Particularly at the beginning of the 1960s, when unemployment rates were exceptionally high in North America, there was a widespread belief that technological changes and, in particular, the spread of automation were altering dramatically the demand for particular types of labor and were producing a chronic deficiency in job opportunities. The proportionately larger increases in the labor force during the past decade have caused, in the views of some people, more serious problems than normal in absorbing new entrants into the labor force.

Whatever may be the merits of these and other arguments about the longer-term structural changes taking place in labor markets, unemployment rates have been strongly influenced by the direction of monetary, fiscal and exchange rate policies. Much of the gloom about the structural failings of the system in the early 1960s faded as more expansionary policies in North America brought the unemployment rates down from a high in Canada of 7.1 per cent in 1961 to 3.6 per cent in 1966 and from a high in the United States of 6.7 per cent in 1961 to 3.5 per cent in 1969. At the end of the 1960s more restrictive policies were initiated in both Canada and the United States. They have been accompanied, with a lag, by substantial increases in the unemployment rates. In Canada the unemployment rate averaged 6.4 per cent in 1971 and in the United States it averaged 5.9 per cent.

Periods of above normal unemployment rates are also periods of lower actual total output and incomes than of potential total output and incomes. The loss of income cannot be measured precisely and the time span over which the loss is measured will be important. But, A. M. Okun, the former chairman of the President's Council of Economic Advisers, has suggested for the United States that, for each extra percentage point in the unemployment rate above 4 per cent, the gross national product in real terms will be about 3 per cent lower than it would otherwise be.[2] Similar estimates of the relationship between actual and potential output and income, as unemployment rates vary, have been made for Canada. For example, it has been suggested that in the first half of 1971 actual income and output in Canada was about 3.5 per cent below potential which would mean a shortfall of about $3 billion.[3] Despite the inevitable inaccuracies of quantitative estimates of the gap, it

2. Arthur M. Okun, *The Political Economy of Prosperity* (New York: W. W. Norton & Co., 1970), p. 135.
3. Economic Council of Canada, *Performance in Perspective 1971* (Ottawa: Information Canada, 1971), p. 19.

is clear that greater success in managing aggregate demand policies to maintain high employment levels would have a high payoff not only in reducing the human misery associated directly with unemployment but also in sustaining the rise in average incomes, in decreasing the transfer of resources to compensate the unemployed, and in increasing the available resources for economic and social welfare policies.

Governments do not like to create more unemployment; such action is not the best route to success at the polls. The dilemma that has faced many governments is that, at high employment levels, rates of inflation have been encountered which have been judged to be too high. A rate of change of average prices may be judged too high because of its alleged costs; because it is above a popular conception of what is a normal or natural rate for the economy; because of a fear that the rate will accelerate, causing at a later stage a greater waste of resources if corrective action is not taken now; or because balance of payments difficulties are encountered which are ascribed to an excessive rate of domestic inflation. Attempts to curb inflation through more restrictive monetary and fiscal policies have involved costs in terms of higher unemployment.

The concept of a policy "trade-off" relationship has become a popular summary of the dilemma facing governments that try to maintain high employment levels with a reasonable degree of price stability. The relationship means that, if governments follow more expansionary monetary and fiscal policies to lower the unemployment rate, a higher rate of average price increases will occur; conversely, if more restrictive policies are followed to reduce the rate of price increases, a higher unemployment rate will occur. Such a relationship has been observed over time in many countries.

The trade-off relationship has not been so stable as to provide a precise forecast of the effects of changes in the direction of monetary and fiscal policies. Moreover, observations based on past experience when unemployment rates and prices have fluctuated do not necessarily tell us very much about the consequences of trying to keep the unemployment rate or the rate of price increases fixed at a roughly constant rate. If expectations of wage and price increases adjust upwards, the trade-off relationship will appear less favorable; a higher rate of price increases will be associated with given rates of unemployment. Thus, let us suppose a government commits itself to maintaining a very low rate of unemployment and will create whatever expansionary monetary and fiscal policies are necessary to maintain that low rate. If price increases become higher for long, expectations of future price increases will rise which will make the trade-off relationship less favorable and induce a more expansionary monetary and fiscal policy in order to preserve the lower unemployment rate. Inflation could thus become even more serious than would have been predicted on the basis of past experience when a less ambitious, variable employment goal had been pursued. The inflationary consequences of this approach will depend on how zealous the government is in trying to lower the unemployment rate permanently through reliance on monetary and fiscal policies.

A different strategy would be to direct monetary and fiscal policies towards preserving a fixed modest or zero rate of average price changes, to bring these policies to bear solely on the maintenance of price stability and thus to divorce them from employment issues. The rate of unemployment which naturally emerges over time would have to be accepted.

Neither approach is, in practice, an appealing option for public policy. An acceleration in the rate of inflation is likely to deflect monetary and fiscal policies from a fixed target rate of unemployment. If unemployment increases to levels generally regarded as unacceptable, monetary and fiscal policies are liable to be deflected from a fixed target rate of price stability. Further, a high degree of economic interdependence among countries in movements in prices and employment levels limits the extent to which independent national targets can be pursued through monetary and fiscal policies.

In a highly uncertain world in which there are strong political pressures on governments to show that they have tried to secure both higher employment and greater price stability, shifts in monetary and fiscal policies have tended to have a strong short-run bias and to alternate between promoting the goal of full employment and that of price stability. Because of lags in the system, the result has been a policy-induced cycle. If the rate of price increases is judged too high, monetary and fiscal policies are switched towards a restraint position. The effects of the change take a long time to work through the system; perhaps it is a couple of years or so before most of the effects are felt. The initial impacts of the restraint tend to fall heavily on output and employment levels. By the time price increases are beginning to show a marked slowdown, public concern about rising unemployment mounts and pressures rise for shifting monetary and fiscal policies towards an expansion position. Again, with substantial lags, the system responds. Unemployment declines, but growing evidence of an acceleration in price increases strengthens the case for changing again the direction of economic policies. The cycle begins again. Over time, however, the economic system can become less responsive to shifts in the direction of policies. When restraint is imposed, people begin to remember that previous periods of restraint did not last long and that prices soon began their upward course again. Thus, expectations of wage and price changes do not adjust down as much, and both higher rates of price increases and higher unemployment are experienced than previously. The earlier postwar confidence that the new techniques of macroeconomic policy management would resolve the problems of maintaining high employment and stable prices becomes undermined.

The worker, housewife, political leader and economic adviser have all become perplexed and frustrated by the failures of stabilization policies in Western industrialized countries. The failures have not been as great as many people feared and sometimes still fear. There have not been the soaring unemployment rates of the great depression, the soaring price increases of earlier hyperinflations such as in Germany after the First World War, or inflations more recently experienced in some Latin American countries. Severe economic shocks from a collapse of the international monetary system have been averted, although strains remain in the system. Nevertheless the problems have been sufficiently serious to require a basic rethinking of the techniques of stabilization policies.

Solutions to the problems remain unclear. Efforts may be made to increase the responsiveness of prices, wages and employment to shifts in stabilization policies by developing techniques permitting governments to affect expectations more directly; by policies with shorter lags; and by stronger attacks on abuses of economic power which inhibit and distort adjustments in an economy. The policy-induced cycle might be reduced both through improvements in forecasting the consequences of policy changes and by setting the policies with a somewhat longer time horizon. The limits on stabilization policies in keeping the unemployment rate as low as may be economically and socially desirable need to be recognized, and the opportunities for further reductions in unemployment lie mainly in the development of improved labor market policies. It would be unduly optimistic to expect, however, that all vestiges of the trade-off problem will disappear, never again to haunt the policy maker. In his recent presidential address to the American Economic Association, Professor James Tobin argued:

. . . a substantial amount of the unemployment compatible with zero inflation is involuntary and non-optimal. This is, in my opinion, true whether or not the inflations associated with lower rates of unemployment are steady or ever-accelerating. Neither macroeconomic policy makers, nor the elected officials and electorates to whom they are responsible, can avoid weighing the costs of unemployment against those of inflation.[4]

---

4. James Tobin, "Inflation and Unemployment," presidential address delivered at the Eighty-Fourth Annual Meeting of the American Economic Association, New Orleans, Louisiana, December 27–29, 1971 (mimeographed), p. 35.

Stabilization Policies and the Distribution of Income to the Poor

If policy makers cannot escape the trade-off choice, it is important to consider, in view of the subject of this seminar, the impacts the choice will have on the distribution of income to the poor. Clearly one of the great popular fears about opting for some inflation is that the distribution of income will be distorted in an inequitable manner.

The modest but prolonged postwar inflations in many Western countries have not had the serious, dramatic consequences many people predicted; economic damnation has not overtaken those who have flirted with inflation. Trends in productivity do not appear to have been adversely affected. The evidence does not indicate that inflation has caused major shifts in the distribution of income among wages, profits and other sources of income or major shifts in the distribution of income by size of income. Yields on debt have adjusted as expectations of price increases became reflected in interest rates; anticipated inflation has led to adjustments in yields of various forms of wealth.

More specific information is needed, however, on the implications of the trade-off choice for the distribution of income to the poor. When prices are rising, does the price index tend to rise relatively more rapidly for items purchased by the poor? If so, the real purchasing power of their incomes would suffer relative to other groups in society. Do the incomes and wealth of the low-income groups gain both absolutely and in relative terms if unemployment rates are lower and price increases higher or if unemployment rates are higher and price increases lower? Are stronger demand pressures in the labor market a help in dissolving some of the barriers to the poor in obtaining employment at non-poverty wages?

Data and research are lacking for conclusive answers to these questions. With present knowledge and in terms of the recent experience with unemployment and inflation in North America it appears that, on balance, low-income groups do not suffer and probably gain when the economy is operated at high employment levels, despite the inflationary consequences. The low-income group is not homogeneous, however, in age, sources of income and expenditure patterns. The group as a whole may benefit but some sub-groups, such as the aged poor, would benefit less from the stimulation of employment opportunities and suffer more from the price increases.

In a study by R. G. Hollister and J. L. Palmer,[5] price indexes for expenditures by the poor and various sub-groups of the poor

---

5. R. G. Hollister and J. L. Palmer, "The Impact of Inflation on the Poor," Institute for Research on Poverty, Discussion Paper 40–69 (Madison, Wis.: Institute for Research on Poverty, University of Wisconsin, 1969).

were estimated. The indexes were calculated for the United States during 1953–1967. The general conclusion is that price indexes for expenditures by the poor as a group, and by various sub-groups of the poor, did not rise faster than the consumer price index and, particularly in the 1960s, rose a little less rapidly. The one qualification is that the higher costs of Medicare moved the price index for the aged poor slightly above the consumer price index in the mid-1960s. The findings confirm the importance of disaggregating the effects of inflation on particular groups but do not support the view that inflation impinges more heavily on the expenditure patterns of the poor.

The problems of sorting out impacts of changes in employment conditions and the rate of inflation on the distribution of incomes are much more complex. For example, the relative importance of the various sources of income shifts with changes in economic activity and differs by income class. We know that the ratio of profits to wages has tended to fall when an economy moves into a recession and unemployment grows, and has tended to rise in a boom period when unemployment has declined and prices increased more rapidly. On the other hand it is not at all clear that inflation has had any longer-run impact on the ratio. Consequently, the short- and the long-run relations between inflation and the distribution of incomes need to be distinguished.

Transfer payments are typically a higher proportion of income in the lower-income groups. We would expect higher employment levels to reduce directly the payments of unemployment compensation and to reduce indirectly some other forms of income maintenance due to higher average incomes. The impact of inflation on transfer payments is less certain when they are not linked to movements in a price index. Evidence for a number of countries indicates that transfer payments have been adjusted in line with inflation but the timing and reasons for government action in making the adjustments are difficult to predict. Further, data are inadequate or not available for making precise calculations of the effects of changes in unemployment on the distribution of income. In her analysis of the 1961 census data for Canada, Sylvia Ostry noted that "no data presently available provide direct information on the income losses sustained by unemployed individuals and their families,"[6] and that "much more detailed information on work history and income is required in order to distinguish the impact of unemployment per se from that of other economic causes of poverty."[7]

6. Sylvia Ostry, *Unemployment in Canada*, 1961 Census Monograph (Ottawa: Dominion Bureau of Statistics, 1968), p. 55.
7. Ostry, *Unemployment in Canada*, p. 62.

Empirical studies have been made which do not attempt a detailed sorting out of the many relationships but relate the size distribution of income to changes in the level of economic activity.[8] Measures of the inequality in income distribution have been calculated and then related to measures of the general performance of the economy – such as employment conditions. The findings support the view that improvements in employment conditions, despite a more rapid increase in prices, have a relatively more favorable effect on low-income groups. The results do not imply, of course, that inflation is a sufficient or efficient anti-poverty program.

The empirical results of recent research on the distributional effects of the trade-off choice thus cast doubt on the popular assertion that governments must stop inflation in order to help the poor. The inequities of inflation appear to lie more in "horizontal" problems of equity because some groups are more vulnerable to inflation than others, particularly if pensions and various forms of transfer payments adjust only incompletely or with significant lags to changes in the price level. A remedy would be to link these sources of income to a price index in order to provide a full automatic offset to inflation. If society is seriously concerned about ensuring income support for economically disadvantaged or vulnerable groups, it is presumably real income – money income adjusted for changes in the price level – which is relevant; full, automatic adjustments of income support to changes in the price level would, therefore, be a recognition that real income is the relevant concept.

A further consideration in discussions of the distributional effects of the trade-off choice is the impact of stronger demand pressures in the labor market on reducing discriminatory barriers. As H. G. Johnson has pointed out, emphasis should be placed on "the importance of maintaining full employment for the reduction of poverty, on the grounds that a tight labor market is a powerful long-run solvent of discriminatory barriers to participation in the labor market at non-poverty wages."[9] In addition, the advancement of a low-paid worker is affected by his opportunities to "learn by doing" and by intermittent and prolonged periods of unemployment, lowering the prospects of escaping from poverty.

---

8. See in particular, Charles E. Metcalf, "The Size Distribution of Personal Income During the Business Cycle," *American Economic Review,* LIX (September, 1969), 657–68. Other studies include: Lester C. Thurow, "Analyzing the American Income Distribution," *American Economic Review,* LX (May, 1970), 261–79; Hollister and Palmer, "The Impact of Inflation on the Poor," and unpublished research by Charles M. Beach at Princeton University.

9. H. G. Johnson, "Approaches to the Reduction of Poverty," *Inequality and Poverty,* ed. by Edward C. Budd (New York: W. W. Norton & Co., 1967), p. 185.

Full Employment and Labor Market Policies

Difficulties in achieving what are regarded as satisfactory employment levels through reliance exclusively on monetary and fiscal policies were discussed earlier. Below some unemployment rates the inflationary consequences of stronger demand policies become unacceptable; to try to keep pushing the unemployment rate lower through monetary and fiscal policies is to invite a sharp acceleration in inflation without significant benefits – and possibly adverse consequences – to the unemployment rate, even if the effects on international trade and capital flows permit this degree of independence in domestic policies. The lower limit will depend in part on the dynamic path of adjustment the economy is currently following and the time horizon over which policies are established. In view of the long lags in the adjustment of the economy to changes in monetary and fiscal policies, a current situation of relatively high unemployment and rising prices may be largely a reflection of the past direction of policies rather than of where unemployment rates and the rate of inflation would settle if the current direction of policies were held steady for a time. The lower limit, it was also suggested, is not a fixed hard floor but a rather more elastic range over which policy makers have to weigh the costs of unemployment and inflation. Further, there is not a fixed, long-term normal rate which can be referred to as *the* full employment rate and which prevails among countries and within countries over time, because changing institutional features on both the demand and supply sides of labor markets affect the unemployment rate.

Opportunities for special policies to affect specifically the composition of the demand for and supply of labor and to facilitate and promote adjustment processes in the labor market broaden the scope for full employment policies beyond aggregate demand policies. These labor market policies cover a wide range of possible measures.

First, there are those which seek to shift the composition of demand for labor to slack seasons of the year, to regions of above-average unemployment and, in general, to those sections of the labor market in which labor surpluses seem to have emerged. Examples of these measures lie in winter works programs, regional incentives for industrial location and special measures to shore up faltering businesses and industries.

Second, greater interest has been shown in many countries in measures to alter the composition of the supply of labor. The measures include mobility programs to help move labor to areas where employment opportunities are greater and manpower retraining programs to help provide the skills that are in greater demand.

Third, there are measures aimed at improving information on

job opportunities and reducing the private costs and time involved in searching for new employment. A reduction in the unemployment rate is made possible by methods that more efficiently transmit knowledge about job openings and available supplies of labor. Improvements in national employment services are an example.

Finally, the functioning of labor markets can be affected by public policies to correct abuses of economic power on both the demand and supply sides of labor markets. New restrictive practices, whether initiated by management or by labor organizations, decrease the amount of employment in the affected areas and increase the problems of absorbing labor in other areas. Monopolistic practices in the production and sale of commodities increase the relative price and curb the expansion of output and employment in the production and distribution of the commodities. Similarly, labor organizations, including professional organizations, frequently have an interest in curbing new entrants and securing restrictions on work practices that will create an artificial scarcity of labor in their occupations and lead to higher relative pay. The noticeable growth in public concern about these restrictive activities in recent years has been largely channelled – I believe mistakenly – into the fight against inflation. The practices distort the pattern of job opportunities, raise barriers to the escape from poverty wages and reduce average real incomes in the society. To link policies to deal with them to the on-again, off-again fight against inflation is to seriously underestimate their enduring and more fundamental importance.

Public policies in these four areas do not guarantee a lowering of the unemployment rate. Some measures to shift the composition of the demand for and supply of labor may simply redistribute unemployment, evening it out by region, occupation, sex, age and duration, without significant effects on the average rate, but the measures could still promote other social goals of reducing distress associated with particularly high incidences of unemployment. Income maintenance and mobility measures to assist workers in the search for new jobs could increase turnover rates of labor and thus increase the average number looking for new jobs. Manpower forecasting is unfortunately such an inexact matter that training programs tied to such forecasts could aggravate areas of surplus skills. In Canada in 1969–70 only 3.9 per cent of the federal manpower training program was spent on training-in-industry and the balance was spent on institutional training whereas in the United States, 76.8 per cent of the federal manpower training program was spent on on-the-job training.[10] The implications for this type of support for manpower training have been insufficiently explored. Finally,

10. Economic Council of Canada, *Design for Decision-Making*, Eighth Annual Review (Ottawa: Information Canada, 1971), p. 105.

efforts to shore up particular businesses or industries to maintain specific demands for labor may not only be inefficient and costly but also postpone and aggravate at a later date unemployment problems in these areas.

Success with public policies in these four areas depends on success with other public policies. For example, much of the impetus for expanded labor market policies has come at times of above-average unemployment. They are advanced as solutions to what is really a failing of aggregate demand policies. As a result, they face the double threat of waning public support if unemployment rates decline and of growing public disillusionment if unemployment rates fail to respond. Much of their contribution lies in facilitating adjustment processes, in reducing unemployment with less inflationary consequences, when demand pressures in the labor market are generally high.

Policies in these four areas are, in addition, particularly difficult to coordinate. Objectives in launching them vary. A reduction in the unemployment rate is not necessarily the principal objective. Sometimes the intention is to promote greater economic efficiency and higher economic growth and, at other times, it is to secure a more equitable distribution of jobs and incomes. Moreover, expanded government expenditures in these areas undoubtedly provide opportunities for subsidization of particular groups for electoral rather than economic and social advantage.

The large number and complexity of possible measures and the differences in objectives make systems for studying and evaluating inter-relationships among actual and potential measures more urgent and difficult. Improvements in technical appraisals of individual measures have been advancing rapidly as the growth of cost-benefit literature attests. The most serious challenges lie in better public evaluations of how the various pieces of policy fit together, in greater coordination and integration of individual measures and in improved forms of economic planning and review mechanisms.

A New Approach to Work
and the Problem of Economic Instability

by Melville J. Ulmer
Professor, College of Business and Public Administration,
Department of Economics,
University of Maryland

Conventional ideas about work, which in turn underlie public policies toward the poor and the unemployed, derive in part from the treatment of labor in orthodox economic theory. They also share, therefore, some of the limitations of that theory, in particular its failure to rise entirely above the class biases of its authors. Thus, work is commonly considered as the service of a "factor of production," a mere tool, a means to an end, on the same footing as the services of land and capital; and like them it can be directed one way or the other, turned on or turned off, with equal ease as profit calculations dictate. Again, it is held that for maximum efficiency labor must be joined with other "factors" in a "least cost" combination, though in the latter are included only the pecuniary outlays of business and none of the costs, pecuniary or otherwise, of labor. Formulas that meet the narrow interests of a profit-seeking corporation are in this way uncritically extended to society.

Wherever culture has become business oriented, as it is in western democracies, these and similar notions are more or less firmly embedded in everyday thinking. They are likewise carefully enshrined in contemporary textbooks, so that quarreling with them may seem about as fruitful as disputing the multiplication table. Nevertheless, this paper raises some critical questions. In particular, it presents a revised approach to the position of work and labor in society, and explores its implications for public policies on unemployment, inflation, poverty, and the spreading malaise that some believe is alienating broad sectors of people from prevailing western institutions.

The Work-Life Dichotomy and Its Consequences

One of the familiar intellectual currents bearing on individual productive activity is the so-called Puritan ethic. In its crudest form it implies that man lives in order to work, and thereby serves God through the industry and forebearance that He values. Crude as it is, the notion has deep roots in modern institutions, which become strengthened all the more wherever maintaining high employment is taken as a goal of public policy, as it commonly is. The evidence appears in statements such as: "We've got to keep the space program going because it provides so many jobs." Or: "Military expenditures may be dangerous, but at least they boost the level of employment." Such thoughts, and the underlying practices, link the old Puritan ethic to the relatively modern theory of John Maynard Keynes, who at one point (in the 1930s) remarked that building pyramids was better than nothing. They both establish work as an end product of life.

The opposite point of view suggests that we work in order to live. Here, work enters as a disutility, in the neoclassical sense, in return for which one obtains the sustenance required for living. Note that it implies a definite compulsion for economic activity: work or starve. In modern times, it is true, the sharp alternatives are powerfully modified, but even today, with the exception of pensioners and the very wealthy, no one can live with reasonable comfort anywhere without employment. Such incentives to participate in productive activity are nearly universal and I am not suggesting that their use, with proper moderation, is morally wrong or socially pointless. Nor do I deny Keynes' assumption that there is solid reason for maintaining a prosperous community.

The contention here, instead, is that the Puritan-Keynesian and neoclassical approaches suffer from a common and serious ailment: both make a false distinction between means and ends, which in turn has led to questionable practices in business and government. Work is an integral *part* of life, occupying an important proportion of the hours most of us are destined to spend on this globe, and a critical element in itself of whatever happiness or sorrow, satisfaction or frustration, may be our lot. It is not a means to life, therefore, nor an end product, but rather one significant component of living, yielding its own direct contribution, positive or negative, to our welfare.

Such comments, perhaps, may seem like rarefied quibbling, until it is realized that the alternatives distinguished have important consequences for private and public policy. Here are a few examples.

1 *Psychic labor costs and production techniques*
The method of production commonly selected by administrators, with the approval of practically all authorities, is the one that produces output at the least cost. In such calculations, labor inputs are graded on the same scale as capital and natural resource inputs. The more net output derived from given resources, it is reasoned, the greater the national welfare. But the method of production has a *direct* impact on the welfare of people – specifically, the workers

employed. National welfare is reduced insofar as a production technique subjects workers to danger, disease, monotony, boredom or frustration; welfare is expanded when productive activity is creative, purposeful, interesting, and varied. Because labor is treated, simply, as a factor of production – inanimate in this context – such effects are ignored in the least cost combination. Logically, they could not be so ignored if it were acknowledged that work is one facet of human activity, rather than simply a means to living as neoclassicists would have it, or as a sacrifice offered for higher objectives (possibly divine) in accord with the Puritan-Keynesian ethic.

If direct yields to the worker (positive or negative) of his activity were counted along with pecuniary costs, no doubt prevailing techniques of production in many industries would be revolutionized. It is also possible that workers would be encouraged to shift from one job to another occasionally, merely for the sake of variety. On balance, if the corrected calculations to include worker reactions were made, and the production technique were itself treated as a relevant variable, society would be significantly better off; in the terminology of economics, a true "Pareto optimal" would be reached.[1]

2 *Psychic labor costs and service to society*
The returns an individual receives from his work activity, directly, depend not only on the nature of the task – the inherent interest, for example, that the operations may have for him – but also on the purposes to which it is directed. Many people sense intuitively a truism that has been all but completely submerged under the camouflage of modern business and government institutions: work is a contribution to the needs of society and is required for that reason alone.

---

1. By making the appropriate postulates, however unreal they may be, it is possible in orthodox theory to eliminate the problem discussed in this paragraph purely by assumption. For example, let us suppose perfect competition, perfect knowledge, perfect, frictionless mobility of all resources, and an absence of technological change. Then competitive firms would be induced to try a wide variety of the available techniques of production, offering in each case wage rates to workers that reflected the value of their marginal product. The wage rates would differ from firm to firm, as would the production techniques and the "psychic" returns to workers from the labor they were performing. Workers would base their choice of jobs on the conditions of employment offered by each firm as well as on the monetary returns. The firms that provided the best combination of working conditions and wages would get most or all of the workers and prosper. But of course none of the assumptions made is even approximated in practice; and in any given line of work, virtually at all times, employees confront a single prevailing technique of production rather than a multiplicity of choices. (A "Pareto optimal" is achieved in the economic system when no one individual can be made better off without reducing the economic welfare of some other individual.)

Now it is true that work is a personal need for some individuals, perhaps in a degree for all individuals, but especially so for the artist. Even here, however, a little thought discloses that the social contribution element is always, or nearly always fundamental. Very few artists, even if they had the financial support, could go on contentedly and forever painting pictures that no other person sees, making music that no one else hears, writing stories that no one else reads. Similarly, a scientist may pursue the truth unswervingly, and with real joy, but normally not if his findings are systematically tossed to the winds and forgotten before any one else can see them. It is rare that the personal satisfaction derived from creativity can be maintained for long without some inkling that the fruits will somehow, some day be observed and shared by others. Creativity becomes something more than that – it becomes work, however joyful or painful it may be – when it helps to satisfy the needs of others.

What, then, may one conclude of the more lowly member of the labor force, not the artist, scientist, or craftsman, but one whose work may be humdrum, or at best not especially engrossing or exciting? Let us suppose that he is producing food of questionable purity, drugs of questionable efficacy, advertisements of questionable truth, parts for nuclear warheads, or less dramatically any one of the many thousands of goods that satisfy the frivolous, transient, artificial demands, ingeniously whipped up by TV commercials, for expensive status symbols, youthful vigor, or surefire guarantees of success in sex. Such workers are not supported in their endeavors by the firm knowledge that their activities are worthwhile, make any particular contribution to anybody, or can in any sense be a source of pride. Their psychic returns from productive activity may be zero or negative. In the more severe cases, they may feel alienated from established institutions and attempt to escape somehow in the kind of understandable but futile flight from reality described by Charles Reich.[2] A redistribution of the product-mix, a reallocation of resources that eliminated wasteful, dangerous, or useless forms of output would make a nation better off in more ways than one. The one particular way of interest here is in the improvement of the morale of workers.

3 *Fixed social labor costs and their significance*
The replacement of an obsolescent machine or tool by a more efficient model is a common occurrence in business and one sign of progress. Whenever the introduction of the new capital equipment, and the discarding of the old, results on balance in a net addition to profit, it pays to make the changeover, by definition. In the requisite calculation, the costs of maintaining the old equipment – of oiling,

---

2. *The Greening of America* (New York: Random House, 1970).

repairing, replacing parts, etc. – are counted as a saving, and properly so; once the machine or tool is discarded, the need for maintenance obviously vanishes. There are no fixed costs that go on even when equipment ceases to be used.

Erroneously, at least from society's viewpoint, exactly the same calculations are applied to "obsolescent" workers. In determining whether human beings are to be replaced by a machine, wages of the workers are counted in full as a potential saving, since once the workers are fired they need not be paid. Severance pay, if required by union contract or custom, is treated as a one-time cost, tantamount to that of ripping out, transporting, and scrapping a machine when it is replaced by another. But from society's point of view, human beings cannot be scrapped. They bear a fixed cost of maintenance that must be met, temporarily by unemployment insurance perhaps, later on by "welfare" or similar payments, but continuously in any event by one means or another. We may add to these the psychic blow to the employee and his family when his skills are no longer wanted. There may also be substantial costs of moving in an effort to find another job or of retraining if the individuals involved are willing and able to utilize it. In any case, technological unemployment is typically expensive in a variety of ways that do not enter business calculations; moreover, it is long-term in most instances, sometimes lasting for life. Were such costs, especially the fixed costs of maintaining humans, taken into account it would no doubt turn out that much of the world's technological "progress" has in fact been regress; that in other words, new labor-saving devices have in general been introduced too abruptly and too fast and that the net gains to society are in the aggregate much smaller than generally supposed and in some instances probably negative.

The foregoing observations have a direct relationship to the potential economic role of public employment programs, to which we now turn.

Unemployment and Public Employment

All western democracies struggle with the problem of unemployment, which undulates through recessions and inflations but practically never disappears entirely. The connection between cyclical unemployment and inflation, which must be taken into account in any program for stabilization, will be discussed in the next section. For the moment it is sufficient to recognize that a small but considerable proportion of the labor force, especially in the United States and Canada, is particularly vulnerable to fluctuations in demand and is idle a large part of the time. Indeed full employment – a situation in which all who want jobs can get them – is an extremely rare occurrence; its last appearance in the United States was during the Second World War.

The great majority of the especially vulnerable group – the hard core unemployed – are the unskilled and the semiskilled. But in addition to these there is also a significant proportion, always, of the skilled, sometimes the very highly trained, who are thrown out of jobs by technological change or by enduring shifts in the national demand pattern. An example of the latter is the cutback in the aerospace program in the United States a year ago (1971) which displaced thousands of specialized engineers and physicists. True full employment, which except for major wars is practically never achieved, would imply an unemployment rate in the United States of about 2 per cent. Actual unemployment between 1948 and 1971 has averaged nearly 5 per cent as a minimal estimate. On this basis it may be calculated that we lost an average of $50 billion in output per year in the United States since 1948, through not maintaining full employment.[3] That output foregone, and never to be regained, over the last quarter of a century, is approximately equal to the actual gross national products during the same period of India and Pakistan together.

This huge loss in production is of interest because it suggests the tremendous advances that can be made in the future by giving the unemployed the opportunity to work. Indeed, the dollar figures just cited probably understate the potential social gains. For if the idle manpower were put to work in the private sector, a large proportion of the additional output would consist of articles of narrowly limited social utility, marginal goods that are a tribute primarily to the cultivated art of advertising. It is in the public sector, as John Kenneth Galbraith has never tired of emphasizing, that unsatisfied social needs are extremely urgent and sometimes alarmingly so – in medical attention, crime prevention, mass transportation, environmental control, education, public facilities for recreation and the arts, care of the aged and infirm, and others. If resources otherwise idle – that is, the unemployed – were given the opportunity to work in the public sector, the social contribution would be substantial and no doubt materially greater than the estimate of private output lost, as given above.

The contribution would be substantial not only for society as a whole, but also for the unemployed themselves. The considerations I advanced in the previous section of this paper help to show why a program of this kind would be especially advantageous. In the

3. My estimate utilized the relationship between increments in the GNP and in labor inputs developed in George L. Perry, "Labor Force Structure, Potential Output, and Productivity," *Brookings Papers on Economic Activity,* No. 3 (1971), pp. 533–78.

first place, its operation would be highly economical. Although the new public employees might be paid union or market wages for their trades or professions, as I think they should, their net cost to government would be very much less. To determine the net cost we would have to deduct from their wages the unemployment insurance, welfare payments, or other public benefits they would have received if idle. Thus, guaranteeing jobs for all, or recruiting the unemployed for public service, is in fact a public economy. It can enhance a nation's output by an amount much greater than the cost.

This economy in the net social cost of labor would show up also in the way in which the factors of production would be combined, at least if government administrators used the proper accounting. Since the net cost of a man-year of labor would be lower than its actual wage by the amount of its foregone social benefits, the relationship between its productivity and its cost would be substantially improved vis-à-vis that of capital and natural resources. It would pay, and would be truly more efficient in many instances, to use less mechanized, more labor-intensive techniques of production than are common in industry. Thus expenses for capital would be minimized, provided also that government officials could resist the blandishments of industry's high-pressure marketers and lobbyists.

Guaranteeing public employment for all those able to work would be for many individuals and families an alternative to gradual deterioration on the dole. For workers, along with higher incomes, this would be the central benefit – an escape from the miasma of idleness, from the sense of worthlessness that unemployment commonly brings. But there would also be potential side benefits that, at its best, public employment can provide. If indeed the techniques of production were in general less capital intensive than those found in industry, the result could possibly be more interesting, less monotonous work. If projects were properly directed and well managed, employees would be made keenly aware of the significance of their objectives and the essential role of the individual in their achievement. Pride in one's work is itself a material benefit, to employees and to the success of their projects. Recent experiments in Canada in the Opportunities for Youth program show how even small, inexpensive projects, usually engaging youth without previous employment experience, can be organized to capture the enthusiastic participation of employees and imaginatively directed toward useful social objectives.

Unemployment and Inflation

We have mentioned the fact that in all western democracies, and perhaps especially in the United States and Canada, there is a submerged group of people who are unemployed a large part of the time and in some instances permanently. They are the reluctant draftees in a reserve army that expands and contracts with the business cycle, a minority without political power of its own and yet the object of ceaseless parliamentary debates and economic maneuvers. The maneuvers consist of Keynesian fiscal and monetary measures which raise or lower the level of business activity, as authorities deem necessary; in the nearly three decades since the Second World War, they have succeeded in providing a roller coaster pattern in output, employment, and prices, a pattern of periodic switching that in Britain inspired the term "stop-go economy."

By now the occasion for the pattern, the reason for the ups and downs, is familiar to most people. When business expands, output and employment naturally increase. But long before full employment is closely approached, prices also rise and advance more and more steeply as the expansion continues. At some point short of full employment the inflation is officially adjudged intolerable, disruptive of orderly economic activity at home and of the nation's trade abroad. The advance is therefore checked by some combination of Keynesian restraining measures: higher taxes, a cutback in government expenditures, or a boost in interest rates. As business activity drops, the inflation normally subsides more or less, depending upon the duration and severity of the slump; but just as regularly, and in roughly the same degree, unemployment increases. Practically always the more inflation retreats, the more unemployment advances. It turns out, in effect, that those who lead the war against inflation, those who are thrust in the front lines however reluctantly, are the involuntary recruits in the reserve army of the unemployed. They are normally mobilized there, in full force, until inflation drifts down to an "acceptable" level. Meanwhile, of course, the political party out of office is scandalized by the depression and expressions of dismay and shock become increasingly common.

In time, particularly since after a while corporate profits and stock prices are weakened, a turnabout is executed. Taxes are reduced, public outlays are liberalized and credit is made more easily available. With such conventional Keynesian amelioratives, the economy normally recovers with output and employment on the rise and, unfortunately, inflation picking up too. As the expansion proceeds and inflation intensifies, the pressures for restraint, for a "corrective" recession arise once again and ultimately grow irresistible. In short, unemployment and inflation remain on a perpetually activated see-saw. When one goes up, the other goes down and they alternate in direction continuously.[4]

4. Some have supposed that an exception to this general rule occurred in the U.S. during 1970–72 but a careful analysis would reveal that the period is no exception. As unemployment rose, the inflation did diminish, although not as rapidly as would have been expected from previous experience. Ap-

Thus, fiscal and monetary measures, no matter how cleverly administered, are incapable by themselves of achieving true economic stability. All they do is move the economy from one unpleasant combination of unemployment and inflation to another – in the jargon of economists, from one point on the Phillips curve (the typical relationship between prices and unemployment) to another. It was for this reason, some years ago, that I first advocated an approach to stability that goes beyond the conventional Keynesian measures, one section of which I now summarize and extend somewhat.

Earlier we mentioned that the bulk of the unemployed commonly consist of unskilled and semiskilled workers, with a sprinkling of the technologically displaced. In fact, unemployment rates in the United States are usually from three to five times as great for the unskilled as for the highly trained, as shown in the table, p. 74; apparently much the same situation prevails in Canada. Even in recession, when the overall rate of unemployment is very high, many types of professional and other skilled personnel remain in scarce supply, as the table indicates for 1961, 1968 and 1971. In other words, there is a disparity between the structure of the demand for labor and its supply – a disparity that has great significance for inflation.

When an effort is made through expansionary fiscal and monetary policies to reduce unemployment, the effect is to intensify the scarcity of skilled personnel, bringing upward pressure on their wages and salaries and subsequently on prices. Only when inflation mounts to a socially intolerable pitch does it pay private industry to hire many of the unskilled or other idle members of the labor force, whose capabilities do not meet industry's prime needs. The roller coaster pattern of economic activity is essentially the result of such periodic and futile efforts to pump up the economy, each inflationary upsurge being followed by a "corrective" recession. No way has yet been discovered to get the unskilled and the technologically displaced into jobs without stimulating an inflation that cannot be maintained; nor would it appear that any way can possibly be found so long as nations restrict themselves to aggregative fiscal and monetary policies. It is on these grounds, in part, that I have advocated a system of tax-financed public employment.[5]

---

parently the "Phillips curve" had shifted, reflecting in part a deepening of inflationary psychology which in turn, no doubt, was strengthened by the longest business expansion on record (1960–69) during which inflation was permitted to accelerate continuously. (The Phillips curve is a statistical relationship between the level of unemployment and the rate of price increase, examples of which, for different countries, are shown in the chart, p. 77).
5. Presented originally, though in a different form, in my book *The Welfare State: U.S.A.* (Boston: Houghton Mifflin, 1969).

Unemployment by Occupation Expressed as Rates and as Percentage of Civilian Labor Force and Total Unemployment

	1956a			1961			1968			1971		
	% of CLF	Rate	% of U.	% of CLF	Rate	% of U.	% of CLF	Rate	% of U.	% of CLF	Rate	% of U.
Total	100.0	3.8	100.0	100.0	6.7	100.0	100.0	3.6	100.0	100.0	5.9	100.0
White-collar	38.6	1.7	17.4	42.4	3.3	21.0	46.1	2.0	25.7	47.1	3.5(3.3)b	27.8
Prof. & tech.	9.1	1.0	2.4	11.1	2.0	3.4	13.3	1.2	4.5	13.6	2.9(2.2)b	6.7
Mgrs., officials & proprietors	9.8	0.8	2.0	10.3	1.8	2.8	10.0	1.0	2.7	10.5	1.6	2.9
Clerical	13.4	2.4	8.6	14.6	4.6	10.1	16.8	3.0	13.9	16.8	4.8	13.7
Sales	6.3	2.7	4.5	6.3	4.9	4.6	6.1	2.8	4.7	6.3	4.3	4.5
Blue-collar	39.3	5.1	52.5	37.0	9.2	51.1	36.4	4.1	41.7	34.9	7.4	43.6
Craftsmen & foremen	13.3	3.2	11.3	13.1	6.3	12.4	13.0	2.4	8.7	12.7	4.7	10.2
Operatives	20.1	5.4	28.5	18.4	9.6	26.5	18.6	4.5	23.2	16.8	8.3	23.7
Nonfarm laborers	5.9	8.2	12.8	5.6	14.7	12.3	4.9	7.2	9.8	5.4	10.8	9.8
Service workers	11.8	4.6	14.4	12.6	7.2	13.6	12.5	4.4	15.5	13.5	6.3	14.4
Farm workers	9.9	1.9	4.9	7.2	2.8	3.1	4.5	2.1	2.6	3.8	2.6	1.6
Inexperienced workers	0.4		10.8	0.8		11.3	0.5		14.5	0.7		12.6

a. 14 years of age and over.
b. Figures in parentheses adjusted for defence cutback.

Source: Based on data from the United States Department of Labor.

The key phrase in the last sentence is "tax-financed." Let us suppose a situation prevails such as that in the United States in 1961 when nearly 7 per cent of the labor force was unemployed and inflation, in the presence of this serious recession, was virtually at a standstill. Under such circumstances, if government were to provide jobs for the idle and raise taxes by appropriate amounts at the same time, full employment could be achieved without inflation. The taxes would insure that overall spending in the private sector would not rise above its prevailing noninflationary level. But at the same time production in the public sector would be substantially expanded, using otherwise idle labor for the satisfaction of the nation's most urgent social needs.

A little arithmetic would suggest that the magnitude of the public employment program required might be formidable, perhaps too great for all practical purposes. If 7 per cent of the labor were unemployed and my own goal of a maximum unemployment rate of 2 per cent were accepted, jobs would have to be provided for 5 per cent of the labor force or more than four million men and women. Furthermore, the Phillips curve in the United States has shifted since 1961 so that instead of 7 per cent, perhaps 8 per cent of the labor force would have to be unemployed to induce a noninflationary behavior of prices. But such a view neglects several important offsetting factors.

(1) The degree of inflation that develops at any level of business activity (and any level of unemployment) is in part the result of an inflationary psychology that has been amply nurtured by experience since the Second World War. Prices have advanced constantly over the past 30 years, differing only from time to time in the rate of increase. Understandably, business and labor have adapted to the environment, with each group in society sensitively alert for opportunities to boost its price, wage, salary, or fee to maintain or enlarge its share of the national income. That is what is meant by inflationary psychology and its effect is obviously to intensify the upward slant of the price level. Born of a particular environment, however, the psychology of inflation would no doubt subside if that environment were changed. A determined government program to maintain full employment *without* inflating the economy would itself represent a signal alteration in the environment and, through its impact on the bargaining attitudes of business, labor, and others, would make the government's job easier. In particular, it would lower the rate of inflation compatible (in the absence of the government's program) with a given level of unemployment.

(2) The relationship between unemployment and inflation could be further improved by temporary use of direct price and wage controls. For a year or two, while the vestigial expressions of inflationary

psychology remained, these would be highly useful. As the new environment of guaranteed jobs and stable prices was created, the direct controls could be gradually abandoned.

(3) A gradual build-up of the public employment program and the taxes that go along with it would also help business and the public to adapt to the new situation. Effective achievement of the goals of stabilization as well as the principles of good management would suggest that the employment program be started on a small scale and slowly extended to full size in perhaps a two- or three-year period.

(4) If properly organized, the public employment program would operate in conjunction with opportunities for systematic on-the-job training. Particularly for youth, for whom unemployment rates are extraordinarily high, such instruction could hardly avoid being useful. Part of the training would naturally be directed toward fulfilling the scarce skill requirements of the public projects. But at the same time some of the training could be directed at increasing the supply of types of skilled workers notably scarce in private industry. Insofar as this was accomplished successfully, it would help to reduce the potentialities for bottleneck inflation.

In technical terms, all four of these factors would help shift the Phillips curve to the left so that any given level of aggregate demand in the private sector would be commensurate with a lower rate of inflation. The accompanying chart shows Phillips curves for some leading industrial nations, with the United States and Canada in the least favorable situations. If the United States curve were gradually shifted half the distance now separating it from those of Germany and Sweden, it would mean that inflation could be kept to a level of between 0 and 1 per cent per annum with a level of aggregate demand consistent with 5 or 5.5 per cent unemployment. Under these circumstances, a 2 per cent unemployment rate (implying ideal "full employment") could be achieved with public employment of about 2.5 million men and women. The cost of this program, on a net basis, might come to some $6 billion to $7 billion per year, about equivalent to the amounts we have spent in recent years on space and military research.

The Myth of Declining Employment Opportunities

One writer recently likened the position of man in the production process today to that of the horse in 1909. In the period of tranquil prosperity preceding the First World War, equine hours of work declined appreciably and material returns in the form of feed and shelter improved. Yet in a few years the horse as a source of energy in transportation, farming or elsewhere was eliminated almost entirely. The writer contends that in a similar way man will soon be

Unemployment and Inflation Rates, Selected Industrial Countries
(in per cent)

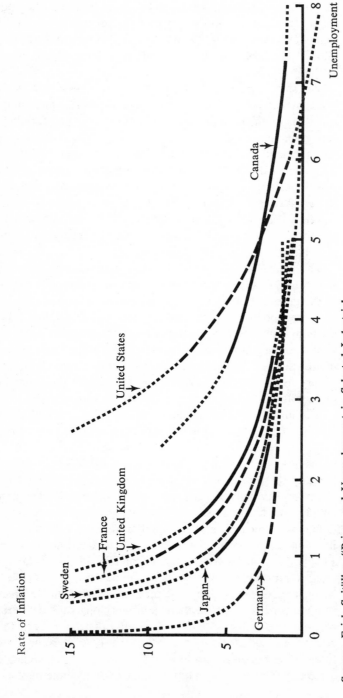

Source: Erich Spitäller, "Prices and Unemployment in Selected Industrial Countries," *International Monetary Fund Staff Papers* (November, 1971).

displaced by automation and cybernation in the bulk of all jobs ranging from assembly-line worker to middle-management decision-maker. Some utopian idealists may welcome this prospect as a promise that the productive burdens of mankind are soon to be lifted. Others, with an eye to institutional lags, may be concerned for the social disruption, the class divisions and the general misery that could evolve before the nirvana of plenitude and free goods for all is reached. My own concern here is with the degree of accuracy of the prospect.

The slender basis of fact on which the forecast rests is the constant increase in output per man hour as usually measured in the material producing industries – manufacturing and farming. What it neglects are:

(1) The substantial errors in the conventional measures of production,
(2) The role of diminishing returns as population expands, and
(3) The wide range of services in which shortages exist and are likely to persist or even deepen.

When account is taken of these, it becomes apparent that the need for human labor is virtually certain to expand in the foreseeable future.

The errors in published estimates of production spring from a failure to give any weight at all to negative outputs. For every dollar of the gross national product as measured, a certain amount of air and water pollution, defacement of the countryside and similar deductions from the real income stream are also produced. Another way of looking at negative output is as costs that are not now being met by society. To make up for past omissions and offset contemporary social costs as they occur would require the expenditure of many billions of dollars and many millions of man-years of labor.

The influence of diminishing returns is related and has similar effects. The gradual, inevitable depletion of some natural resources as population expands means that we shall have to pay more in terms of labor for future increments in output. Some scholars, particularly those at the Massachusetts Institute of Technology, have taken an especially gloomy view of the prospects, even predicting an absolute decline in standards of living before the century is out. Opinions on such extrapolations differ widely but the high probability of increasing costs of production in certain lines is undeniable. Finally, it is well known that demand in advanced countries increases substantially for services, in contrast to tangible goods. Medicine, education, the arts, mass transportation and recreation represent areas in which there are enormous gaps between social requirements and availability. In short, there is no dearth in the economic needs of society nor is there likely to be in the foreseeable future. The important problem is how to apply the available labor force fully and effectively to the satisfaction of these needs.

Poverty and
Direct Forms of Income Security in Canada

by Tom Philbrook
Professor, Faculty of Environmental Studies,
York University, Toronto, Ontario

It must be obvious that we as a nation have never really tried to eliminate poverty. Even in our rhetoric we tend to be circumspect, neither promising much nor little. We speak often, for example, about equality but seldom about the injustice of some people being massively wealthy while many others are extremely poor. That might be unseemly.

Our policies and programs try to assure that people do not suffer too severely from having very limited resources or as a result of events beyond their control such as floods, locusts, recessions, and large families. Yet in seeking to improve their lot, we do so without making an undue charge on the wealthy – either individuals or corporations – and thereby shift much of the burden to the barely better off middle-class wage and salary earners. Most tellingly, programs to combat poverty and income insecurity must never be put ahead of, or conflict with the interests of private enterprise.

In what follows, I shall first look at direct forms of income security in Canada, both operating and proposed. From there I shall look statistically and qualitatively at poverty in Canada. The final section will comment on the first two sections, with specific references to guaranteed annual income.

1 Forms of Income Security

When one looks at our social welfare system, one sees what is apparently a carefully designed, rational system implemented as revenue became increasingly available and for the purpose of achieving a basic and adequate welfare and income standard for every Canadian. However, when we look at the dollar values paid out through income security measures, we find them below even the most minimal standards.

Towards the end of the Second World War, federal politicians and officials began working out new programs of income security.

Much of the thinking was derived from Britain's Beveridge report on welfare and income security.[1] In addition, these efforts certainly reflected plans and programs put forward by the CCF party in the Thirties which were in some respects soon to be implemented by the CCF government in Saskatchewan. Most influential was the Marsh report[2] which in a way brought forward to government the policy recommendations of these sources. Finally, the thinking was also heavily influenced by Keynesian economic theory.

Equalization was perhaps the single most dominant thrust in welfare planning at this time. One cannot doubt that these men and those coming after them sincerely wanted to eliminate poverty. But there were also other facets of Canadian economic life that they felt were untouchable. Hence the inherent contradiction which made it impossible to eliminate poverty: great accumulations of capital were to have a higher priority than a decent minimum redistribution of the nation's wealth – the maintenance of a class and status system underpinned by industrialism as against a human distribution of wealth.

Equalization did, however, serve a significant purpose for federal policy-makers. It provided the justification for federal intervention into a policy and program field taken to be, under the BNA Act, of sole provincial concern. It was now assumed that the federal government had a responsibility to ensure that every Canadian had the same opportunities for employment and welfare benefits regardless of where he lived. It was judged that this could only be accomplished by federal financial involvement in income security programs. Programs universally available were to be covered by the federal government while selective programs were to be operated jointly by the federal and provincial governments to ensure the province's influence on social welfare and policies.

The federal government first entered the social welfare field in 1927 with an old age pension scheme. The next major entry, which did not come until 1940, was the introduction of unemployment insurance. But it was in 1944 that the federal government entered the income security field in a big way by introducing family allowances.[3] It was a program enacted to give recognition to the fact that families with children had greater needs and to bring to children a measure of equality of opportunity by ensuring that their mothers had at least some money with which to maintain them. It was also looked upon as an economic stabilization measure that would keep

1. William Beveridge, *Social Insurance and Allied Services* (London: H.M.S.O., 1942).
2. L.C. Marsh, *Social Security for Canada* (Ottawa: Printer to the King, 1943).
3. In 1964, youth allowances were introduced which in effect extended family allowance coverage to children up to age 17.

a significant amount of dollars flowing into the consumer spending stream.

From 1945 to the late Fifties, the federal government enacted a number of categorical programs in addition to the various veterans' pensions and allowances which were not considered "welfare." The three categorical programs established were old age assistance, blind persons' allowances and disabled persons' allowances. An unemployment assistance program (not the same as the unemployment insurance program) was also established. It did not specify eligibility conditions other than that the person had to be unemployed and in need. These programs were based on the income of the applicant and required a 10-year categorical residency. While portions of these categorical programs are still in operation in some provinces, they are being phased out. A number of provinces now have taken the option of providing for these recipients under a general assistance program, the Canada Assistance Plan.

The Canada Assistance Plan (CAP) has provided federal support for the development of rationalized and professionalized provincial welfare departments. The federal contribution is 50 per cent of organization expenses and 50 per cent of assistance payments.

There are two major types of assistance payments made under CAP. First is that for basic needs – including food, clothing, shelter and fuel – and needs arising from special circumstances. Second, recipients are provided with health and, where available, rehabilitation services.

The provincial welfare departments determine the nature of what constitutes need and benefit levels. However, the federal act stipulates certain conditions for eligibility, mainly by applying what is called a needs test consisting of an assessment of the budgetary requirements of the individual or family as well as the income and resources available to them. The provinces are not allowed to impose residence as a condition of eligibility.

With each province determining its own benefit levels as well as the method of determining them, there is little consistency across Canada. In fact, it is virtually impossible to find out just what benefit levels an individual or family has available to it. Members of the Special Senate Committee on Poverty had an extremely difficult time with this and were told about similar difficulties by a large number of organizations which either represented or were composed of the poor. The committee also found in talking to provincial welfare officials that the officials themselves were unwilling to reveal their benefit levels. The reason given was that the calculation of benefits is an extremely complex matter tailored to the particular circumstances of each applicant and they therefore could not indicate in a general way what the benefit levels were.

Not surprisingly, the provinces all have a number of quarrels with the Canada Assistance Plan and therefore the federal government. High among these is the argument, made chiefly by the Atlantic provinces that, because they do not have a great deal of revenue of their own, the federal government should pay a greater portion of their general welfare assistance costs. The federal government argues that these provinces already receive substantial equalization grants from the national purse. The second argument – heard mainly from British Columbia but also Ontario to some extent – is that because of migration from the poorer provinces, they must carry a substantial burden of welfare needs generated in other provinces. Finally, all provinces have severally disputed just what should be included or excluded for cost-sharing purposes. The latter argument is, of course, endless and time-consuming in any cost-sharing agreement between levels of government.

It is worth looking, briefly, at the organizational meaning of the federal/provincial agreement embodied in the Canada Assistance Plan. Most of the best talent in the departments involved go into the negotiation and management of these agreements. Moreover, usually the closer one is to the centre of these agreements, the higher the salary and the more secure the position. This picture is typical in the social services; security of tenure and size of salary are inversely proportional to how closely one works with people who are the concern of the service policies.

What often appear to be quarrels between the two levels of government are more political imagery than real conflict. Working relationships are established between administrative officials of the respective departments and are nurtured and protected since they become the mainline channels for communication, administration, and negotiation. Without these channels, the routine implementation and operation of the policies could not occur.

These administrative activities of officials supply an essential continuity. Indeed, a large portion of the work of senior officials of both provincial and federal departments involves continuing negotiation and adjustment of the administrative cost-sharing agreement. For the most part, changes in policy stem from changes first, in the financial picture and second, in difficulties encountered in the administration of the agreement. Seldom in these negotiations and operations does an official really concern himself with the objectives and goals of a particular policy unless it is to justify a particular change his department feels is necessary. In short, as people on welfare have experienced, their interests have little, if anything, to do with the operations of these programs.

Finally, the picture the public receives through the media is often one of extreme contention between provinces and the federal government. The public seldom is made aware of the administrative continuity and agreement that exists in the official operation of cost-sharing programs.

Provision for assistance to the elderly is the last major element in Canada's repertoire of income security programs. This assistance includes old age security, guaranteed income supplement, and the Canada Pension Plan.

Old age security is a universal program guaranteeing a flat rate of $82.88 a month to anyone over the age of 65. Until 1970, the payment had a 2 per cent cost-of-living escalator attached to it. However, the escalator clause was eliminated that year.[4]

When this clause was removed by Parliament, the government stressed the importance of the guaranteed income supplement, enacted in 1967. This is taken to be a form of a guaranteed annual income whereby pensioners who have little income other than old age security can receive an additional benefit to a maximum of $67.12 for single pensioners and $59.62 for married pensioners. The maximum supplement is reduced by one dollar for every two dollars a month of income over and above the old age security pension and any other supplement that may have been received. Thus, a pensioner with no outside resources is guaranteed the impressive income of $150 a month if he is single; a married couple receives $285. If the pensioner is fortunate, he will have already paid for his house and acquired enough clothing to last him the rest of his life; he can then devote his monthly sum chiefly to food and keeping himself alive.

Related in a rather well articulated way to these two programs is the Canada Pension Plan, enacted in 1965. This program provides those 65 and over with pensions of approximately 25 per cent of adjusted pensionable earnings since the beginning of the program or from the age of 18, whichever comes later. During his period of employment, the individual will contribute 1.8 per cent of his contributable earnings to the pension fund and his employer another 1.8 per cent. If the individual is self-employed, however, he will contribute 3.6 per cent. The plan also provides for benefits to survivors, orphans, disabled widows and so on – all rather standard provisions in pension plans. Since in years to come there will be literally hundreds of thousands of Canadians whose pensionable earnings will average well under $10,000 a year, we need not fear that Canadians on the pension plan will be basking in southern Florida or the West Indies during the winter. Neither will they be travelling abroad sight-seeing and so on. In short, we can rest assured that these perquisites will continue to be enjoyed largely by those of us who manage to reach and remain in the upper tenth or fifteenth percentile of our national income distribution.

---

4. In May 1972, Parliament raised the old-age security benefit to $82.88 a month and, as of April 1, 1973, the old age security pension and its guaranteed income supplement will be fully escalated in accordance with the Consumer Price Index.

One final proposed program needs to be mentioned. The federal government has had legislation before Parliament to substantially change the family allowance program. These policy proposals, called the Family Income Security Plan (FISP), do away with the universality of present family allowances, substituting selectivity based on family income. FISP will provide maximum payments of $15 for children under age 12 and $20 for children aged 12 to 17. A family with one child must have an income of $4,500 or less to receive the maximum. This ceiling rises by $500 for each additional child. For each $100 of family income above this ceiling, family allowance payments are reduced by 33 cents a month.

Had the family allowance payments kept pace with the growth in personal per capita income since 1944, the allowances would be nearly as high as those now proposed in the Family Income Security Plan. This means that we are not achieving anything but, in fact, taking a step backward by making what was the universal plan available to all families in Canada now only available to a certain portion. But what they get is of no greater value than what families got back in 1944.

Our niggardliness in spending on income security is also revealed in the growth of government expenditure for social welfare.

While growth in public expenditures on health and welfare has increased steadily during the Sixties – from $3 billion in 1959–60 to $7.4 billion in 1968–69 (a growth of just under 150 per cent), growth in social welfare expenditures has been only two-thirds of this rate. Social welfare expenditure growth in the same period has gone from $2.2 billion to $4.5 billion (an increase of about 105 per cent), and per capita spending has gone from $128 per person to $219 per person, an increase of 71 per cent. This expenditure has gone up from 6 per cent to 6.2 per cent of the gross national product and 8.2 per cent to 8.9 per cent of the net national income during this past decade.

These rates of growth, when looked at in relation to the GNP and national income, do not reveal any spectacular increase in expenditure for income security in Canada. Even though there has been some real growth in income security expenditure, it cannot be assumed that anyone is really better off.

Moreover, welfare caseloads throughout most of the Sixties remained at a more-or-less stable and acceptable level of about 24 cases per thousand people. There was considerable variation between provinces from lows of 17 or so in Ontario to highs approaching 50 in Newfoundland. However, the last two years have seen a considerable growth in the welfare caseload throughout Canada. What this means is difficult to say, for the definition of a welfare case is vague at best.

Keeping in mind, then, the nature of these programs, we can look at the extent of poverty in Canada and from these two pictures get some insight into the absence of any real anti-poverty efforts in this country.

2 Poverty in Canada

Two matters need to be considered before we describe poverty in Canada.

a   In the early Sixties, economists and others in the United States began counting the poor. Shortly afterwards we in Canada began similar activities. To a large extent this counting motivated the U.S. president's economic advisers to press for anti-poverty programs. In much the same way, the chapter on poverty in the *Fifth Annual Review* of the Economic Council of Canada[5] had some influence on Canadian policy – at least it brought about the Special Senate Committee on Poverty.

Counting the poor and measuring poverty must be seen in light of the still significant physical science approach to human and social matters. It has been said many times by physical scientists that if you can't measure it, it probably doesn't exist. While recognizing the importance of measuring, we must remember that when we do so, we remove much of the intimacy with human affairs that we need in order to understand and influence them.

b   The second matter relates to a distinction frequently made between absolute and relative poverty. To put these notions in perspective it is necessary to recognize that, from an income point of view, the majority of Canadians are essentially poor. For example, in Toronto, Canada's largest metropolitan area, an income of about $10,000 a year is required to buy a house. Yet the average income in Metro Toronto is about $7,000 John Porter, in his *Vertical Mosaic*,[6] estimated that in 1955, middle-class lifestyle really started at about $8,000 a year. The 1971 equivalent to that salary would be about $18,000 which takes in only the highest 20 per cent of families. Ferdinand Lundberg has noted:

Anyone who does not own a fairly substantial amount of income-producing property or does not receive an earned income sufficiently large to make substantial regular savings, or does not hold a well-paid, securely tenured job is poor. He may be healthy, handsome,

---

5.   Economic Council of Canada, "The Problem of Poverty," in *The Challenge of Growth and Change, Fifth Annual Review* (Ottawa: Queen's Printer, 1968), pp. 103–40.

6.   (Toronto: University of Toronto Press, 1965), pp. 131–32.

and a delight to his friends – but he is poor.[7]

In some ways the emphasis on the distinction between absolute and relative poverty reflects the complacent but still present view of the Fifties that we have come into an affluent society where absolute poverty no longer exists. That a family need not starve or go without minimal clothing or shelter misses the point. In reality, poverty is always both absolute and relative. For to be poor, relatively speaking, is to be absolutely poor. The fundamental qualities that define poverty are related to style of life. In our consumer-oriented society lifestyle is publicly visible and privately felt according to access to consumer goods. This means that poverty is intrinsic to the operation of our industrial economy as long as there is maldistribution of its benefits, for not only does it set pay scales of its laborers, but it also sets the dominant consumer ethos.

With these points in mind, we can take a brief look at the nature and size of poverty in Canada. It is also necessary to keep in mind all of the weaknesses, flaws and limits in the data which have been well enunciated in many reports and need not be reported here. Most of the quantitative material in this section comes from three recent reports:

(1) *Poverty in Canada,* A Report of the Special Senate Committee;[8]
(2) The renegade poverty report called *The Real Poverty Report* by Ian Adams and others;[9] and
(3) *Urban Canada* by N. H. Lithwick, prepared for Robert Andras, when he was the federal minister responsible for Central Mortgage and Housing Corporation.[10]

The Real Poverty Report estimated that there are about 4,550,-000 poor people in Canada. This estimate was based on a poverty line which consists of one-half the average living standard enjoyed by Canadians.[11] Out of this 4.5 million, approximately 900,000

---

7. Ferdinand Lundberg, *The Rich and the Super Rich* (New York: Bantam Books, 1968), p. 23.
8. (Ottawa: Queen's Printer, 1971).
9. (Edmonton: M. G. Hurtig Limited, 1971.)
10. (Ottawa: Central Mortgage and Housing Corporation, 1971.)
11. *The Real Poverty Report* uses what they have termed a relative poverty line based on average standard of living for Canada as a whole. This is based on a twofold operation. This first consists of establishing living standard points by family size. This, they set up as follows: for an individual, they give three living standard points, for a family of two, five living standard points; and then one living standard point for each additional dependent. The value of the living standard point is based on average income for a given period for a particular family size. Hence, if the average income for a family of four was $7,000, the living standard point would be $1,000. The relative poverty line is then set at one-half this value, or one-half of one living standard point – or $500 × 7 for a family of four equals $3,500; for an individual, 3 × $500 or $1,500. Obviously, one would want to check

were women and 3,650,000 were men. A total of 250,000 of the single persons were men and 400,000 were women. Of the family heads, 850,000 were men and 150,000 were women. The remainder was made up of children and other dependants. In short, something like one-fifth of our population is estimated to live at one-half or less the average standard of living.[12]

The Lithwick report focused chiefly on urban poverty, but made extensive calculations based on size of place. He found a major difference between rural and small urban centres on the one hand and large urban centres on the other. There was greater poverty among families in the former, and a predominance of poverty among the aged in the latter.

In metropolitan areas, roughly 40 per cent of the poverty was accounted for by elderly people, another 30 per cent by families where the head was not in the labor force, and the remainder among the employable. Of these, about 12 per cent were working poor with families of more than five members.

In urban centres of 100,000 or less, we find a shift from individual poverty to family poverty and from younger to older age groups among families in which a woman is the head. In addition, we find low employment rates among individuals and an increase, particularly among the aged, of those not in the labor force. Overall, the incidence of poverty is higher in the smaller urban centres and the rural areas than it is in the major metropolitan centres.

Finally, in the rural areas poverty is most common among large families where the man is either self-employed or seasonally employed. This group typifies the rural poor and distinguishes rural poverty statistically from urban forms.

Regional differences, in large measure, reflect these urban place differences. Not surprisingly, provinces with a high concentration of people in large urban centres also have the highest annual personal income per capita, the highest average weekly salaries and wages and the highest percentage of employed among the working age population. These characteristics are illustrated in table 1.

Overall, the Atlantic region is, in terms of these statistics, the poorest, has the lowest per capita income, the smallest percentage of employed among the working age population, and the lowest average weekly wages. Quebec is rather close to the Atlantic provinces, in respect of these measurements. Both Ontario and British

---

to see whether the living standard point would be the same if it were based on the average income of an individual as against an average income of a family of two, three, four, and so on. They should be roughly the same. The value of this concept of a relative poverty line is that it takes into account differing family size and relates the poverty line explicitly to average income by size of family.

12. Adams, *The Real Poverty Report*, Table 1.4.iv, p. 22.

Table 1

Regional and Provincial Disparities, 1969

Province	Annual personal income per capita	(Canada = 100)	Average weekly wages and salaries	(Canada = 100)	Employed as % of working-age population	Unemployment rate
Newfoundland	$1,613	56	$106	90	38.8%	10.3%
P.E.I.	1,818	63	81	69	48.6	5.3
Nova Scotia	2,304	79	96	81	47.0	5.4
New Brunswick	2,080	72	97	82	45.1	8.5
Atlantic region	2,032	70	n.a.	n.a.	44.5	7.6
Quebec	2,626	90	115	98	50.8	6.9
Ontario	3,365	116	122	103	56.1	3.1
Manitoba	2,842	98	108	91	54.1	3.7
Saskatchewan	2,516	87	108	92	51.6	3.1
Alberta	2,913	100	118	100	58.5	2.7
Prairie region	2,784	96	n.a.	n.a.	55.3	2.9
B.C.	3,116	107	129	110	53.9	5.0
Territories	2,542	87	n.a.	n.a.	n.a.	n.a.
Canada	2,906*	100	118	100	53.1	4.7

*Excluding the personal income of Canadian non-residents.

Source: Canada, Parliament, Senate, Committee on Poverty, *Poverty in Canada* (Ottawa: Information Canada, 1971), p. 51.

Table 2

The Distribution of Wage Rates in Jobs Covered by the Federal Department of Labor's Survey, 1969

Hourly earnings*	Distribution of wage-and-salary earners
Up to $1.00	0.6%
1.01–1.50	8.5
1.51–2.00	18.4
2.01–2.50	20.5
2.51–3.00	20.3
3.01–3.50	16.9
3.51–4.00	8.7
4.01–4.50	3.5
4.51–5.00	1.3
5.01–6.00	0.8
6.01 +	0.5
Total	100.0

*Wages and salaries paid on a basis other than hourly were converted to their equivalent.

Source: Ian Adams and others, *The Real Poverty Report* (Edmonton: M. G. Hurtig Limited, 1971), p. 29.

Table 3

Shares of Total Non-farm-family Income Received by Non-farm Families Ranked by Income, 1951–1969

	Lowest fifth	Second fifth	Middle fifth	Fourth fifth	Highest fifth	Total
Shares of total income						
1951	6.1%	12.9%	17.4%	22.4%	41.1%	100.0%
1954	6.5	13.5	18.1	24.4	37.5	100.0
1957	6.3	13.1	18.1	23.4	39.1	100.0
1959	6.8	13.4	17.8	23.0	39.0	100.0
1961	6.6	13.5	18.3	23.4	38.4	100.0
1965	6.6	13.3	18.0	23.5	38.6	100.0
1967*	6.9	13.3	17.9	23.5	38.4	100.0
1969*	6.9	13.0	18.0	23.4	38.7	100.0

Upper limits						**Average**
1951	$1,820	$2,700	$3,480	$ 4,640		$3,535
1954	2,220	3,240	4,150	5,680		4,143
1957	2,380	3,600	4,680	6,350		4,644
1959	2,650	3,920	5,000	6,690		4,968
1961	2,800	4,370	5,460	7,180		5,317
1965	3,500	5,250	6,810	9,030		6,669
1967*	4,090	6,060	7,930	10,650		7,756
1969*	4,600	7,050	9,280	12,110		9,056

*Estimated on the assumptions that families are evenly distributed within the published income classes and that the proportionate relationships between non-farm and total-relative income shares and non-farm and total-upper limits and averages that prevailed in 1965 also applied in 1967 and 1969.

Source: Ian Adams and others, *The Real Poverty Report* (Edmonton: M. G. Hurtig Limited, 1971), Table 1.4.iii, p. 21.

Columbia are considerably better off than the national averages, while the Prairie provinces, with the exception of Saskatchewan, are close to the national averages. Saskatchewan is at about the same level as Quebec. While the incidence of poverty is highest in the Atlantic provinces, it should be kept in mind that over half of all low-income families live in either Quebec or Ontario.

In almost two-thirds of the low-income families, the heads worked for at least part of the year. About 40 per cent gained their income from wages and salaries, and another 20 per cent or so were self-employed. Nearly 40 per cent of the low-income family heads worked throughout the year. Somewhat over 25 per cent of all low-income families were headed by people over the age of 65.

These figures reveal the extent to which poverty is related to low wages. Our views on wages are well reflected by our current minimum wage rates. The federal government has [April 1972] the highest rate of $1.75 an hour. The Prairie provinces, B.C. and Ontario come in at around $1.65 an hour, while the Atlantic provinces are still between $1.25 and $1.40 an hour, and they make a distinction between men and women, with the women's minimum wage rate being 25 cents or so less than men's. At $1.75 an hour a man working full time earns a salary of about $3,600 a year, while the person working at $1.25 an hour earns $2,600 a year. It should also be remembered that those working at or near the minimum wage are liable not to be working full time and to be subject to frequent layoffs. Table 2 shows the distribution of wage rates covered in the federal Department of Labor Survey for 1969. It is significant here that nearly 70 per cent of the labor force covered by the survey earned $3.00 an hour or less. At $3.00 an hour working full time, one earns $6,200 a year. This is not a sufficient annual income to obtain a mortgage from CMHC to purchase a home.

These data on wage rates in turn reflect the distributions of income in Canada. The overall picture is shown in table 3.

In sum, this statistical picture of poverty, as lean as it may be, shows that poverty has been a constant phenomenon in Canada over at least two decades. Although the data on income distribution do not permit us to go much further back than 1951, it seems a fairly strong assumption that this distribution of income has been true in Canada for at least the last seven or eight decades, if not all the way back to the beginning of Confederation. In spite of the rhetoric about the expanding economy and increasing personal disposable income, it really doesn't change much for most Canadians.

There is another way of understanding the nature of poverty that is seldom done in Canada or elsewhere. This is essentially to look at its institutional sources which in turn means to look at the relationship between work, poverty, local institutions and broad civilization patterns. I have been doing this for some years in my own research with special reference to the Atlantic provinces.

It is important to realize that during the 19th century the Atlantic provinces were, for the most part, prosperous growing regions with an economy based largely on lumbering, shipbuilding and trade. When these activities declined by the end of the 19th century, the first phase of industrialism, which had begun earlier, levelled off and it never really expanded significantly thereafter.

Over the last 50 years the local economies were still largely based on lumbering, agriculture or the fisheries and a high proportion of those engaged in them were self-employed. Government policies have had a disastrous effect largely because officials and politicians neglected to tailor the intersection of industrial development and existing local economies and social institutions.

Regional economic development policies aim at increasing the rate of economic growth in the lagging regions. These policies have not, however, achieved a significant increase in growth rates for a number of reasons, but have managed to destroy or greatly curtail the existing local and resource-based industries. Thus the work style of a large portion of the labor force has become unmarketable. It was a work style based on doing a multiplicity of tasks for varying periods of time during the year. Some people have shifted from essentially pre-industrial work to industrial work, but they do so at lower wage rates than those in more highly developed areas.

This lower wage rate then becomes a principal attraction for industry and, with the entry of industry pressure, mounts to raise wages to national levels. This in turn tends to make the area less attractive for industry because of disadvantages of location and the lack of metropolitan social amenities for its management. Since new industries have obtained much of their capital through public grants, they can withdraw to greener pastures with little loss. Hence, little economic growth is achieved, the existing labor force is disturbed and conditions become worse for the average family to the point now of crisis in some districts.

For the industrialized and urbanized sectors of Canada, the picture is not quite so bleak. Generally, there has been continuous increase in the wages of semi-skilled and skilled workers. But these increases in wages have tended only to match overall growth and personal income. In terms of human cost we must count the circumstance that even with a steady increase in wages the urban worker faces a continuing decline of control over his destiny.

These examples merely touch upon what should be a full institutional analysis of the life of working people.

The statistical profiles of poverty not only lack the meaningfulness and completeness possible with institutional analysis, but they also serve an extremely limited purpose. Statistical analysis mainly serves an accounting or regulatory function that is applicable only if we have decided that the system of income security, more broadly, of social services and anti-poverty policy are the correct ones. Institutional and historical analysis serves the more fundamental purpose of raising, and to some extent suggesting answers to, the question of where we are going and what we should be doing. In light of the persistence of poverty in Canada, these fundamental questions must be faced.

3   Toward Social Equalization

Let us turn now to the matter of the guaranteed annual income (GAI) and its implications for income security policy in Canada. Two factors are obvious. The first is that at present we cannot afford it. This is true for reasons associated with both political and financial costs. The important thing to keep in mind is that the financial costs are closely related to the political costs. Senator Croll is probably making an accurate assessment of Canadian public opinion in seeking to tie the GAI to increases in the GNP.[13]

It is equally true that within the next five years or so a form of guaranteed annual income, probably using the negative income tax mechanism, will be adopted by the federal government partly because the guaranteed annual income is an almost inevitable evolution of our present income security system. It is also true that within the next few years the necessary shift in public opinion will occur so that politicians will be able to bring in legislation for such a program. With this shift in public opinion, the necessary additional revenue for such a program will be found.

We must not look at such a happening, however, with either excitement or satisfaction. A guaranteed annual income scheme should be viewed primarily as a way of making direct transfers to the individual in the form of allowances that overlap with earned income. It means administratively that we are saying that an individual should not be compelled to choose between earning an income or obtaining it through welfare. In short, the GAI is really a technique of phasing out transfer income as earned income rises. It is attractive because it does away with some of the more messy problems present in our current welfare assistance programs, particularly those surrounding the judgments concerning how much an individual or family should get. An additional advantage central to our present economic thinking is that it permits the economy to draw more readily on the lower class for labor in times of expansion. Finally, it will probably be a way of quelling the rising discontent of the poor with the present system. The one major prob-

---

13.   Senator David Croll was chairman of the Senate's Special Committee on Poverty.

lem now for both politician and economist alike is fear of the effect of a GAI on work incentive. This problem should simply disappear almost automatically, since politicians and the public at large are likely to become aware that working and being poor are synonymous. Poor people always work!

Yet with a form of guaranteed annual income as the major element of the income security program we cannot assume any real diminution of poverty. This is because guaranteed annual income levels will be set sufficiently low so as not to change the present distribution of income. There may be a slight shift of 1 to 2 per cent of total personal income to the lowest 20 per cent of the income-earning population. Such a shift, of course, will make very little difference to the present class structure. A meaningful change in the distribution of income and therefore the class structure of our society requires far greater changes.

Canada is still basically a capitalist and liberal political economy. An economy such as this, as George Lichtheim pointed out, maintains a class division between the wealthy few and the many without property. It is an economy responding only to "effective demand" that relies, in turn, on actual purchasing power. It fails to satisfy basic material needs except in a tortuous way that is seldom to everyone's satisfaction. It produces luxury goods for the few and then endeavors by large-scale production to make many of these goods saleable to a larger portion of the population.

The result is that social inequalities are constantly reproduced and even rendered more acute, even though society grows richer and there is some rise in real income. The built-in automatism is such that those who start off with material advantages (including advantages in skill, training and education) secure a proportionate share of the social product.[14]

W. Arthur Lewis addresses this point by bringing in the role of what we have come to know as the welfare state. "The price mechanism rewards people according to the scarcity of resources (labor and property) that they possess, but it does not itself contain any mechanism for equalizing the distribution of scarcities. For justice in distribution, we clearly have to summon the forces of the state."[15]

In turn, the welfare state offers little possibility for a real solution to the problems of poverty. It operates on the basis of taxation of the rich and the expansion of the public sector, including education, health, housing, and welfare. Regardless of the importance of

---

14. George Lichtheim, *A Short History of Socialism* (New York: Praeger Publishers, 1970), p. 316.
15. W. Arthur Lewis, *The Principles of Economic Planning* (London: Dennis Dobson, 1949), p. 12.

these benefits, they still fall short of altering the overall class structure and income distribution. They do not alter at all the status of wage and salary earners, since this wage relationship is dictated by who owns the means of production. If wage and salary earners did own these, it would not mean that they would no longer have to work, but it would mean that profits would be distributed far more generally, bringing about a far narrower income-spread distribution of income and thereby an elimination of poverty.[16]

Obviously, the demands for a more equitable distribution of income rest upon the paramouncty of non-economic considerations over economic ones. While this is a conceivable state of affairs, it is obviously not yet probable. We have not yet been able to remove the topic of economic growth from the top of our policy agendas. "Unless and until the majority of the electorate in a democratically-governed country is prepared to do without a continuous rise in living standards . . . economic considerations will take precedence over social and cultural claims."[17] Hence, to build a new, equitable society requires not a new philosophy or more theory but encouraging people to look at their political economy in new ways. It can be called anything but it is likely to be socialism that centres on common or social (not state) ownership.

In any discussion about a guaranteed annual income, we must recognize that, even in its most generous forms, it is still going to be just an efficient way of maintaining our present socioeconomic conditions. However, if the real goal is to make an impact on present poverty and mounting uneasiness in society, we must talk of many other things – such as cabbages and kings.

Our present policies and the institutions which they influence do not reveal integrity but rather an effort at make-believe, to try to conceive of the world as it is not.

This means that those of us who have acquired some historical, psychological and political depth to our perspective must turn to those around us, our colleagues, and work with them. In many ways intellectuals have more to contribute to fellow intellectuals than they do to the people at large. There are fundamental class distinctions that make it almost impossible for middle- or upper-middle-class intellectuals to talk meaningfully with working-class people. We can only hope that there will be a few who can bridge this social psychological chasm. Yet intellectuals in politics and administration, and indeed even as enlightened corporate executives, can begin reorienting their policies and programs in a way that

---

16. Lichtheim, *A Short History of Socialism*, p. 317.
17. Lichtheim, *A Short History of Socialism*, p. 325.

liberates working-class people and permits them to begin revitalizing and changing their own lives. One example would be policies of industrial development that do not destroy local economies but support them and permit them to survive a decade or two or three, until such time as the people themselves change their lifestyles. We even have a name for this notion: it is called intermediate technology.

Beyond this, we must endeavor as conditions permit to seek government policies that give greater direction to the use of capital, both private and public. Underlying this direction should be a willingness to change the patterns of ownership. This does not mean the shifting of ownership from private hands to state control but varying kinds of cooperatives, so that those involved in the uses of the objects of ownership maintain a measure of control over them. One example of this is the increasing movement towards cooperative living, a form of ownership that is neither private nor public.

We must begin concentrating on wage policies in far more complex ways. Such primitive notions as setting a 5 or 6 per cent limit on annual wage increases are foolish. Obviously in the labor force at any given time there are those who require 12, 18, and 24 per cent or more increase in wages. There are obviously others who require nothing more than a cost-of-living raise. In short, we should force the increase of wages in some spheres of the economy and hold them down in others.

In a sense we are striving for an ecological theory of value. Such a theory of value is not man or growth oriented but life-enhancing. There is a tremendous job to be done in developing in a clear and persuasive way the meaning and application of such a theory of value. This truly is our prime immediate task.

Social Services and the Guaranteed Annual Income

by Nicolas Zay
Director, School of Social Work,
Laval University, Quebec

Much has been said and written about the relationships between income maintenance programs and social services since a group of United Nations experts pointed up the necessity of coordinating them, inasmuch as no program or service by itself can "raise and maintain the real standard of living of the population."[1] The report goes on to say:

Whatever form of social security is introduced and whatever stage of development it has reached, the association of social service with programs of social security should be ensured.[2]

The Canadian Welfare Council[3] had the same thing in mind when it stated in its report on the principles of a social policy for Canada that:

Social security and social services, of necessity, are complementary. Sufficient income for an adequate standard of living is not enough, in itself, to ensure well-being. An appropriate range of social services is also necessary, both to prevent problems arising and to help solve them where they exist.[4]

The standard of living referred to in the United Nations report has the same meaning as the term "well-being" used by the council,

---

1. United Nations, Department of Economics and Social Affairs, *The Development of National Social Service Programmes* (ST/SOA/40), 1959, p. 32. (Hereinafter referred to as *Social Service Programmes.*)
2. United Nations, Department of Economics and Social Affairs, *Social Service Programmes,* p. 32. Under "social service" (the definition of which is given in the report and quoted on page 6, note 5) the group of experts include all services normally provided in welfare institutions (family and children's services, services for persons with social, physical or mental handicaps, community services, etc.) and services provided by social workers in institutions belonging to other service systems (such as health, education and recreation). The term "social security" covers insurance programs as well as social assistance programs or universal benefit programs (demogrants).
3. Now The Canadian Council on Social Development.
4. Canadian Welfare Council, *Social Policies for Canada* (Ottawa, 1969), p. 41.

but the latter uses the term "social services" in a broader sense, including in it the services provided under welfare, health, education and other systems.

The difficulty we encounter when we try to study this relationship or make it operational arises from three sources:

(1) The ambiguity of the objectives of income maintenance programs and in particular of social assistance programs which quite often serve to promote values other than the raising and maintenance of the actual living standards of individuals and families. (These values, which officially or unofficially underlie the operations of the program, affect not only the criteria used to asses its effectiveness, but also the relationships between the program and the beneficiaries.);

(2) The ambiguity of the concept of "social services";

(3) The difficulty in differentiating between coordination at the program conception level (planning) and at the organization and implementation levels.

To a large extent, these ambiguities account for the different approaches that have been taken to the question.

As a result of the recommendations made by the group of experts referred to, the United Nations Social Affairs Committee decided to give priority to a study of the relationships between social services and social security. Accordingly, the International Social Security Association placed the study on the agenda of its 14th general meeting held in Istanbul in 1961. The study was resumed at the Washington general meeting, held three years later, at which Ida Merriam gave the findings of a survey conducted by the association among the member states. The most important conclusion was perhaps the one that noted that the relationship between social security programs and social services is affected by the overall objectives of social policy.[5] At a subsequent meeting of the association held in Leningrad in 1967, a panel discussion was organized on the subject, and Richard Titmuss presented a report dealing with all aspects of the question.[6] In particular, he examined the advantages and disadvantages of different practices both from the angle of the administration, which is concerned with operational efficiency, and from that of the user, who is anxious above all to satisfy his needs.

A quite different school has concerned itself more with problems that arise when both the benefits and services are provided within a social assistance program.

---

5. "Social Services Provided by Social Security Agencies, Members of the I.S.S.A.," *Bulletin of the International Social Security Association,* XVII, 10-12 (October-December, 1964), 358.

6. Richard M. Titmuss, "The Relationship Between Income Maintenance and Social Service Benefits, an Overview," *International Social Security Review,* XX, 1 (1967), 57-66.

Gordon,[7] Schwartz,[8] Burns,[9] Kahn,[10] McEntire and Haworth,[11] among others, investigated this question and came by different paths to the conclusion that the welfare system needed to be reorganized and that payment of benefits should be kept separate from the provision of services. The same view was expressed by the Task Force on Organization of Social Services which emphasizes in its report that:

Separation of cash assistance under our public assistance programs and social services is a desirable step and should proceed.[12]

Since then, this policy of separation has been applied fairly generally in the United States. The anticipated advantages have been summarized in these six points: elimination of all confusion over the function of each program; freedom of choice for the user in the selection and use of services; improvement in the standard of administration; more efficient use of manpower; ease in evaluating the effectiveness of both social services and income maintenance programs; and greater development of social services.[13]

In Canada, no systematic study has ever been made of the relationship between social security programs linked to risk and the provision of services but the tendency has always been to keep them separate, except in certain programs – such as workmen's compensation – that offer rehabilitation services to their users. Some plans, such as family allowances, maintain welfare services but their role is relatively limited. The relationship between social services and assistance plans is dealt with in a recent report by a federal-provincial group of experts charged with examining the possibilities of simplifying the procedure used to determine eligibility for benefits.[14] The report, written primarily with a view to

7. Gordon Hamilton, Editorial, *Social Work,* VII, 1 (January, 1962), 2.
8. Edward E. Schwartz, "A Way to End the Means Test," *Social Work,* IX, 3 (July, 1964), 3–12.
9. Eveline Burns, "What's Wrong with Public Welfare," *Social Service Review,* XXXVI, 2 (June, 1962), 111–22.
10. Alfred J. Kahn, "Social Services in Relation to Income Security: Introductory Notes," *Social Service Review,* XXXIX, 4 (December, 1965), 381–89.
11. Davis McEntire and Joanne Haworth, "The Two Functions of Public Welfare: Income Maintenance and Social Services," *Social Work,* XII, 1 (January, 1967), 22–31.
12. U.S., Department of Health, Education and Welfare, Task Force on Organization of Social Services, *Services for People* (Washington, D.C.: Preliminary Report of Task Force, 1968), p. ii.
13. U.S., Department of Health, Education and Welfare, Social and Rehabilitation Service, "The Separation of Services from the Determination of Eligibility for Assistance Payments" (Washington, 1970), p. 49.
14. Federal-Provincial Task Force on a Developmental Approach to Public Assistance, *Final Report to the Federal-Provincial Conference of Ministers of Welfare* (Ottawa, 1971).

improving the efficiency of the system, states the problem in the traditional perspective of a residual assistance program whose purpose is to restore the beneficiaries to a place in the social system. The report suggests that access to the program should be made easier by making admission procedures more flexible but stipulates that persons who are fit to work should not be eligible unless they use the professional rehabilitation and placement services. In fact, it does not raise the problem of social development – that is, improvement of the quality of life – or of the gaps between actual standards of living.

These two schools of thought, centred on the relationship of the social services to insurance programs on the one hand and welfare systems on the other, have very different concerns and indicate problems of coordinating planning and management and distribution of services.

The chief concern in planning is to determine the relative importance of the income maintenance programs and allocate resources accordingly. For instance, at the management level the problem consists of the advantages and drawbacks of an institutional integration; the problem in distribution is to find out how to make it easier for users to gain access to the different programs so they can derive the maximum benefit and improve their standard of living. Of course, there is a close connection between these different concerns, but at the operational level one should differentiate between them, just as one should make a distinction between income maintenance plans based on risk and those based on need. The connecting link between social services and income maintenance programs based on risk is the risk itself.

The very circumstances which lead to payment of a cash benefit may give rise to special needs which can only be met by means of supplementary services.[15]

Coordination of these services and programs, as well as the points of view of the authorities and beneficiaries, can be reconciled fairly easily since the occurrence of the risk can be forecast fairly objectively and the consequences predicted with relative accuracy, with the result that we can make the required services available to the beneficiaries. We can even incorporate in these programs some preventive services. Extending services may of course lead to controversy but this never involves the relationship between the risk and the beneficiary's situation.

The case is quite different when the integrating link is need. Not only is it impossible to predict when and how need will arise, but

15. Ida C. Merriam, "The Relations of Social Security and Social Welfare Services," *Bulletin of the International Social Security Association,* XV, 3-4 (March-April, 1962), 7.

it is quite difficult to determine its causes. Thus we find, side by side, explanations that in all seriousness attribute the state of need to factors as contradictory as individual laziness, the functioning of the social system, the maladjustment of the individual to change or the rigidity of social structures in the face of human need.

In a situation where the lines are so blurred, integration of services and income maintenance programs is hardly desirable. There is danger that such integration will not only limit access to benefits or services but also create conflict between the users and the program administrators owing to differences of interpretation. In this perspective, we shall consider the role and relationship of the social services with a guaranteed annual income program.

Guaranteed Annual Income

The term "guaranteed annual income" may be taken to mean a plan whereby the individual is assured of a minimum income that will enable him to attain a predetermined standard of living. Understood in this way, the guaranteed annual income is the result of a body of policies designed to achieve this state. These policies may include measures concerning minimum wages, a guaranteed job or annual salary, and a certain number of insurance programs that protect the individual or his family against the various risks of life, as well as a residual program for those who, in spite of all existing measures, fail to procure the income regarded as a minimum.

But the guaranteed annual income, taken in a technical sense, may refer exclusively to a residual program. In a recent article, Gilles Beausoleil showed the similarities between social assistance and the guaranteed annual income (GAI), which differ from one another only in their coverage:

In the case of the guaranteed annual income, at least theoretically, every individual or head of a family is entitled to a guaranteed annual income whether he is deprived of his livelihood or not and regardless of his performance in the labor market. Social assistance is limited to unemployed persons. In the case of assistance, participation in the labor market means withdrawal of benefits. This is the basic difference between the two programs.[16]

As far as relations with the social services are concerned, there is a fundamental difference between the GAI[17] and traditional social assistance, since the GAI has no eligibility requirements other than that of insufficient income; consequently the question of making the

---

16. Gilles Beausoleil, "Le revenu annuel garanti," *Bien-être social canadien*, XXII, 5 (November-December, 1970), 142.
17. We assume that the eventual GAI program will be based on a tested, and not a presumed, state of need (like universal benefit programs).

provision of benefits subject to use of the services cannot arise as such.

There is every reason for supporting such a program although, contrary to expectations, it will only go a very short way towards eliminating poverty (in the broad sense of the term). The amount of an individual's or family's income is just as superficial an indicator of the real standard of living as the gross national product or the national revenue is of social conditions prevailing in a country at a given time.

There is no doubt that the proposed mechanism may narrow the gap between the incomes of the different population groups, and this is highly desirable. But for all that, it will not, as some people seem to think, reduce automatically the disparities in actual living standards. Reduction of these disparities can only be brought about by social services together with health, education, recreation and similar services.

Social Services

The term "social services" is used in such a variety of senses, some of them contradictory, that it is impossible to suggest a definition without giving the impression of trying to perpetuate the existing chaotic situation.

The confusion arises from the fact that this expression is used one time for activities defined in terms of the methods used,[18] another for institutions defined in terms of their functions,[19] and still another for a system of services defined in terms of the public or private authority responsible for managing it. In addition, it is used to designate a whole body of social activities which have almost nothing in common except that they serve human needs. This is why the term social services has come to include education, health, welfare, recreation, housing and even social security.

In this paper the term "social services" will be restricted to a

---

18. United Nations, Department of Economics and Social Affairs, *Social Service Programmes*, p. 6. This report defines social service "as an organized activity that aims at helping towards a mutual adjustment of individuals and their social environment. This objective is achieved through the use of techniques and methods which are designed to enable individuals, groups and committees to meet their needs . . ."

19. Alfred J. Kahn, "Social Services as Social Utilities," *Urban Development, Its Implications for Social Welfare*, Proceedings of the XIII International Conference of Social Work, Washington, D.C., 1966 (New York: Columbia University Press, 1967), p. 193. "A social utility is a social invention, a resource or facility, designed to meet a generally experienced need in social living. It is defined as so vital that the broader community suffers from the results of the deprivation faced by an individual."

number of well-defined activities classified according to their operational objectives, although admittedly this is an arbitrary definition. Since these objectives are an organic part of the ultimate purposes of social policy, an attempt will be made to list them, although this is a rash thing to do since there is no consensus on this subject and these objectives are constantly changing.

For the purposes of this study, these objectives are grouped in seven categories which are neither exclusive nor exhaustive.

1 *Promotion of greater social justice by a more equitable distribution of income and goods with a view to reducing the disparities between living standards of the various sections of the population and improving the living standard of social classes that live just outside the dynamic sections of society.* This objective[20] is important as there is every reason to believe that, without suitable corrective measures, the gap between those who benefit by progress and those who do not will continue to widen.

2 *Improvement in the educational level of the population to give everyone an equal chance in life.*[21] This measure also seeks to facilitate adjustment by individuals to a swiftly-changing society.

3 *Protection and improvement of health for the good of the individual and of society.*[22] In this area the most spectacular changes now are seen because of scientific advances, and it is here that the elimination of inequality is most urgent.

4 *Prevention of deviance*[23] *in all its forms and the elimination as far as*

20. Notably found in: Canada, Parliament, Senate, Special Committee on Poverty, *Poverty in Canada* (Ottawa: Information Canada, 1971); Canada, Royal Commission on Taxation, *Report* (Ottawa: Queen's Printer, 1966–67); Quebec (Province) Commission of Inquiry on Health and Social Welfare, *Report* (Quebec: Official Publisher, 1967, 1970–71–).

21. This objective is emphasized in several reports, including: Ontario, Commission on Post-Secondary Education in Ontario, *Draft Report* (Toronto: Queen's Printer, 1972).

22. This objective is stressed in: Canada, Royal Commission on Health Services, *Report* (Ottawa: Queen's Printer, 1964–65); and Quebec (Province) Commission of Inquiry on Health and Social Welfare, *Report*.

23. This objective is emphasized in: Canada, Department of Justice, Committee on Juvenile Delinquency, *Juvenile Delinquency in Canada* (Ottawa: Queen's Printer, 1965); Canada, Committee on Corrections, *Toward Unity, Criminal Justice and Corrections* (Ottawa: Queen's Printer, 1969); Quebec (Province) Commission of Inquiry into the Administration of Justice on Criminal and Penal Matters in Quebec, *Crime, Justice and Society* (Quebec: Official Publisher, 1969); and Canada, Commission of Inquiry into the Non-Medical Use of Drugs, *Interim Report* (Ottawa: Queen's Printer, 1970).

possible of its most harmful consequences both for the individual and society. In speaking of deviance, the meaning given by Cohen[24] is used. According to Cohen, the behavior of a deviant is "one which transgresses the normative rules" and in this sense, without being good or bad in itself, represents a threat to social organization. Even though deviance does not necessarily destroy that organization and may, in certain cases, make a positive contribution to the vitality of the system, some of its more extreme manifestations represent a danger both for the individual and the community and may on that account warrant action by the public authorities.

5 *Promotion of personal development and measures to combat alienation.* This objective is perhaps the most difficult to define in operational terms; it is the hardest to understand and probably the most important objective in terms of development centred on human growth. At the risk of oversimplifying, it could be said that this means optimizing the individual's potential for functioning socially in an increasingly complex world by helping him to discover his needs and satisfy them by appropriate activities, taking into account his abilities, his resources and the social restraints. This objective differs from the preceding one in that it is directed not towards elimination of the factors that cause dysfunctioning but towards optimum development of individual potential.[25]

6 *Improvement of the environment in all its forms: housing, town and region.* A housing policy can be summed up in very simple terms: it must provide each citizen with decent housing appropriate to his needs and at a rent he can afford to pay without unduly straining his budget. Moreover, the tenants of some 500,000 or 600,000 dwellings in Canada which are considered substandard (most of them slums) must be rehoused.[26]

The housing problem and in particular the provision of housing for low-income families, is inseparable from the problem of urban renewal. At the symposium on urban housing held by the Canadian Institute of Public Affairs, Blumenfeld[27] quoted town planner Pat-

24. Albert K. Cohen, *Deviance and Control* (Englewood Cliffs, N.J.: Prentice-Hall, 1966), pp. 1–11.

25. Great Britain, Committee on Local Authority and Allied Personal Social Services, *Report* (London: H.M.S.O., 1968) and U.S., Department of Health, Education and Welfare, Task Force on Organization of Social Services, *Services for People.*

26. The first Canadian Conference on Housing, in 1968, made a series of recommendations on this subject which were published with the lectures and deliberations in: Michael Wheeler, ed., *The Right to Housing* (Montreal: Harvest House, 1969).

27. Hans Blumenfeld, "Est-il possible de loger convenablement tout le monde?" in *Une Ville à vivre: un Colloque sur l'Habitat urbain d'aujourd'hui*

rick Geddes who said more than half a century ago that the policy of sweeping slum clearance is one of the most disastrous and pernicious blunders; the large population thus expelled would be drawn into worse conditions in other quarters. The speaker added that tearing down slums does not mean abolishing them but enlarging them; it is not a socially progressive step – it is criminal madness.

A recent study by the Conseil de Développement social du Montréal métropolitain on public housing[28] in the Saint Martin district amply confirms Blumenfeld's hypothesis: the residents, without being given any choice in the matter, have to allocate a larger portion of their income to rent, and this has a greater impact on families that spend proportionately less on housing. It is not surprising, therefore, that there is no perceptible improvement in the morale of the relocated families and that, in spite of all material advantages, there is dissatisfaction among the residents who "probably feel just as poor and exploited as before."

Closely linked to the question of urban renewal is that of regional redevelopment which is supposed to encourage equalization of living conditions.

7 *Better adaptation of people to their work, especially to changes in working conditions resulting from technological progress.* Very often this objective is expressed in terms of full employment, but there is a static aspect about this notion which is increasingly a subject of debate.[29] There are at least four sets of phenomena contributing to discrimination in the labor market:

a The difference in the level of development in different regions, increasing the disparity in economic activity and number of available jobs;

b Sectorial displacements resulting from the decline in certain branches of activity simultaneously with the expansion of others;

c The development in geometric progression of technology in its most advanced forms;

d As a partial effect, at least, of the three preceding categories, an increased selectivity which raises particular problems for certain classes of workers such as the young, women, the elderly, the physically and mentally handicapped, persons with behavior problems and immigrants.

In the context of these fundamental objectives, the programs related to social services may be grouped into four main categories.[30]

---

et de demain (Montreal: Editions du jour, 1968), pp. 17–18.

28. "Consultation populaire: le logement public" (Montreal, 1971), p. 47.

29. A comprehensive treatment of this problem is found in the publications of the Organization for Economic Co-operation and Development.

30. These categories are based on the report of the Task Force on Organization of Social Services, *Services for People.*

(1) *Services designed to close the gap between actual standards of living.* Although they are universal, they are essentially oriented towards providing services which will be of most benefit to the marginal population or the handicapped. In particular, these include protection services for persons incapable of looking after themselves either because they suffer from physical or mental handicaps or because they belong to groups which are the target of discrimination (Indians, Eskimos, immigrants, delinquents, alcoholics). The accent is not so much on the services themselves as on the coordination of services to deal with the specific needs of the users.

(2) *Services emphasizing personal development and the reduction of alienation* by referring individuals to services they need; serving as a go-between in their dealings with the institutions providing these services; and helping individuals and groups promote their social rights.

These services facilitate the achievement of several of the social objectives, especially raising the education level and improving health. This is done by helping people, through personal or mediation services, to make maximum use of welfare, health and education services. Services which fall into this category are individualized information services,[31] referral services, legal aid, and consumer protection services.

(3) *Treatment services of all kinds:* consultation, rehabilitation, individual or family therapy, vocational guidance, preparation for employment, etc. These services are mainly aimed at prevention of deviance, promotion of personal development and better adaptation to work.

(4) *Socialization and development services.* These services contribute to the achievement of most of the major social objectives. They include a wide range of services, some of which complement those provided by the family, the health or educational systems, while others supplement these services if necessary. Some concrete examples are: various types of foster homes for children and adults; day care centres (the increasing need for these and their expansion were mentioned in several recent reports);[32] visiting homemaker services[33]

---

31. Not to be confused with mass information services as proposed in: Canada, Task Force on Government Information, *To Know and Be Known* (Ottawa: Queen's Printer, 1969).

32. Among others: Canada, Royal Commission on the Status of Women in Canada, *Report* (Ottawa: Information Canada, 1970). A study of day care centres in Montreal estimated a need for four times as many places as there are now available: Montreal Council of Social Agencies, *A Survey of Day Care Facilities for Children of Metropolitan Montreal* (Montreal, 1969). Also, Canadian Council on Social Development, *Day Care*: Report of a National Study (Ottawa, 1972).

33. Canadian Council on Social Development, Advisory Committee on

and other help in the home for families, the elderly, the disabled and sick; meals on wheels for the sick, disabled and elderly;[34] different types of drop-in centres for persons leaving hospital or suffering from loneliness; recreation services and certain education and cultural services. All these are social utilities in the sense that their use increases the collective well-being and social development of the population.

Complementary Role of Social Services

The role of the social services may be considered either in relation to the guaranteed annual income itself or together with the guaranteed annual income in relation to the achievement of the ultimate social goals. In relation to the guaranteed annual income, social services can have three possible roles: supplementary, supportive and substitutive.

1 *Supplementary Role*
In this role, the services supplement benefits to raise the actual standard of living. The lower the benefits, the more important the supplemental role. Most GAI plans suggested so far in the United States and Canada provide an income definitely below the poverty line;[35] this line itself is subject to debate. Thus, in 1967 the Social Planning Council of Metropolitan Toronto[36] set the basic minimum for a family of four (two adults and two children) at $4,861.08, while the Montreal Diet Dispensary[37] set it at $3,297.77, a difference of 45 per cent. One would have to be naive to think that a GAI program based on a more or less arbitrary poverty line can in itself provide the beneficiaries with an adequate standard of living. This is true for several reasons.

The first reason is that there can be no general consensus concerning the standard of living that should be provided for each member of society. If the poverty lines suggested by the Social Planning Council of Metropolitan Toronto and the Montreal Diet

Visiting Homemaker Services, *Visiting Homemaker Services in Canada* (Ottawa, 1971). The report deals with this problem and makes a series of recommendations for the extension and improvement of this service.
34. Canada, Parliament, Senate, Special Committee on Aging, *Final Report* (Ottawa: Queen's Printer, 1966). The report made a series of recommendations on this subject.
35. Special Committee on Poverty, *Poverty in Canada,* proposes benefits set at 70 per cent of the committee's poverty line. In the United States, the Family Assistance Act of 1969 rejected by the Senate set the guaranteed annual income at less than 50 per cent of the poverty line for a family of four.
36. *Guides for Family Budgeting* (Toronto, 1967).
37. *Budgeting for Basic Needs* (Montreal, 1967).

Dispensary differ so widely, it is because there are differences in the basic assumptions about the nature and quantity of consumer goods included in the budget. As we move away from a strictly survival budget, we can expect these differences to grow.

The second reason is that benefits based on need, even if they are provided by right, encounter popular prejudice which is difficult to stamp out. These prejudices, which spring from the principle "to each according to his work," are rationalized in a variety of attempts to find a formula that will provide an adequate income for everyone without discouraging the incentive to work. It is particularly significant that a group of welfare recipients in Montreal felt the need to advertise in a daily newspaper, giving statistics tending to prove that the majority of people receiving social assistance are not capable of working.

The third reason is that benefits provided by right are necessarily based on an "average" need and consequently do not correspond to the "actual" need of an individual or family. Hence, there is a gap which must be filled in one way or another; to the extent that a system of services (health, housing, social services) is available on a universal basis to provide for the satisfaction of a number of basic needs, the gap between the "average" need and the "actual" need can be significantly reduced. For example the provision of universal health services, according to some estimates, increases income from 7 to 9 per cent, raising the actual standard of living proportionately. Similarly, by providing housing it is possible to raise the actual standard of living by 20 to 30 per cent.

As far as social services are concerned, in the restricted sense in which we use the term, their contribution cannot now be measured with any accuracy; in fact these services have to do with social performance, the indicators of which, insofar as they exist, are debatable to say the least. An information service, a referral service or even a social consultation service can only be evaluated in terms of either the satisfaction felt by the user or the rate of use. None of these criteria is really satisfactory. Therefore, the necessity for a service can only be judged qualitatively by the demand shown for it.

2 Supportive Role

The second role of social services consists in supporting the GAI. The services in this category differ considerably from one another but all have one thing in common: the potential to reinforce the program. Some enable the users to raise their actual standard of living by helping them make the most effective use of their benefits; others can help them become more self-reliant and better able to provide for themselves.

A good example of the first type of services is guardianship. This service is relatively undeveloped in Canada owing to the complexity of the underlying legal problems. All income maintenance plans[38] provide for the appointment of a trustee responsible for seeing that the benefits are used wisely in cases where the beneficiary is incapable of providing for himself because he has a physical or mental handicap. The service is generally restricted to managing benefits on behalf of the beneficiary. If it were enlarged to provide more comprehensive protection, it would no doubt give better results. Whatever its scope, however, its basic role is always to support the income maintenance programs. Budget consultation and consumer education services have almost identical roles. Their objective is to help individuals and families develop skills in using the resources at their disposal. Some interesting experiments have been tried in this field in recent years but they fall far short of meeting the need for such services.

A second category includes all support services designed to motivate individuals to work and help them find and keep a job adapted to their potentialities. This category may also include services aimed at explaining to employers the advantages of hiring such people. Quite a few programs in Canada are designed to help welfare recipients get back in the labor market.[39] With the establishment of a guaranteed annual income program and the disappearance of the concept of welfare recipient, these services may become more universal, with greater emphasis on the needs of individuals than on their status in relation to a social assistance program. At the same time it will be possible to assess the effectiveness of the programs much more objectively.

3 *Substitutive Role*
The third role the social services can play is that of substitution. In some cases, indeed, the recipient's needs cannot be satisfied by cash benefits so services have to be substituted for them. The best example of this type of service is placement in private homes or institutions. The importance of placement is shown by the fact that an estimated 92,482 children and 60,433 adults were placed in Canada in 1968–69. This is a marked increase over 1960–61, representing 56 per cent for children[40] and 50 per cent for adults.[41]

38. Notably the old age security plan, the Canada Pension Plan, the veterans' income maintenance plans, provincial workmen's compensation schemes, etc.
39. For example, the Employment Opportunities Program in Alberta and the Two-Way Agency Referral Service in Vancouver.
40. Federal-Provincial Working Group on the Costs of Welfare Programs, *Final Report of the Federal-Provincial Conference of Ministers of Welfare* (Ottawa, 1971), pp. 55, 71.
41. Federal-Provincial Working Group on the Costs of Welfare Programs, *Final Report to the Federal-Provincial Conference of Ministers of Welfare,* pp. 55, 65.

However, placement methods are changing, with fewer children being placed in institutions and more in foster homes. Also, foster homes are beginning to become diversified and new types, such as group homes, are appearing. There is a trend in adult placement to specialization of institutions to meet diversified needs.

The advantages of placement could be debated at length and the question arises whether it should be avoided as much as possible by substituting other types of services. In any case the substitution role is due to the fact that these types of services achieve some objectives of a guaranteed annual income program by providing for the recipient's maintenance.

These services now are administered by the same authority that provides assistance benefits. This brings advantages and disadvantages that have never been studied systematically. The establishment of a guaranteed annual income if it is administered, as would be desirable, by an authority independent of the one managing social services, should produce new patterns of coordination and cooperation. The details of this are difficult to predict but the basic principle is that the cash benefits program should provide a basic subsistence for recipients, while the social services are responsible for raising people above the subsistence level, promoting better personal adjustment and a better balance between the individual and society.

The classification of services according to their role in relation to the GAI is to some extent arbitrary because some services may fit into more than one category. Moreover, such a classification may appear theoretical at first glance, but its full significance appears when we approach the problem at the organizational level. Before doing this, however, it may be advisable to examine the right to social services.

The Right to Social Services

All services mentioned as examples contribute, with many others, to realizing the great goals of Canadian society and should be available to the whole population indiscriminately. This justifies the efforts being made to give them a status comparable to health and education services and make them available to people by right. The idea of recognizing the right of individuals to social services is not a new one. It springs from the Universal Declaration of Human Rights proclaimed by the United Nations and is slowly making its way in Canada.[12] But the basic problem is how to ensure enjoyment

42. The Quebec Commission of Inquiry on Health and Social Welfare devoted a whole chapter to human rights and the right to social services but did not deal with the question of how to implement this right. Quebec (Prov-

of this right and not make it obligatory.[43] In order for people to exercise their rights, services must exist; their use should not be subject to any other criterion than that of need. This brings us to the question of the resources and organization of social services.

Organizing and Financing Social Services

Organizational programs can be summed up in three main questions: what services must be provided? to whom? how?

1 *Providing Services and Setting Priorities*
The choice of services to be provided is difficult in a society that is seen as being in constant evolution and whose social goals are being transformed quickly. It is difficult, not only because needs are changing but also because the resources available to provide services are, and always will be, limited. There must be priorities for choosing services to be provided, especially if we agree that every service should be provided on a universal basis. The order of priorities is especially important since the creation and development of different types of services affect the order in which overall social policy goals can be achieved.

As Richard M. Titmuss rightly pointed out, "some social programs favor the rich over the poor and others favor the poor over the rich."[44] The writer has taken the view that the number one goal is to attack poverty. The priorities suggested by the Task Force on Organization of Social Services in the United States are centred first on the poor, then on children and youth.[45] In Canada, we have not tried to lay down such hard and fast priorities. We should be glad of this because it is not desirable – and probably not possible – to base social policy on such limited objectives. A social policy that seeks the support of public opinion should aim at changes that improve general conditions and benefit some members of society without worsening the lot of any.[46]

ince) Commission of Inquiry on Health and Social Welfare, "Human Development," in *Development,* Vol. III, Tome I, of the *Report* (Quebec: Official Publisher, 1971), pp. 157–85.

43. The Task Force on Employment Opportunities for Welfare Recipients in Ontario, for example, recognizes the right to certain social services but at the same time makes it an obligation by making the payment of benefits subject to use of the services. Ontario, Task Force on Employment Opportunities for Welfare Recipients, *Report* (Toronto, 1972).

44. Titmuss, "The Relationship between Income Maintenance and Social Service Benefits, an Overview," p. 61.

45. Task Force on Organization of Social Services, *Services for People,* p. 59.

46. David A. Hardcastle, "A Welfare Transfer for the Poor," *Social Service Review,* XLV, 4 (December, 1971), 427.

So long as responsibility for establishing priorities and determining the kind of services depends on the private sector, the problem is not particularly acute since, at the local level, the necessary compromises are relatively easy. But when the question involves services seeking to meet universal needs in the interest of all members of society, the problem becomes much more complex. The opposing views of different groups of the population, different geographical regions and different cultures must be reconciled. This being so, establishment of priorities acceptable to the population as a whole calls for far more sophisticated machinery and procedures than we now have. The search for such machinery will no doubt continue. Meanwhile, it would be preferable to speak of relative priorities, not absolute ones.

On the other hand, the order of these priorities may be based on social groups, problems or services. Social services, unlike other services, have always been group- and problem-centred. There is a tendency now to try to develop models centred more on services – a good thing in itself, provided the model embodies the principle of temporal and spatial relativity.

2 Scope of Services

The second problem involves the scope of services: who is to receive them? In view of the importance attached to the equalization of opportunity and the levelling of social inequalities, it might be concluded that services should be provided on a selective basis – that is, to a well-defined group in accordance with predetermined criteria. Nothing could be further from the truth, because the effectiveness of the services is closely linked to their universality.

A service is said to be universal when it is available to all who wish to take advantage of it – that is, all who feel the need for it. A service is sectorial or selective when it is available only to certain groups of the population defined according to criteria other than that of need. The criteria now used to determine eligibility reflect a variety of considerations: moral (services to veterans), occupational (rehabilitation of workers in firms covered by the Workmen's Compensation Act), political (nationality), ecological (place of residence), socio-cultural (services for Indians and Eskimos), economic (services to the poor), or administrative (services for delinquents).

The universal system is better adapted to a policy aimed at standardizing services (that is to say, a policy centred on improving the quality of life), whereas the selective system is better adapted to a policy slanted towards equalizing actual standards of living. These aproaches are far from irreconcilable, provided they can be judiciously weighted.

If a guaranteed annual income is introduced, the problem of the scope of social services will probably arise in a different way from what it now does with regard to social assistance programs, since recipients will be somewhat different. The GAI will include the working poor and casual workers as well as persons unfit to work.

Providing services on a universal basis also improves their quality. It is a well-known fact that services organized only for the poor are usually of lower quality and, as a result, not valued by the users. The Task Force on Organization of Social Services in the United States emphasized the difficulty of adequately financing services for the poor and recruiting qualified staff to provide these services.[47] This is explained by society's hostility to diverting too much money to marginal groups and by the natural dependency of the users, who let themselves be satisfied with inferior services.

3   Provision of Services

The third factor is how the services are provided. If the right to social services is to be more than a mere declaration of principle and if we consider that the use of such services is in the public interest, the general organization of these services should reflect this attitude by ensuring their availability, accessibility, flexibility and diversification.

Availability means that everything is done to see that the services are at people's disposal. For a long time we have thought that the demand for a service could be met more or less automatically in accordance with the law of supply and demand. We know today that this is not true. In the field of social services there is no automatic adjustment, and if we want the services to be available to people in sufficient quantity, we must create the appropriate resources.

In Canada the private sector has always taken the initiative in satisfying this demand but it is clear that it is no longer equal to the task. Action by the federal and provincial governments is needed, because they are the only ones that can generate the necessary resources. They can do the job in several ways and the way in which they do it will undoubtedly affect the quality of services.

Accessibility means that the services are made available to people so each user can have them when he needs them. Obstacles to access may be physical, psychological or social. A centralized service, a service insufficiently publicized or interpreted to the people, or one that does not take into account the need its users feel for self-determination, consciously or unconsciously raises barriers between itself and the population.

Diversity means that the services are organized to give the user

---

47. Task Force on Organization of Social Services, *Services for People*, p. 38.

a number of choices. There are several ways of satisfying any need and it is up to the user to determine which one suits him best. The necessity of choice as an organizing principle for social services rests on the idea that self-determination is indispensable to ensure optimal use of services. The rationale underlying this principle is centred on the user rather than the service offered. There should be a choice not only of a particular service (for example, among different types of housing) but also among different types of services that enable a person to achieve the same goal (for example, between assistance in the home and institutional assistance). Choice also implies that the user, except in very special cases, does not have to use a service he feels he does not need.

Flexibility means that services are organized to be adaptable to change; no one can predict the future or how needs for social services will change. As a result, serious long-range planning is not possible. It is perhaps this temporal relativity of social services which distinguishes them most from all other systems of services less subject to change. The problem of flexibility is perhaps the most difficult to solve in a context of technocratic planning. Attempts being made by welfare institutions, both public and private, to operate on the basis of projects may solve this problem, but we certainly cannot give an opinion on the value of such attempts at present.

4 *Management of Social Services*
The need to put social services on a public basis may lead us to promote a network of services managed by the public authorities. Although it is advisable to make distinctions between different social services (some of them being of such a nature that they should be managed by the public authorities), generally it is not desirable that the state, which is responsible for providing the resources, should have exclusive responsibility for providing such services. There are several reasons for this:

a Because a monolithic system of social services would lower the quality of services provided, owing to the absence of competition;
b Because a monolithic system would give the user little or no choice, and choice is as important as the service itself;
c Because in such a system there would be almost no room for creativeness or spontaneity; and
d Because a public system, by itself, could never cope with the rapid development of social services.

5 *Financing Social Services*
Starting from the assumptions that the GAI provides everyone with a minimum income and that social services are provided by a network of public and private institutions and agencies, the problem of financing can be stated in the following terms: to what extent

and by what means should services be financed by a GAI plan bearing in mind that some of the services are in lieu of cash benefits, others enhance the value of such benefits, and others are added to the GAI to improve the quality of life.

It is obviously impossible to answer this question in detail without knowing what form the GAI plan will take. There are several alternatives.

a The plan may be required to finance services up to the amount due to an individual, the balance being charged to the budget of the social services.

b The plan may be required to fully finance the social services provided to its beneficiaries.

c The monetary value of social services provided persons eligible for the GAI is deducted from the benefits.

Each of these methods has its advantages and drawbacks, but the first is probably the easiest to apply.

Many suggestions have been made about methods for financing social services provided by private organizations. We shall consider only two of them: the voucher system and the subsidy system.

The subsidy system can only be used if the same authority administers both the GAI and the social services. It has the advantage of ensuring control over the quality of services but, to the extent that the social services are provided on a universal basis, it may possibly subsidize services to persons other than beneficiaries of the GAI.

The voucher system, now the most popular method, bears no relation to the former system in which the recipient was given allowances in kind instead of cash. Vouchers can only be used to finance complementary services or substitute services where the person's status calls for such a form of service.

Two forms of vouchers may be provided: those with a fixed value and those with a variable value. With the latter, the amount is set so the individual can procure the basic service he needs, although it is possible for him to get something better if he has the desire and means. This system was proposed in Britain by the Institute of Economic Affairs, which suggests that vouchers be issued to low-income families to enable them to pay for a whole series of services such as education, medical care and recreation. Voucher prices would be on a sliding scale corresponding to the income of the individuals.

This system is now used in the food coupon program in the United States. Thus, for example, a family of four with a monthly income of $100 can buy food coupons with a market value of $78 for $44. If the family's monthly income is below $30 it can buy $52 worth of coupons for $8.

A variant of the voucher system for individuals is that of vouchers given to groups who become responsible for seeing that the vouchers are used as efficiently as possible.

Conclusion

At the close of this brief survey, it is only natural to consider the future of social services.

The introduction of a guaranteed annual income should bring some fairly radical changes in the welfare system. This system, devised as a necessary evil, aims at keeping the number of welfare recipients as low as possible and providing them with the bare minimum income compatible with prevailing social standards. The procedures used to do this vary from one province to another. Some stress efficiency of administrative controls and thus cut the average per capita cost of assistance. Others attach more importance to "rehabilitation" programs. These objectives, however valid, cannot contribute significantly to achieving the great social goals. There is no program based on improving social development and the quality of life *per se*. The existence of social development cannot be deduced from either the employment rate or the unemployment rate.

The effectiveness of the system of social services seen in the light of a guaranteed annual income will depend on the following.

(1) *The amount of the benefits provided by the GAI plan.* This amount will determine to what extent services will have to fill gaps between the GAI and the real needs of individuals and to what extent the services can be directed toward social development.

(2) *How successful we are in reconciling the rapid expansion of services to meet rising needs with improvement in the quality of services.*

(3) *How successful we are at the management level in separating the provision of cash benefits and social services.* If the allowances are administered by the welfare departments, we can expect very few changes from the present situation.

(4) *How successful we are in reconciling the necessity for maintaining high standards of services with that of leaving as much initiative as possible to the organizations that supply the services.*

(5) *How successful we are in harmonizing traditional, static planning with planning that seeks to promote and accelerate change.*

(6) *How successful we are in involving the users in the planning, management and provision of services so that the services will be adapted to changing needs.*

The Possibilities of Income Transformation

by S. M. Miller
Director, Urban Center,
New York University, New York

and Martin Rein
Professor, Department of Urban Studies and Planning,
Massachusetts Institute of Technology, Cambridge

Recently in many countries signs have appeared of dissatisfaction with the distribution of income and the limited effects of social policies. In this paper we illustrate the kinds of observations which have led many social policy experts to conclude that inequalities have persisted.

Some "welfare state" countries committed to the ideals of reducing inequalities seem perversely unable to achieve this aim effectively. A vigorous debate in Britain was launched when Peter Townsend, a leading Labour intellectual, charged that the poor became poorer during the five years of Wilson's Labour government. This erosion in the relative position of the poor arose despite the government's success in raising family allowances and increasing welfare payments (supplementary benefits) more rapidly than prices and net average wages. Price inflation, wage increases, rising levels of taxation, lowered tax thresholds, and effects of deflation seem to have nullified the most determined efforts of Britain's Labour government to improve the relative economic well-being of the poorest segment of its working population.

In Sweden, wage solidarity policies explicitly designed to narrow the distribution of wages have produced social unrest which found expression in prolonged strikes among mining and white-collar workers in the summer of 1971. The better-off seem threatened by the economic advances of the low-wage sector especially when their real income failed to increase because of inflation. The outcome of the struggle seems less discouraging since the demands of the white-collar unions to undermine solidarity policy were thwarted.

The recent economic reforms in some Eastern European nations have sometimes deliberately been aimed at widening wage differentials in order to promote greater incentives for efficiency and productivity. If income redistribution is not taking place in socialist and welfare state countries, then what is the likelihood of greater equality occurring in countries such as the United States that have no explicitly egalitarian ethic?

A review by the Organization for Economic Cooperation and Development (OECD) of a number of countries suggests that despite dramatic increases in the proportion of the population enrolled in higher education, there has been no appreciable increase in the composition of working-class students among all university students.

The 1965 economic survey of *Incomes in Postwar Europe*[1] concludes that:

Between the prewar and immediate postwar years, there appears to have been some reduction in primary income dispersion but the factors reducing income inequality seem to have weakened considerably over the last decade or so . . . Taking all households, a slight reduction in income dispersal has continued in some countries, but not in all . . . Broadly speaking, households in the highest income groups have suffered a deterioration in their relative position in a number of countries, though not in all; yet at the same time the income gap between the poorest groups and middle income ranges, has, if anything, increased. [*emphasis added*]

The startling recognition of the existence of poverty is not the only source of dismay, for increasingly the feeling emerges that there is something undesirable and mystifying, perhaps unreasonable, about the income distribution of the particular nation in question, whether it is the United States, Canada or Sweden. Some of the reasons for this disquiet are worth exploring.

One source of unease is the awareness that the facts about income distribution are not what they were believed to be. Two powerful and complacency-inducing myths withered as poverty was rediscovered and inequality persisted: that "affluence" described the state of the consumers in high-industrial societies and that economic growth was producing not only a larger but a more equitably shared pie. When economic growth proved an inadequate solution to the recurring problem of inequality and affluence was dethroned as the panacea, a disquiet followed.

A second disturbing factor has been the recognition of externalities, the social (and usually unrecognized) cost of producing the gross national product (GNP). Environmental and ecological fears have brought an awareness of the disutilities involved in producing what purport to be the utilities of the private economy. If one looks at the actual conditions of people, their real money income may rise while their quality of life may deteriorate because

---

1. U.N. Economic Commission for Europe, *Incomes in Postwar Europe: A Study of Policies, Groups and Distribution*, Economic Survey of Europe in 1965, Part 3 (E/ECE/613/add. 1), 1967, Chap. 11, p. 5.

of pollution and other factors. The way in which GNP is produced is, therefore, very significant and is one of the refrains of this paper.

Third, gross monetary income becomes increasingly a poor indicator of the command over resources. The great expansion in services raises the question of how they are distributed and what benefits they have for people in different kinds of economic and social situations. The exchange between income and wealth and the importance of taxation and how to avoid it affect very deeply individuals' command over resources over time.

For these reasons, the apparent stability of income distribution in many countries probably misrepresents the important long-term trends because, when the more subtle evidences such as in-kind benefits and tax forgiveness are taken into account, income inequalities must surely have grown in high-income nations.

A fourth important dawning is that government policies affect or should affect the distribution of income. We are not dealing with immutable market forces with the possibility of great harm if there is interference. Whatever government does – as increasingly in most countries it does a great deal – affects income distribution. Whether by omission or commission, through purchases from manufacturers or contractors, manipulation of interest rates, tariffs and quotas or investment incentives, government activity is a crucial molder of the character of production and the distribution of income in a nation. Consequently, the overall distribution of income, not just the humanitarian policies considered to be welfare-stateism (such as social security or unemployment insurance) are products of government action or inaction. Thus, there is someone to hold responsible for the distribution of income instead of a market which presumably has an automatism that should not be questioned.

It is disappointing to realize that social policies have played only a modest role in redistributing resources in the aggregate. Although the relative position of some specialized groups in society (such as the aged) has improved, they have been largely financed by their own past payments through social insurance and general taxation. Particularly disturbing is that the relative position of others, such as the working poor, has declined.

Fifth, there is a loss of confidence that the distribution of income makes sense. Indeed, it is not even clear what the rationale is. Two basic principles usually adduced to explain the distribution have limited explanatory power. One is that the return is proportionate to the contribution an individual makes. It is hard to think of what these contributions are when some of the highest paid people in the society receive these rewards for their efforts to enable even richer people to evade the impact of tax and other laws. One can multiply examples of people with high returns in terms of income who are really misusers of wealth and destroyers of resources rather than developers of them. A favorite example is that ditch-diggers probably benefit a society more than most of its lawyers. But their returns do not mirror their differential contributions.

The other principle is that of the meritocracy – that people of higher ability are educated with emotional and economic costs in order to perform more important jobs and therefore should be re-warded for their ability and educational investment. The assump-tion is that the meritocracy coincides with social and economic con-tribution, a doubtful belief. But even assuming its validity, educa-tion fails to explain much about the distribution of income in most countries; a variety of other factors are at work, including genetic and environmental ones, the ability of an occupational group to protect itself against competition, and the like.

Thus it is not an exaggeration to say that increasing numbers doubt that a rational basis for current income distribution exists. The legitimacy of the unequal distribution is breaking down al-though there is not widespread acceptance of alternatives.

Finally, it becomes increasingly clear that the issues of distribu-tion are not questions of adding or modifying a program to improve some minor deficiency which has been discovered in a health or social insurance scheme but go to the very character of the society that is desired. Our goals for a society are predicated in the deci-sions made about the composition of product and the distribution of income in that society, whether those decisions are made con-sciously or unconsciously, deliberately or inadvertently. The big questions of purpose and content are usually pushed to the side as possible incremental changes compel attention. The search for what we really want is overwhelmed by the shock at what we can really get. But income distribution questions are fundamental and more likely to resist the push towards minor achievement.

Measurement as a Substantive Problem

The way of measuring is a way of thinking. Increasingly, the in-adequacy of GNP and national income (NI) as indicators of well-being becomes apparent. Decades ago, Pigou[2] illustrated the mis-leading character of calculations in his discussion of the house-keeper turned wife. When she is a housekeeper and unmarried, her wages are a contribution to GNP and NI. Married and provided the same income as before from her former employer turned hus-band, performing the same services perhaps even more carefully, she has reduced the GNP and NI because she no longer receives

---

2.   Arthur Cecil Pigou, *The Economics of Welfare,* 4th ed. (London: Mac-millan, 1952).

her income as wages. More recently, the examples of misleading calculations revolve around pollution. While an enterprise is worsening conditions for citizens, all its activities are considered contributions to GNP and the diminution in our well-being because of pollution is not considered. If the government spends money to clean up the environmental harm that has been done, GNP increases. Achieving what we had before is an advance; losing what we had is not calculated as a loss.

What has happened is that the convenient practices economists adopted in order to avoid value judgments have become an obstacle to systematic and clear thinking about the processes of production and distribution. Economists have tried to avoid really defining a contribution by saying that it is anything for which a price is paid and therefore should be considered in total production. (Soviet economists in their desire to follow Marxian concepts of value have excluded some items from the calculation of national product.) There is no easy solution to the calculation of national well-being. But obviously we need a variety of different kinds of measures of it. What we now have is one system of measurement used in different ways (gross national product, net national product, national income, disposable income) but it is still only one stream of analysis. Many different cuts into the ways of analyzing what is happening within a society are obviously needed. The simple system that we have adopted in the national accounts is clearly inadequate for the multiple purposes we now wish to use. These are purposes of well-being over time, recognition of various secondary effects or unintended effects on the environment and society, and concerns about the distribution of services as well as income.

It now has become a major political as well as an intellectual concern to demystify GNP and NI and provide a variety of ways of looking at the processes and products of the economy. To explain why we get these outcomes now is the cardinal task of radical (in the sense of root) economic, social and political analysis.

Economists have been mainly concerned with one aspect of the issue of inequality, namely, that of income. (The distribution of wealth has been much less studied than the distribution of income.) In the analysis of trends in the distribution of income, one major measure has been featured. This is the Gini coefficient and the Lorenz curve[3] which underlies the coefficient. But this particular

---

3. The Lorenz curve is formed by plotting the cumulative frequency distribution of the amount of income against the cumulative frequency distribution of the population. It shows the total amount of variation from complete equality. The Gini coefficient is a summary measure of the Lorenz curve and varies between zero (complete income equality) and unity (complete income inequality).

measure is limited because it fails to discern whether changes in the coefficient are due to shifts in the share of income received by higher-income groups, middle-income groups or lower-income groups. The same coefficient of income inequality can mask quite different profiles and pyramids of income distribution. For example, when the Lorenz curves intersect, the result can be a distribution which is more equal at the top and with greater inequality at the bottom or the reverse. Atkinson perceptively notes that:

the Gini coefficient is often presented as a purely "scientific" measure of inequality, but it is clear that it must implicitly embody values about the distribution of income, since without introducing such values one cannot weigh the lesser inequality at the top against the greater inequality at the bottom of the distribution.[4]

There are still other troublesome problems of measurement including difficult decisions about the unit of analysis (individuals, families, or households); the resources to be measured (income expenditures, wealth, transfers, subsidies, or still other measures of well-being); and the time to be covered (weekly, monthly, yearly, lifetime income).

Important as these technical considerations are, they are overshadowed by the inadequacies of the concept of income as a measure of well-being and social stratification. Two lines of development have emerged which in some respects overlap.

First is the effort to distinguish between economic, political and social inequalities based on Max Weber's influential essay[5] in which he differentiates the basic dimensions of stratification in terms of class, status and power. The usefulness of differentiating these dimensions is based on the assumption that they are not coterminous and that public policy may serve "to equalize rewards without equalizing status, or vice versa, [or] . . . to increase or diminish inequality of power independently of either status or class."[6]

The second development is illustrated in the recommendation of the minority report of the Royal Commission on Taxation in Britain which pressed for a more encompassing definition of income. It argued that:

no concept of income can be really equitable that stops short of the comprehensive definition which embraces all receipts which increase an individual's command over the use of society's scarce resources – in other words, his "net accretion of economic power between two points of time."

4. A. B. Atkinson, "The Measurement of Economic Inequality in Britain – A Survey," in *Poverty and Inequality,* ed. by Dorothy Wedderburn (London, forthcoming).

5. Max Weber, "Class, Status, Party," in *From Max Weber,* ed. by H. H. Gerth and C. W. Mills (London: Oxford University Press, 1946).

6. W. G. Runciman, *Relative Deprivation and Social Justice* (London: Routledge and Kegan Paul, 1956), p. 41.

Richard Titmuss, building on these concepts for his criticisms of the official measure of the distribution of income, has defined income as the command over resources over time.[7] This concept of resources permits a more comprehensive definition of the dimensions of well-being, while the emphasis on "over time" calls attention to more than the year-to-year changes in income.

A number of writers in the United States and Europe have been influenced by the ideas of Weber, the Minority Report on Taxation and the writings of Titmuss. Miller and Roby have developed six dimensions of well-being: income, assets, services, education and social mobility, political participation and power, status and self-respect.[8] The implicit argument in such typologies is that improvement of one dimension of inequality does not insure improvement in other dimensions. It follows, therefore, that it is important to examine more than a single dimension of inequality focusing on both positive and negative developments along many dimensions. This framework poses awkward problems in reaching a composite index of well-being, since there is no consensus on how these dimensions should be weighted. Moreover there are multiple measurements for each dimension and innumerable problems of relating the resources to each other. This broadened perspective makes the task of interpreting trends more difficult, partly because data on the non-economic dimensions are scanty but also because the trends on different dimensions conflict, inhibiting general conclusions. One reason there is quite frequently a great deal of disagreement about the facts is that different dimensions are studied and different groups are compared. There is no way of avoiding such problems except to state clearly *what* is to be compared with *whom* and to attempt to get a more comprehensive rather than a single-vision understanding of the trends within a society. Refinements and elaborations of these issues are under way and will contribute much to the future study of inequality. In summary, then, we conclude that while income obviously remains a crucial dimension, it is not the only significant one. There has been increasing acceptance of the position that we must study more than one simple dimension of inequality and that more than one simple measure of each dimension is required. This paper does not discuss these broader dimensions and concentrates on income and, to some extent, services.[9]

---

7. Richard M. Titmuss, *Income Distribution and Social Change* (London: George Allen and Unwin, 1962), p. 68.
8. S. M. Miller and Pamela Roby, *The Future of Inequality* (New York: Basic Books, 1970).
9. For a broader attempt, see S. M. Miller and Martin Rein, "The Possibilities and Limits of Social Policy" (prepared for the Working Meeting of the Research Committee on Poverty, Social Welfare and Social Policy, International Sociological Association, Bucharest, December 16–18, 1971).

Much less systematic attention has been devoted to the issues surrounding the selection of a unit of measurement. The choice of family and household units assumes income sharing and thus defines away the interesting problems of how smaller units pool resources and on what principle these resources are distributed. At a broader level, the choice of a unit raises the issue of which groups are to be compared. In the United States, politically acceptable comparisons are made between the incomes of blacks and whites while there is much less concern about how income deciles fare relative to each other. Regional differences in both income and the other dimensions of inequality are very significant where countries have lagging regional development, for example, the Mezzogiorno in Italy; the South and Appalachia in the United States; Slovenia and other provinces in Yugoslavia; the poor North in England; and the Atlantic provinces in Canada. Trends in the economic and social differences among sexes has become in many countries an item on the political agenda. A very delicate issue which is seldom discussed is how to think about the foreign labor in much of Western Europe today.[10] Consider Switzerland and Sweden where foreigners make up high percentages of the manual labor forces; in some countries such as Switzerland, these "guest" workers cannot become citizens. Is their position to be compared with the rest of society and are their conditions to be included in the overall statement of trends within the society?

In the following section, selected data are presented on the distribution of income in Canada. This preliminary review of data is followed by an analysis of the limited effects of taxation and transfers on the original distribution of income. The paper then seeks to explain why these effects are limited and recommends some action.

Pre-Tax Income[11]

As in other countries, the distribution of income in Canada is decidedly skewed and there is no trend toward a reduction in inequalities. Paralleling the pattern of other nations, more than 40 per cent of total income is received by the 20 per cent (top quintile) with the highest income. The two highest quintiles received two-thirds of all income in 1969. The bottom quintile, again like other countries, received 4 per cent of total income in 1969, and the bottom two quintiles received 15 per cent of total income (see table 1).

10. N. M., "International Labor in Crisis," *Foreign Affairs*, XLIX, 3 (April, 1971), 522. The counterpart of the U.S. racial crisis is not ruled out for Western Europe.
11. Material in this and the next section was prepared by Diane Flaherty, a junior fellow, Centre for International Studies, New York University.

Table 1

Percentage Distribution of Total Income of Families and Unattached Individuals by Quintiles Canada, 1951–1969

	Lowest quintile	Second quintile	Third quintile	Fourth quintile	Highest quintile
1951	4.4	11.2	18.3	23.3	42.8
1954	4.4	12.0	17.8	24.0	41.8
1957	4.2	11.9	18.0	24.5	41.4
1959	4.4	11.9	18.0	24.1	41.6
1961	4.2	11.9	18.3	24.5	41.1
1965	4.4	11.5	18.0	24.5	41.4
1967	4.2	11.4	17.8	24.6	42.0
1969	4.0	11.0	18.0	25.0	42.0

Sources: Canada, Dominion Bureau of Statistics, *Income Distributions: Incomes of Non-farm Families and Individuals in Canada, Selected Years 1951–1965*, Catalogue no. 13–529 (Ottawa: Queen's Printer, 1969) p. 78. Canada, Dominion Bureau of Statistics, *Comparative Income Distribution 1965 and 1967*, Catalogue no. 13–539 (Ottawa: Information Canada, 1971), p. 53, and adapted from Canada, Statistics Canada, *Income Distributions by Size in Canada, 1969*, Catalogue no. 13–542 (Ottawa: Information Canada, 1972).

Table 2

Percentage Distribution of Families and Unattached Individuals and Their Aggregate Income Canada, 1951–1969

Income group	1951		1954		1957		1959		1961		1965		1967	
	Pop.	A.I.	Pop.	A.I.	Pop.	A.I.	Pop.	A.I.	Pop.	A.I.	Pop.	A.I.	Pop.	A.I.
Under $1,000	13.1%	1.8%	10.9%	1.5%	10.7%	1.3%	10.1%	1.2%	10.1%	1.1%	7.6%	0.8%	6.8%	0.5%
$1,000– 1,999	15.9	6.6	13.4	4.9	12.6	4.4	11.7	4.0	10.5	3.3	9.4	2.6	10.6	2.7
2,000– 2,999	19.1	14.1	15.5	9.7	13.6	8.0	12.4	7.0	11.7	6.2	10.0	4.6	10.0	2.7
3,000– 3,999	20.1	19.8	17.8	15.5	16.1	13.1	15.7	12.4	13.5	10.1	11.5	7.4	10.0	4.4
4,000– 4,999	13.4	16.8	15.8	17.5	15.0	15.6	16.0	16.1	14.9	14.3	13.0	10.8	10.8	6.7
5,000– 5,999	6.8	10.5	9.6	13.0	10.8	13.7	11.9	14.7	12.7	14.8	12.3	12.4	11.4	9.1
6,000– 6,999	4.4	8.1	6.1	9.7	6.9	10.3	7.1	10.3	9.3	12.8	9.7	11.6	11.5	11.1
7,000– 9,999	4.9	11.2	7.4	14.0	9.9	18.8	10.6	19.4	12.1	21.3	17.4	26.3	9.7	11.2
10,000+	2.3	11.1	3.5	13.4	4.3	14.7	4.5	14.8	8.3	16.0	9.1	23.5	11.2	27.8

Sources: Dominion Bureau of Statistics, *Income Distributions, Incomes of Non-farm Families and Individuals in Canada, Selected Years 1951-1965*, p. 54; and Dominion Bureau of Statistics, *Comparative Income Distribution 1965 and 1967*, p. 28.

Table 3

Distribution of Families and Unattached Individuals and Gross Income of Families and Unattached Individuals, Selected Years Canada, 1951–1961

Income group	1951		1954		1957		1959		1961	
	Families in thousands	Income in millions	Families	Income	Families	Income	Families	Income	Families	Income
Under $1,000	570	$ 294	516	$ 280	474	$ 237	460	$ 233	475	$ 249
$1,000– 1,999	645	980	577	850	590	864	550	824	501	741
2,000– 2,999	861	2,216	730	1,818	649	1,026	599	1,508	575	1,442
3,000– 3,999	673	2,335	783	273	740	2,574	741	2,574	662	2,340
4,000– 4,999	347	1,526	528	2,342	604	2,716	699	3,119	706	3,126
5,000– 5,999	449	2,959	689	445	1,104	7,559	1,352	9,040	1,620	1,836
10,000+	63	1,184	107	1,867	157	2,779	208	3,549	261	4,319

Source: Jenny Podoluk, *Incomes of Canadians*, 1961 Census Monograph (Ottawa: Dominion Bureau of Statistics, 1968), p. 306.

The trends between 1951 and 1969 have not been in the direction of a more equitable distribution. Between 1951 and 1969, the lowest quintile and the second lowest have had a reduction in their share while the two top quintiles increased their portion.

Table 2 permits a different type of comparison; instead of five quintiles, it presents nine groupings by size of income.

From 1951 to 1967 the lowest two income groups (under $1,000; $1,000–$1,999) showed a trend towards, at best, limited reduction of inequalities (using the percentage of population figures) and, with some measure of change (using the percentage of income going to the groups), a worsening. But the two top groups also showed improvement in the ratio of the change of population to change of income to those groups. Since the two income groups above the lowest are also below the poverty lines defined by the Senate Committee on Poverty,[12] the gains of the top group have been at the expense of groups that cannot afford to have their position weakened.

Distribution of population among income groups has also changed since 1951. The number of families in the lowest three income groups (table 3) declined from 1951 to 1961 and the number of families in the top three groups increased. But the increase in the population of the upper group was larger both in percentage and absolute terms than the decline in the number of families in the lowest income group. From 1951 to 1961, 95,000 families moved out of the under $1,000 group and 198,000 moved into the $10,000 and above group. This means that more people are getting rich than are moving out of the most intense level of poverty. If a relative, moving poverty line is considered, then the movement of more people into the highest income group means that those in the lowest group have become relatively worse off, further below a standard of living which has shifted upwards.

Wealth

The distributions of financial assets are even less equal than the distribution of aggregate income for the one year (1963) for which data are available (table 4).

The percentage of financial assets commanded by each of the three lowest income groups is slightly higher than the percentage of aggregate income received by each group, but the percentage of

12. These poverty lines are per annum by family unit size: 1–$2,140; 2–$3,570; 3–$4,290; 4–$5,000; 5–$5,710; 6–$6,430; 7–$7,140; 10–$9,290. Canada, Parliament, Senate, Special Committee on Poverty, *Poverty in Canada* (Ottawa: Information Canada, 1971), Table 1, p. 8.

Table 4

Percentage Distribution of Families and Unattached Individuals, Aggregate Income, Total Assets, Financial Assets, Canada, 1963

Income group	Population	Aggregate income	Total assets[a]	Financial assets[b]
Under $1,000	8.0%	0.9%	2.7%	3.5%
$ 1,000– 1,999	9.9	2.8	2.7	6.5
2,000– 2,999	10.7	5.2	5.7	6.1
3,000– 3,999	12.4	8.3	7.1	6.9
4,000– 4,999	14.0	12.0	11.0	10.5
5,000– 5,999	14.0	14.7	14.0	9.7
6,000– 6,999	10.1	12.5	12.0	9.7
7,000– 9,999	11.6	17.9	14.0	14.0
10,000+	9.3	25.7	26.0	34.0

a. Total assets include liquid asset holdings, investments in mortgages, loans to other persons plus estimated value of home.
b. Financial assets are total assets minus estimated value of home.

Source: Adapted from Canada, Dominion Bureau of Statistics, *Incomes, Assets and Indebtedness of Non-farm Families in Canada*, 1963, Catalogue no. 13–525 (Ottawa: Queen's Printer, 1966), pp. 30, 40, 50.

financial assets controlled by the highest income group is much greater than the percentage of income to that group. The distribution of income, then, understates the degree of control of the resources of the economy exercised by the top group.

Regional Distribution

As in other countries, regional disparities in income distribution are pronounced. As table 5 shows, 45 per cent of families in the Atlantic provinces received low incomes compared with the overall Canadian figure that 25.3 per cent of families had low incomes in 1961.

Small towns (populations of 1,000–9,999) and rural areas were particularly likely to have low-income families (31.8 per cent and 45.9 per cent) as well as families headed by women (42.6 per cent).

The long-term trends presented in table 6 show a general decline in regional income differentials. The range in income for the provinces was between 57 per cent of the Canadian average and 121 per cent in 1926; in 1965 the range was reduced to 59 per cent to 115 per cent. While all the lower-income provinces increased their relative standing in the 39-year period, Quebec and New Brunswick made the smallest gains (Quebec, from 85 per cent to 88 per cent of the national average; New Brunswick, from 64 per cent to 69 per cent.

Taxation Effects

Does taxation lead to a more equal distribution of income? The answer seems to be for Canada, as for other countries, only slightly. Table 7 compares the Gini coefficient before and after taxes for five years between 1951 and 1961. For each year there is a somewhat lower coefficient after taxes than before. On the other hand, there has been very little change in the after-tax coefficient in this 10-year period; indeed, the pre-tax coefficient declined just slightly more than the post-tax.

The burden of taxes (see table 8), in terms of the ratio of taxes to income for income groups and the percentage of total taxes paid by each group, has improved slightly from 1951 to 1961, with the burden smaller at the lower end as well as at the upper end and the $5,000–$9,999 group bearing the cost of the change.

The Canadian tax structure, again like that of many countries, is not particularly progressive, something which helps explain its limited ability to reduce the inequalities in the distribution of income.

Table 5

Selected Characteristics of All Families and of Low-Income Families, Canada, Year Ended May 31, 1961

	Number of families		% of total		Incidence of low income
	Total	Low-income	All families	Low-income families	
Total	3,626,964*	916,050*	100.0%	100.0%	25.3%
Region					
Atlantic provinces	348,887	157,938	9.7	17.3	45.3
Quebec	988,307	275,505	27.2	30.1	27.9
Ontario	1,362,618	253,760	37.6	27.7	18.6
Prairie provinces	556,251	149,998	15.3	16.4	27.0
British Columbia	368,116	78,359	10.1	8.6	21.3
Place of residence					
Metropolitan centres	1,901,221	314,540	52.4	34.3	16.5
Other urban municipalities	958,767	249,713	26.4	27.3	26.0
30,000–99,999	276,397	54,162	7.6	5.9	19.6
10,000–29,999	270,001	64,573	7.4	7.1	23.9
1,000–9,999	412,369	130,978	11.4	14.3	31.8
Rural	766,856	351,797	21.1	38.4	45.9
Size of family					
Two	960,421	280,199	26.5	30.6	29.2
Three	734,111	147,991	20.2	16.2	20.2
Four	757,883	157,283	20.9	17.2	20.8
Five or more	1,174,549	330,577	32.4	36.1	28.1
Sex of head					
Male	3,343,756	795,494	92.2	86.8	23.8
Female	283,208	120,556	7.8	13.2	42.6
Number of children under age 16					
None	1,382,913	329,949	38.1	36.0	23.9
One	699,114	143,571	19.3	15.7	20.5
Two	678,546	155,849	18.7	17.0	23.0
Three or more	868,391	288,681	23.9	31.3	33.1

*Includes Yukon.

Source: Jenny Podoluk, "Low Income and Poverty," *Poverty in Canada*, ed. by J. Harp and J. H. Hofley (Scarborough, Ont.: Prentice-Hall, 1971), p. 128.

Table 6

Personal Income[a] Expressed as a Per Cent of the Canadian Average 1926 to 1965 (various years)

	1926	1929	1933	1939	1946	1950	1955	1959	1961	1963	1965
Newfoundland						51	54	55	60	58	59
Prince Edward Island	57	59	51	53	58	56	55	62	62	63	69
Nova Scotia	67	71	77	76	86	74	73	75	77	74	75
New Brunswick	64	65	66	65	75	69	65	66	68	66	69
Quebec	85	92	94	88	82	85	85	85	88	87	88
Ontario	114	122	129	124	115	121	120	119	118	117	115
Manitoba	109	98	93	90	103	100	95	100	97	97	97
Saskatchewan	102	67	47	77	97	87	93	87	78	107	99
Alberta	113	92	74	87	108	103	103	104	102	100	99
British Columbia[b]	121	128	132	125	114	123	122	118	116	114	115

a. Includes all transfer payments and imputed net income of farmers.
b. Includes Yukon and Northwest Territories, 1926 to 1950.

Source: T. N. Brewis, "Spatial Characteristics of the Economy," *Poverty in Canada*, ed. by J. Harp and J. P. Hofley(Scarborough, Ont.: Prentice-Hall, 1971), p. 157, calculated from Canada, Dominion Bureau of Statistics, *National Accounts, Income and Expenditure*, Catalogue no. 13–201, Ottawa, Queen's Printer, various years.

Regressive or Progressive?

A study for the Royal Commission on Taxation has estimated that
federal taxes are regressive below $2,000 and progressive above
that level, and provincial and local taxes are regressive below
$3,000 and proportional above that.[13]

When indirect taxes, which in 1961 accounted for $8.2 billion
of the net revenue of $10.3 billion to federal, provincial and muni-
cipal governments are considered, the incidence of taxes is greatest
for the lowest income classes.[14] Families with under $2,000 pay
60 per cent of their income in taxes; families over $10,000 pay
only 38.4 per cent.

Transfer Effect

Cash transfers reduce only slightly the Gini coefficients: for all
family units in 1961, the coefficient was .429 without transfers and
.395 after transfers. As table 9 reveals, there was a more inequitable distribution of post-transfer income, as measured by the Gini
coefficient, in 1961 than in 1951.

Diane Flaherty has made some rough calculations of the effects
of cash transfer on the gross income of families in the income class
of $2,000–$3,000.[15] From 1951 to 1961, gross income increased by
100 per cent and the average transfer payment to a family in this
income class advanced by 160 per cent. The gain is not as significant as it appears, for in no year does the transfer payment bring
total income to the poverty line for a family of four ($5,000) sug-
gested by the Senate Committee on Poverty.[16] The increase in
transfer payment may bring total income closer to the poverty line
with an increase in the average transfer payment, but the poverty
line should also be moving, so the real comparison is between
changes in income including transfer payments and changes in the
poverty line.

13. Jenny R. Podoluk, *Incomes of Canadians*, 1961 Census Monograph
(Ottawa: Queen's Printer, 1968), p. 285; citing W. Irwin Gillespie, *The
Incidence of Taxes and Public Expenditures in the Canadian Economy*, Royal
Commission on Taxation, Studies No. 2 (Ottawa: Queen's Printer, 1966),
Chap. 4, pp. 164–91.
14. Special Committee on Poverty, *Poverty in Canada*, Table 18, p. 47, citing, Gillespie, *The Incidence of Taxes and Public Expenditures*, Tables 2, 3,
p. 65.
15. Calculations based on Podoluk, *Incomes of Canadians*, p. 306. The assumption is that the average income of a family in the $2,000–$3,000 income
group was close to $2,500. This class is chosen because it is the low-income
class with the best chance of being increased above the poverty line through
redistributive transfers. If transfers do not lift this class out of poverty, they
are even less likely to do so for lower income groups.
16. Special Committee on Poverty, *Poverty in Canada*, Table 1, p. 8.

Table 7

Effects of Taxation on Income Inequality, Gini Coefficients, Canada, 1951–1961

	Gross income (pre-tax)	Gross income (after taxes)
1951	.390	.369
1954	.388	.377
1957	.397	.378
1959	.386	.367
1961	.385	.366

Source: Podoluk, *Incomes of Canadians*, p. 287.

Table 8

Change in Burden of Taxes, Canada, 1951–1961

Income	Change in ratio of tax to income	Change in % of total taxes paid
Under $1,000	–	–
$1,000– 1,999	−2.7	−2.3
2,000– 2,999	−3.0	−6.1
3,000– 3,999	−4.9	−6.9
4,000– 4,999	−6.3	−0.6
5,000– 9,999	+22.5	+14.3
10,000+	+9.7	+1.8

Source: Podoluk, *Incomes of Canadians*, p. 288.

Table 9

Gini Coefficients, Pre- and Post-Cash Transfer, Canada, 1951–1961

	Total income (post-transfer)	Income exclusive of transfer payments
All family units		
1951	.384	.413
1961	.395	.425
Unattached individuals		
1951	.433	.483
1961	.454	.532
Families		
1951	.337	.366
1961	.346	.380

Source: Podoluk, *Incomes of Canadians*, p. 291.

Some other information on Canadian transfers:

(1) In 1961, only $2.2 billion of government expenditures of $11.8 billion were for direct cash transfers. If the other government expenditures are redistributive to higher income classes, then the effects of transfer payment redistribution would be overwhelmed.

(2) In 1967, average transfer payments to low-income families were twice those to other families, while the average income of low-income families was less than a third that of other families.[17]

In 1961, average transfer payments to low-income families were only 1.6 times the average transfer payments to other families while the average income of a low-income family was only one-fourth that of other families.[18]

Public Services

Services are an important, and rapidly increasing component of "the command over resources."[19] They comprise medical, educational (excluded from this discussion) and recreational facilities, housing, personal services or social services narrowly defined. The general reference is to collective consumption, public services, and "income-in-kind" outside the market. Services are an important element in the welfare state and are usually regarded as having a redistributive effect. But data are hard to come by and we have reverted to a general statement rather than an analysis of the Canadian situation.

The services component of the command over resources is exceedingly complicated. The questions involved are:

(1) What services should there be? Different kinds of services probably have differential benefits for different groups in society.

(2) Who uses these services? Availability and actual use may be quite different from what is commonly believed.

(3) How are they paid for? The net effects on redistribution are in terms of this, not only in terms of what kinds of services are used.

(4) How are the services organized? The mode of operation affects very much who uses it and with what kind of benefits.

The actual distribution of services is difficult to assess because of the absence of records on who uses what services over time with what results.[20] Furthermore, patterns of distribution vary for dif-

17. Senate Committee on Poverty, *Poverty in Canada,* p. 21.
18. Podoluk, *Incomes of Canadians,* p. 307.
19. "In some instances, notably education and medical care, a specific egalitarian distribution today may be essential for improving the distribution of human capital and earning capacity tomorrow." James Tobin, "On Limiting the Domain of Inequality," *Journal of Law and Economics,* XIII (October 1970), 276.
20. Since the quality of what purports to be the same service can vary con-

ferent services. For example, in the field of education past use determines future use since the services are organized like a *ladder* – that is, access to college depends on completion of high school. Medical care, by contrast, is a *demand* service unrelated to past use. This is most striking in the case of emergency services because of automobile accidents. Finally, some services are retained over a *lifetime* as in the case of council housing in Britain. Here class bias in the pattern of use must be related to the distribution of income over the life cycle. These observations suggest it cannot be assumed that the actual distribution of benefits is known and that lower-income groups are the principal beneficiaries. This is an empirical question one should study concretely rather than assuming that collective consumption is inherently redistributive.

When services are financed locally, gross inequalities between localities emerge, justified on the principle of local tax effort. Equalizing formulas contribute little to narrowing these inequalities. In these circumstances, we cannot assume equal levels of expenditure or comparable quality of medical care or schooling in different, areas. While it may be a fact that net redistribution occurs within a locality, inter-locality inequalities may grow.

A review of the selected evidence on the use of services and the distribution of expenditures for services[21] suggests that higher-income people know how to use universally available services more effectively than lower-income individuals. A recent article by a noted economist citing evidence from education, medical care and other sectors argues that the distribution of public services favors the middle class and this pattern is so widespread that it virtually amounts to an economic law. Director's Law is named after the reluctant economist who observed the pattern but failed to publish his findings.[22]

A report on Latin America gives further weight to the thesis when it asserts that "the whole society is taxed to provide services that are in practice within the reach only of certain relatively well-off and well-organized elements – as has notoriously occurred in the instances of secondary education and public housing." And a United Nations report summarizing the available literature calls attention to the failure of public services to reach those who are

siderably by region and class (and by other variables), it is no easy research project to estimate who gets what service in what amounts (quantity and quality) in a useful way.

21. Brian Abel-Smith, "Whose Welfare State?" in *Conviction*, ed. by Norman MacKenzie (London: MacGibbon and Kee, 1958), pp. 55–73, raised the possibility that the middle classes benefited more than the working classes from Britain's National Health Service.

22. George J. Stigler, "Director's Law of Public Income Redistribution," *Journal of Law and Economics*, XIII, 1 (April, 1970), 1–10.

most deprived. "A major cause of self-perpetuating poverty is often found to be that social services (education, health, housing, social security, welfare, etc.) . . . do not adequately reach the most needy families in the population."[23]

There is, of course, contention about the universal application of Director's Law. Evidence in the field of medical care suggests that when data on use is examined, it does not apply uniformly to this sector.[24] There is, however, more agreement that the broader the definition of the total subsidies to be distributed in a given sector, the more likely they are to multiply existing advantages. For example, when account is taken of direct subsidies for public housing and special tax treatments (ranging from tax shelters to tax reductions for home mortgages), it is clear that middle- and upper-class families benefit disproportionately from aggregate expenditures in this sector.[25]

This general thesis is further confirmed by evidence from Britain's Central Statistical Office which periodically reviews the relationship between incomes, taxes and social services based on data from the annual Survey of Family Expenditures. The combined estimated cash value in 1968 for such social services as education, health, and public housing was in absolute monetary terms larger for high-income than for low-income families of every type.[26] Even so, these data fail to take account of the value of tax forgiveness provisions and are based on averages rather than the actual volume of services consumed. Only from direct cash transfers (rather than social services) can low-income families benefit more than higher-income families.

We turn in the following sections to explanations of why taxation and cash transfers have not been more redistributive.

Why Taxation Does Not Redistribute

Despite the fact that anywhere from a fifth to more than two-fifths of national income may be taxed, the post-taxation distribution of

23. U.N. Department of Economic and Social Affairs, *Social Policy and Distribution of Income in the Nation* (ST/SOA/88) 1969, p. 105.

24. Myron J. Lefkowitz, "Poverty and Health: Re-examination," September 1971, mimeographed. See Martin Rein, "Social Class and the Utilization of Medical Care Services," *Hospitals,* XLIII (July 1, 1969), 43–53. A shorter version appears as "Social Class and the Health Service," *New Society,* No. 373 (November 20, 1969), pp 807–10. Service questions are complicated because they have to be related to a needs base: what proportion of those in lower-income groups who need hospital (or medical) services get them compared to a similar risk category among higher-income groups?

25. Henry Aaron, "Income Taxes and Housing," *American Economic Review,* LX (December, 1970), 789–806.

26. *Economic Trends,* No. 196 (February, 1970), pp. 29–30.

income differs little, as we analyzed earlier, from the pre-tax distribution of income. Despite the fact that the incomes of higher-income recipients are purportedly taxed at much higher levels than low income – the range is from nothing on low incomes to 70 per cent on the highest levels of income in some countries – the effective tax rates do not vary greatly by income.

Why isn't taxation redistributive? One reason involves how taxation funds are spent. The other is that taxation *practices* differ markedly from what appear to be taxation *policies*.

1 *Exclusion of income*
Much income, especially for higher income groups, is excluded from the definition of income used by the tax collector or is kept from his purview. Fringe benefits (expense accounts, education allowances for children, pensions) which can be large, are excluded from taxation.[27] Sick benefits are not counted in the United States, capital gains are taxed at lower rates and much income is transmuted into wealth in order to reduce taxation (some countries are now talking about wealth taxes). In addition to tax avoidance – which is legitimate – tax evasion occurs in many countries (France, Italy, and Iran have at various times been offered as prime examples).

The result is that while marginal tax rates range from 20 to 91 per cent, effective tax rate on total income may be relatively low. For example, in 1964 in the United States the average rate of tax on $100,000 of taxable income for a couple with two children was only 40 per cent.[28] The effective tax rate for the top 1 per cent of taxable units has declined from 33 per cent in 1952 to 26 per cent in 1967 while the rate for the next 13 per cent has remained roughly constant.[29]

As tax rates go up, in most countries the proportion of total income available for taxation decreases. For example, Stanley Surrey[30] estimates that some $50 billion is lost in federal taxation because of special provisions protecting certain types of income from

---

27. Normally in Canada, pensions are subject to income tax but *contributions* to registered savings plans (up to a certain amount) and war veterans' disability pensions are tax free.
28. Robert J. Lampman, *Ending and Means of Reducing Income Poverty* (Chicago: Markham Publishing, 1971), p. 96.
29. Joseph A. Pechman, "The Rich, the Poor and the Taxes They Pay," *Public Interest*, No. 17 (Fall 1969), p. 33, citing U.S. President, *Economic Report of the President*, 1969 (Washington, D.C.: Government Printing Office, 1969).
30. The material is drawn from Surrey's articles "Tax Incentives as a Device for Implementing Government Policy: a Comparison with Direct Government Expenditures," *Harvard Law Review*, LXXXIII (1970), 705–38 and "Federal Income Tax Reform: the Varied Approaches Necessary to

taxation. This sum amounts to more than 40 per cent of what is collected in federal individual and corporate taxes. This $50 billion figure, what Surrey calls "tax expenditures," does not include the tax losses because of avoidance and evasion.

Through policy and manipulation there probably is a declining share of the total income of high-income recipients that is subject to taxation.

2 Use of regressive taxes

Reliance on regressive taxes has expanded, offsetting the effects of progressive income taxes in countries with income taxes. In the United States, for example, income tax as a proportion of all tax revenues declined from 51 per cent in 1948 to 46 per cent in 1967. Sales and turnover taxes (such as the value-added tax) are not progressive and indeed may be regressive, depending on the items taxed. Property taxes, important for the support of state and local governments, are also not progressive. The increasing reliance on social security taxes is not progressive since the practice is to tax all covered wages at the same rate (proportional tax) and some proportion of the employers' contribution is passed on to the consumer in the form of higher prices.

Since all countries resist higher taxation, the tendency is to use hidden taxes such as sales taxes rather than visible taxes such as income taxes. The result is an erosion in progressivity and the redistribution power of the tax system.

3 Inflation effect

Rising money wages (with rising prices and little increase in real income) has meant that lower-income recipients now are being taxed. Formerly their incomes were not subject to direct income taxation since they fell below the taxable level. The tax threshold has not been raised to keep up with increases in average money income and with the effects of inflation. The result is that many former non-taxpayers now are taxpayers, reducing the overall progressivity of the tax system. This criticism is particularly relevant to Britain. The progressive principle that those below the official definition of poverty should not have to pay income tax requires that the tax threshold be periodically raised.[31]

4 Incentive questions

In many countries the issue is being raised that incentives to work

Replace Tax Expenditures with Direct Government Assistance," *Harvard Law Review*, LXXXIV (1970), 352–408.

31. Canada revised its basic personal income tax exemption in 1972 from $1,000 to $1,500, the first such change since 1949 ($750 to $1,000).

hard, innovate, and take risks have been reduced because of "confiscatory tax rates" inflicted on higher-income recipients especially, but on other groups as well. PEP (Political and Economic Planning) in Britain, after an exhaustive review of the literature, concludes that the only intellectually defensible answer to the question of whether direct taxes have a disincentive effect is *no*.[32] But the notion dies hard and constrains the progressivity of the tax system.

5 *Economic policy*

Since taxation now is a major instrument of national policy for expanding or contracting the economy, the political necessity of getting support for progressivity is more difficult. In the United States in recession days, taxes on higher-income groups are decreased more than those of lower-income groups to expand consumption and investment and win political acceptance of expansion policies. When inflationary pressures threaten, the tendency is to increase taxes more on low-income groups. This is done to reduce demand since, taken as a whole, lower-income groups spend more than higher-income groups. Social justice is sacrificed to political expediency and other national economic goals.

Whatever the commitments to progressive income taxation might be in principle, the tax system as a whole is usually regarded as a means to raise revenue rather than a device for changing the distribution of income. The basis of progressivity is "fairness" or equity of burden, rather than redistribution and equality. Consequently, the effectiveness of the tax structure in redistributing pre-tax incomes has been more limited than it might have been. The form of taxes is as crucial as its level in effecting redistribution.

In order to increase the progressivity of the tax system, the following steps are required.

a The concept of income should be expanded to include all items that increase the command over resources over time.

b Proportional and regressive taxes should be reduced or eliminated and progressive taxes substituted. Where the federal government is the best progressive collector, it can be used, with taxation funds funnelled to lower-level governments.

c Low-income groups should be exempt from taxation which, in countries with high indirect taxes, takes up a high percentage of their income. The exemption level should be a moving one, pegged in relationship to average income.

d Minimal levels of effective tax rates on real gross income levels should be established so that there will not be gross disparities in effective rates.

---

32. C. V. Brown and D. A. Dawson, *Personal Taxation Incentives and Tax Reform* (London: PEP, 1969), p. 66.

e Tax subsidies should be shunned in favor of direct subsidies. Surrey has shown the wasteful nature of much of tax expenditures and that similar national purposes can be served by providing (accountable) direct subsidies rather than tax benefits.

f The progressivity of the tax system should assume more importance. The redistributive as well as revenue-raising goals of the tax system should be treated as more equal concerns than they now are.

The Limits of Cash Transfers

Why haven't transfers been a more powerful instrument for redistribution? A tentative catalogue of possible explanations is offered.

1 *Resistance to taxation*
Since transfers must be paid for (in the absence of a substantial reallocation among programs) the cost must be covered by higher taxation. All countries resist high general taxation, and most come to rely on earmarked insurance schemes that have a net regressive effect. The principles of insurance and user charges typically used in financing these programs are regressive. To concentrate benefits on lower-income groups threatens the principle of equity and fairness to contributors by which such schemes are legitimated.

2 *Universality*
Public services such as education, unemployment insurance, and social security, are required for all groups, not just the low-income population however defined. Consequently there is competition over the spending of funds on different income groups, reducing the possibilities of public transfers' having a high poverty intensity.

3 *Importance of age inequalities*
A high percentage of all cash transfers are devoted to the aged, so that some of the inequality among age groups is reduced. But the result is that inequalities among younger income groups, including the working poor with children, are neglected by cash transfer programs.

4 *Incentives*
The adequacy of cash transfer benefit levels is inhibited by the commitment to maintain work incentives (at least for those regarded either as in the labor market or who should be in it). The result is to place a ceiling on public assistance benefits so they will not exceed low wages and encourage people not to work.

5 *Rationing*

Administrative rationing systems make it difficult to obtain certain transfers (e.g., public assistance) in order to discourage continued reliance on transfer benefits and reduce costs. Devices that promote cost savings discourage the use of transfers among the most disadvantaged groups.

We have recounted the difficulties with taxation and post-taxation devices of cash transfers and services to produce redistribution. Obviously, if taxation were more progressive and higher and if more were spent on cash and non-cash transfers to lower-income groups, much more redistribution could occur. But to rely only on the tax and post-tax routes is to ignore the very production of income that generates the redistributive questions these routes attempt inadequately to deal with. It is our conviction that basic economic policies must be regarded as the essential component of any strategy to redistribute income.

Making Economic Policies Redistributive

It is self-defeating to plan for education, training, and cash transfer systems (social policies) in isolation from economic policies. Policies that determine the level of employment and of wages obviously shape the possibilities and set the limits of social policy. Economic and social policies cannot be placed in separate compartments.[33] We are driven to this conclusion by our observations that cash transfers and service systems cannot adequately offset the more powerful economic policies. There are, of course, those who hold that with a greater political and psychological commitment to redistribution, social policies can be an effective offset to inequalities promoted by economic policies. But our basic feeling is that, when economic policies are not moving in the same direction as social policies, it becomes exceedingly difficult to create a transfer, service or tax system that can really be high enough to offset large differentials in the initial generation of income. Policies must be directed at the generators of inequality. Obviously social policies to offset original income differences, when combined with economic policies to narrow wage differentials and tax policies to provide progressivity, can together have a major impact upon inequalities. But social policies alone will be truncated unless accompanied and reinforced by policies that alter the initial distribution of income.

---

33. Richard M. Titmuss strongly objects to this argument. In his early writings he has stressed the importance of social policies as a counterweight against (less redistributive) economic policies.

It is a mistake to assign to social policies the task of compensating for mischief promoted by the market. The principle of prevention is everywhere accepted except with respect to egalitarian aims. This is fundamental to an assessment of the operation and potential of social policies. Let us state the case frankly. We believe that social policies have been given too large a role. They have often operated as the *poor man's economic policy*: economic policy is concerned with growth; social policies with redistribution and poverty.[34] We think they cannot succeed in this, and that in many countries it is essential to have economic policies reinforce redistribution and to forsake the illusion that taxation and social policies alone can succeed in reducing inequality.

Four important points about social and economic policy follow. First, it is clear now that many social policies are ineffective in the absence of full employment. For example, when training for low-skilled, low-income workers is stymied in a slack economy, training itself becomes the goal, serving as a source of temporary income to individuals, a disguised transfer program rather than a serious program to promote occupational mobility.

As nations face the threat of inflation and stop-go, the issue of full employment may become more urgent, for without it the distributive impact of social policies is nullified. Full employment is not a sufficient condition for redistribution. Nations have experienced full employment over long-term periods without effective gains in the redistribution of income. But it is certain that inequalities would widen in the absence of a full-employment economy.

Second, the general character of government expenditures, not just those on transfers, is important. Government purchases of various kinds of goods and services benefit particular groups. Thus, if the military budget expands, a variety of industries and their higher-income beneficiaries gain. To the contrary, expenditures for other purposes are more likely to benefit lower-income and less-skilled groups.

The income-redistributional effects of governmental actions pervade most, if not all, aspects of governmental economic activity. There are . . . many governmental programs that ostensibly have little or nothing to do with redistributional policy, yet they do bring about distribution effects. Economic stabilization policy and resource-allocation policy – ranging from education to highway to flood control programs – have direct as well as indirect or secondary consequences for the distribution of income. Recognizing the

---

34. Moreover, social policies are identified at least loosely with public intervention and government expenditures and economic policies with action in the private market sector. This dichotomy implies that social policies for the poor drain resources, while economic policies generate wealth.

widespread effects of government actions on the income distribution is the first step in learning how to anticipate these effects, taking them into account, and deciding how to deal with them.[35]
Thus, governmental concern about the distribution of income reflects – or, at least, it ought to reflect – both the undesirable distributional outcome of private sector activities – for that sector is preoccupied with efficiency and profits, not with the distributional consequences – and also any undesirable side effects of the government's own activities in pursuit of the goals of economic efficiency, and stability.[36]

Third, we must recognize the overlap and interpenetration of the cash transfer and wage systems. Though regarded until recently as separate, the level of benefits affects wages (the incentive question) and – a more neglected aspect – the level of wages sets a ceiling on transfer levels. Improving the economic circumstances of the transfer poor is thus constrained by the earning levels of the working poor. It is naive, therefore, to treat the wage and benefit systems in isolation from each other. In some situations, as in France where employers pay the cost of children's allowances directly, transfers are more openly recognized as wage costs. These wage transfer costs are in turn passed on to the consumer in the form of higher prices. All this suggests the need for policies that more explicitly link wages, transfers and prices. In Britain, for example, supplementary benefit levels for one small group, those who are wage-stopped,[37] are tied to the wage negotiations for unskilled workers for the local authority. The fate of the wage-stopped poor is thus explicitly and automatically linked to the low end of the wage structure. Under some circumstances benefit levels plus rent may exceed net wage levels, as appears the case in Britain and the United States. As benefits collide with wages, public opinion becomes anxious about work incentives. Benefit levels are not politically permitted to stay above the low-wage level for extended periods of time. The consequence is that earnings from employment serve as the upper limit of transfer payments, blunting the distributive effects of the transfer system. If redistributive aims are to be

---

35. Burton A. Weisbrod, "Collective Action and the Distribution of Income: A Conceptual Approach," *The Analysis and Evaluation of Public Expenditures: The PPB System,* U.S. Congress, Joint Economic Committee (Washington, D.C.: Government Printing Office, 1969), I, 196–7. Also published as Institute for Research on Poverty, Reprint 34 (Madison: Institute for Research on Poverty, University of Wisconsin, 1969).

36. Joint Economic Committee, *The Analysis and Evaluation of Public Expenditures,* I, 182.

37. An administrative rule which assures that benefit levels for families on welfare (supplementary benefits) do not exceed their potential income from employment.

served, it is necessary first to increase wages in the low-wage sector more rapidly than average wages and second to link transfer benefit levels to changes in wages, thereby also improving the conditions of the transfer-income poor.

Finally, the role of *selective* economic policies must be given priority. These economic policies have as a primary objective economic growth, which tends to be redistributive. Therefore, questions of where growth should take place (a regional problem) are very important in affecting differential gains and losses. Similarly, the selective growth of certain industries and the neglect of others have had differential consequences on employment levels and wage differentials. The general argument calls for selective growth for redistribution, rather than overall aggregate growth. *There is no growth equally beneficial to all groups in a society. Therefore, we need to consider what kind of growth there should be and for whom. The way GNP is achieved may be as important as its level; the same GNP level can have a different distributive impact depending on the composition of the product and the way it is achieved.*

Selective economic policies so defined do not differ much from non-market social policies. Manpower programs can contribute to selective economic growth in order to promote employment opportunities for low-income individuals. The development of new occupational slots to provide jobs for low-income people with relatively limited training and education and the use of subsidies to employers to hire workers (whom they ordinarily wouldn't hire and consider "hard core" employees with poor job motivations) are examples of the way social and economic policies mingle.

Full employment, narrowing wage differentials, integrating low wages and benefit levels and expanding the selective economic policies are among the more important ways that redistribution can be achieved. Still, full employment remains pivotal. It is difficult without it to achieve sufficient economic growth to generate the level of public revenues that make possible redistribution through transfers and service systems. Conversely, when large numbers are unemployed, the size of the transfer system grows. Opportunities for education and mobility are also reduced in a slack economy and we expect that under these circumstances the level of benefits available for cash transfers and services will lag behind net low and average wages. But full employment is insufficient without an explicit commitment to narrow wage differentials.

We believe that social policies can never completely offset the original generation of income differences. If this is so, the issue becomes how to affect the original distribution. *Then the objective is not to develop compensatory social policies to offset economic policies, but to change the latter's role to include both the more narrow economic objectives of growth and stability and the wider social aims of equality, justice, and dignity.* All policies are social and to restrict social policies to transfers and services is misleading.

The Politics of Equality

What would be a more equitable and/or desirable distribution and what are the possibilities of achieving it? There are many different versions of a more egalitarian society, ranging from a minimal practical inequality, nonconvergence of disadvantages, different variations along the same (utility) indifference curve – i.e., variety along dimensions of well-being but limited overall difference in satisfaction, to complete income equality. In this paper, "equality" and "greater equality" have been intermixed and we have avoided discussions of specific goals. In a serious political agenda this specification must occur and attention must also be given to latent conflicts that the pursuit of equality might encourage. Difficult as these issues are, there are intellectual traditions which have explored them.

But the politics of equality are more troublesome. Equality yields a change in the texture of society, Tawney's[38] concern for fraternity and community. But that tends to be a long-run argument, while income redistribution needs a more immediate rationale to win political acceptance.

Now, however, we come back to a question we began with: Can government do anything through legislative action to alter the class structure of society and promote egalitarian aims? Of course that is a tough question.

A sophisticated political analysis of equality has not yet emerged. However, two recent developments hint at the kinds of circumstances that might revive a political debate about equality. As the issues of ecology and environment come to the fore, industrial society may find that it is not uncompromisingly committed to economic growth. Inequalities are tolerated because liberal ideals have accepted an alternative truth – that the benefits of growth itself naturally promote equality and that the margin of growth permits redistribution. Therefore, while everyone gains, the poor gain relatively more, or group relativities are basically less important as long as a larger economic pie enhances the relative well-being of the individual when compared with his own earlier position. But if, as zero growth becomes a new ideal, economic growth is forsaken as the overarching goal of society, then if we are to avoid "an imposition by the rich on the poor . . . a fresh commitment to a decent level of equality" will be required.[39]

---

38. R. H. Tawney, *Equality* (New York: Capricorn Books, 1961).
39. Anthony Lewis, "To Grow and to Die," *New York Times,* February 5, 1972.

The concern about inflation is driving many capitalist countries to accept an administrative approach to income distribution through price, wage, and profit controls. In trying to implement an incomes policy, one inevitably must confront the system of differentials and come to terms with ideas about fairness as well as growth and productivity in wages and salaries. The operation of an incomes policy forces government to arbitrate particular wage claims governed by the principles of a socially just wage. But any group can present a cogent argument that it is being inequitably and unequally treated. In assessing the British experience with incomes policy, Goldthorpe notes that "stable normative order in economic life can *only* be created through norms being underpinned by some minimum degree of value consensus . . . And such consensus in turn cannot be achieved without the distribution of economic resources and rewards, and indeed the entire structure of power and advantage, becoming in some sense 'principled' . . . capable of being given consistent rational and moral justification."[40]

Thus both ecological and economic crises may force a reluctant society to redefine its ideas about equality and submit them to political debate and decision. The politics of instability and crisis may push capitalist nations in more egalitarian directions in spite of themselves.[41]

40. John H. Goldthorpe, "Social Inequality and Social Integration in Modern Britain," *Advancement of Science,* XXVI (December 1969), 190.
41. Obviously, we have not discussed (a) the issues of power, of getting the adoption of greater equality as the goal; nor (b) the questions of the new structure necessary for effective redistributional consequences.

Objectives and Economic Repercussions of the Guaranteed Annual Income

by Nicole Vaillancourt Martin
Professor, National School of Public Administration,
University of Quebec

Despite the proliferation of studies on poverty,[1] we do not seem any closer to a consensus on the future of economic and social policies; yet all the studies agree in their main conclusions. They stress the predominant influence of the structural mechanisms of income distribution on poverty.[2] They point up the responsibility that lies with the performance of our economies. They decry the obsolescence of existing programs and, although social security programs are the prime targets of criticism, the tax system, social and para-social services and economic or multi-purpose programs do not escape the critical scrutiny dictated by the continued existence of poverty.

Obsolescence of Social Security

To judge the merits of the guaranteed annual income (GAI) proposals as a device to replace or complement the present transfer system, it might be useful to re-explore the obsolescent aspects of the social security programs.

One could have expected direct transfer payments to correct the essentially limited nature of the two measures that are supposed to redistribute income: taxation, by its effect on income; and social utilities, by the extent to which they are used and their method of financing. The limited nature of these two measures is because, in

---

1. Among the most recent are: U.S., President's Commission on Income Maintenance Programs, *Poverty Amid Plenty*: The American Paradox (Washington, D.C.: U.S. Government Printing Office, 1971); Canada, Parliament, Senate, Special Committee on Poverty, *Poverty in Canada* (Ottawa: Information Canada, 1971); Ian Adams and others, *The Real Poverty Report* (Edmonton: M. G. Hurtig Limited, 1971); Burton A. Weisbrod, ed., *The Economics of Poverty*: An American Paradox (New York: Prentice-Hall, 1965).
2. Poverty among workers is ascribed either to low productivity in certain sectors of activity or the inability of the individuals to furnish sufficiently high productivity. In both cases it is the income distribution mechanism, in the final analysis, that is involved.

order to benefit from their redistributive effects, it is necessary to have already reached a certain income level.[3] Social security has also never been diverted by an objective such as vertical redistribution of income. Even at the risk of oversimplifying its somewhat complex and many-sided historical development, we should remember that social security was originally a device for pooling social risks. The Beveridge Report tried to broaden this concept. Even in those days, it introduced the idea of a guaranteed annual income by proposing "to maintain all members of the national community above a sociological 'floor' level considered minimal."[4] But this objective was to be achieved by universalizing "protection against the social factors of want." There was, henceforth, justification for maintaining a concept based mainly on protection of income against social risks. This is why social insurance remained a widespread form of social security in Europe. Based on workers' contributions, this system has moved towards broader protection, thus improving the redistribution of workers' incomes among the non-working population. The social insurance system remains ill-equipped to bring about a vertical redistribution of income.

North America borrowed (from England and other European countries) a mixed system in which the government makes the largest contribution, resulting in a greater potential for redistribution. But where, together with financial assistance programs, this system is openly directed to low-income families, it is seen as performing an essentially residual function for the most needy persons. On one hand it copies from social insurance the concept of clearly defined social risks whose consequences must be alleviated. On the other, its financial contribution is not supposed to increase as time goes on (like every service program dedicated to general improvement in the standard of living) but is supposed to fluctuate with economic conditions, exerting a stabilizing influence.

Income Security for Canadians, 1970, still uses this concept,

---

3. W. Irwin Gillespie, *The Incidence of Taxes and Public Expenditures in the Canadian Economy,* Royal Commission on Taxation, Studies No. 2 (Ottawa: Queen's Printer, 1966). Gillespie's studies for the Royal Commission on Taxation (Carter Commission) emphasize the regressive nature of the overall incidence of government measures. This is due to the fact that, as low-income groups do not enjoy the advantages of progressive taxation, they are hit by indirect taxes; moreover, they make proportionately less use of public services than the middle class. A recent Ontario study bears out these findings for education expenditures. According to this study, families with an income of $10,000 or more provide more than 34 per cent of the students in universities and colleges, whereas they pay only 18 per cent of the cost of education at those levels.
4. Guy Perrin, "La Sécurité sociale comme mythe et comme réalité," Revue belge de sécurité sociale, VIII, 10 (October, 1966), 1040. Reprinted in *Droit social,* No. 4 (April, 1967).

stressing the twofold objective of income security.[5] Statistics on low-income families[6] tend more and more to invalidate this philosophy of social risk by showing that poverty is engendered just as much, if not more, by defects in the performance and structure of the economic system as by lack of earning power. This situation, it is true, is modified by economic conditions. In Canada between 1961 and 1967, the average annual rate of unemployment dropped from 7.1 to 4.1 per cent; the incidence of poor families fell from 25 to 18.6 per cent,[7] and the proportion of working poor from 68 to 63 per cent of the total of poor families.[8] But the fact remains that although workers today form the majority of the low-income population, only about one-quarter of the poor population qualifies for financial assistance; and that in 85 per cent of cases, they qualify because of their inability to work.[9] These findings indicate the extent to which redistribution is needed and show that these needs are quite distinct from the ones that income security programs have focused on until now. In short, all our social laws, in their very conception, scrupulously avoid the issue of income redistribution. It will be like this as long as they are based on the concept of socio-economic risk with its assumptions of strictly cyclical or frictional unemployment,[10] equality of job opportunities for all citizens, and a movement of economic growth toward equalization of working conditions, productivity and wages.

A community which says it is prepared to provide each citizen with a basic floor income can hardly maintain that this comes about by itself or will automatically come about by broadening the scope of the traditional income maintenance programs. The philosophy

---

5. "Two income security objectives are relevant to the selection of income security policies. One is the income protection objective. The other is the income support objective." Canada, Department of National Health and Welfare, *Income Security for Canadians* (Ottawa, 1970), p. 15.

6. There are at least as many full-time workers (37 per cent) as unemployed persons or persons unfit to work (37 per cent) among poor families. If we combine full-time and part-time workers, we find that the workers' group (63 per cent) becomes distinctly larger than the group composed of persons who have not worked. Special Committee on Poverty, *Poverty in Canada*, Table 10, p. 29.

7. This decrease is obtained when the poverty lines are kept constant in real value. When they are adjusted in relation to average income, their values fluctuate around a constant according to the economic situation.

8. Economic Council of Canada, *Challenge of Growth and Change*, Fifth Annual Review (Ottawa: Queen's Printer, September, 1968), Table 6-3, p. 118.

9. Special Committee on Poverty, *Poverty in Canada*, p. 31. The information concerning eligibility for assistance applies to the year 1970.

10. It is not so much the type of unemployment that is important but the fact that the philosophy of socioeconomic risk assumes that the probabilities of unemployment are comparable for all workers.

underlying these programs and their methods of application are incompatible with such an objective. In Canada, on the other hand, we already have a guaranteed income plan for the elderly.[11] In addition, a family allowance plan tied to income would also constitute a partial guaranteed income plan.[12] Because of the way these plans are conceived and organized, they tend to aim more directly at vertical redistribution of incomes, taking family responsibilities into account.

In the history of our economic development it is easy to trace the reasons why the idea of income maintenance or protection came before that of redistribution. But the characteristics of our economics strongly suggest that it can just as easily be maintained that, rationally, a reversal of the process would have been better. The evidence of inequalities in job and opportunities and income can be seen on every hand. It should also lead to the conclusion that, as a first step, direct action should be taken to achieve a more equitable distribution of income; we could at the same time eliminate many compelling reasons for income maintenance. This is essentially what the guaranteed income proposes.

On the other hand, there is at least a partial alternative to the guaranteed income as a general mechanism for income redistribution. It consists in making the present rules for income distribution more flexible.[13] This policy, if combined with full employment and a guaranteed employment system, would eliminate the need for redistribution in the vast majority of cases.[14] Therefore, one can argue that the alternative to the guaranteed annual income no longer lies

---

11.   This includes a flat-rate, universal old age security pension and a guaranteed income supplement that assures each person 65 years of age or older of $1,800 annually; or $3,420 for a married couple, both of whom receive the old-age security pension but who have no other income. Starting in April, 1973, the old age pension and guaranteed income supplement will be fully escalated in accordance with the Consumer Price Index.

12.   This appropriation of family allowances by the income security system, as proposed in Canada, is drawing sharp reaction from citizen and family groups and even public welfare administrations.

13.   It may be desirable to replace this course of action by measures designed to raise productivity of workers or industries. Because of the necessary conflict between increased productivity and full employment, it will always be difficult to attain this twofold objective. This is somewhat like the argument put forward in *The Real Poverty Report* that a comprehensive negotiation designed to reduce wage inequalities is imperative. This action would be incorporated in a general incomes policy. Adams, *The Real Poverty Report,* Chapter IV.

14.   Total elimination of the need for redistribution would involve paying a basic wage to all heads of families whether or not they participate in the labor force. That is no longer an alternative to the guaranteed income; it actually is guaranteed income.

in traditional income maintenance programs but in an overhaul of the economic system. Since a guaranteed annual income, however new it may seem, does not necessarily force such an overhaul, it has the same philosophy as every social measure so far: the correction of socially unacceptable effects of the economic system.

How desirable is it for social policy to continue to correct defects in the economic system's performance and how far should it endorse the accepted idea of an absolute relationship between productivity and income, with all the discrimination this involves in the realm of human well-being? The guaranteed income avoids meeting this question head-on.

Objectives and Techniques of a Guaranteed Annual Income

The effect of a guaranteed income in achieving redistribution might be greater than anything we have known so far, both quantitatively and qualitatively. That is the guaranteed annual income's first attractive feature. The second is that the prospect of implementing a guaranteed annual income has enough disturbing factors to upset entrenched rights and set habits of thought and thus impart a new direction for setting the objectives of economic and social policies.

There is no commonly accepted philosophy behind guaranteed annual income proposals. As proof of this, we only have to recall the reciprocal influence of Milton Friedman and Robert Theobald[15] in the development of the guaranteed annual income formulas. On the other hand, both these and later proposals[16] have one objective in common: to improve the income distribution curve in its lowest part, taking family responsibilities into account. The philosophy underlying this option varies according to the author's own philosophy, not only about the role of welfare programs but also about that of economic policies (i.e. the degree of confidence in full employment, the advisability or otherwise of changing the ground rules of the economic system, as well as the direction such change should take).

The different techniques of guaranteed annual income – negative

15. Milton Friedman, *Capitalism and Freedom* (Chicago: University of Chicago Press, 1962); Robert Theobald, *Free Men and Free Markets* (New York: N. C. Potter, 1963).

16. The American proposals include those of Edward E. Schwartz, "A Way to End the Means Test," *Social Work,* IX, 3 (July, 1964), 3–12; Robert Lampman, "Approaches to the Reduction of Poverty," *American Economic Review Papers and Proceedings,* LX (May, 1965) 521–29; James Tobin and others, "Is a Negative Income Tax Practical?" *Yale Law Journal,* LXXVII, 1 (November, 1967) 1–27; Earl R. Rolph, "The Case for a Negative Income Tax Device," in "A Symposium: Negative Income Tax Proposals," *Industrial Relations,* VI (February, 1967), 121–65.

income tax,[17] social dividend and tax credit – are methods of applying a general guaranteed income technique[18] which in fact coincides with that of taxation. In terms of allocating benefits, there are two techniques: the social dividend and the negative income tax. The former brings about redistribution in two operations and the latter in only one. The tax credit can be used with either of these two methods.

On the other hand, there are four different techniques, in terms of particular ways of adapting the present tax system, to make up for inadequate income. The negative income tax is generally seen as an extension of the positive income tax: a proportion of the unused exemptions constitutes the level of guaranteed income. The tax credit was conceived independently of the guaranteed income to replace exemptions[19] or to correct the incidence of indirect taxes on low-income families. In the context of the guaranteed income, it plays the same role as tax exemptions with respect to the negative income tax – that is, a proportion of the unused credits are reimbursed.[20] A third guaranteed income technique does not concern itself with reconciling the two taxation systems – positive and negative – since it sets the guaranteed income in relation to a poverty line rather than to tax exemptions. Finally, the fourth technique, the social dividend, achieves this reconciliation by new rates of positive income tax. However, these distinctions between the techniques become harder to maintain as the number of proposals for a guaranteed annual income increase. Moreover, they are somewhat artificial. Basically, the thing that distinguishes the various guaranteed income proposals from one another is the magnitude of the net redistribution and its effects on each of the income categories. These effects have nothing to do with the technique used; they are

---

17. From the original idea of negative income tax, a more general method "of allowance tied to income" was developed which no longer defines its basic variables in terms of tax exemptions but in terms of a poverty line. "Closely related to and often referred to as negative income plans are guaranteed minimum income plans which . . . would base the guaranteed income payments on some income level that is assumed to lift the individual or family partially or wholly out of poverty." Excerpt from M. G. Murray, *The Role of Unemployment Insurance Under Guaranteed Minimum Income Plans* (Kalamazoo, Mich.: Upjohn Institute for Employment Research, 1969), p. 6. See also J. I. Clark, pp. 274–275.

18. Christopher Green describes this general technique as "transfer by taxation." He says that: "The different types of transfer-by-taxation plans which were discussed . . . are basically similar." Christopher Green, *Negative Taxes and the Poverty Problem* (Washington, D.C.: The Brookings Institution, 1967), p. 62.

19. The superiority of the tax credit over the exemption arises from the fact that, being deducted from tax rather than from income, it retains a constant value, regardless of the scale of income.

20. Rolph, "The Case for a Negative Income Tax Device."

only a function of the values of two variables: the break-even point[21] and the tax rate (or scale of rates) contained in every guaranteed income plan as in every income tax system.

This can be illustrated with the help of a chart reproducing guaranteed income formulas that use the techniques listed. In the accompanying chart we have placed side by side the curves showing the net income after transfer and after tax; these curves result from the application of the proposals (see appendix p. 294) by D. B. Smith (social dividend),[22] James Cutt (negative income tax),[23] the Senate Committee on Poverty (allowance tied to income),[24] and the tax credit proposal developed by the Ontario government.[25] The example is that of a family of two adults and two children.[26]

Let us compare the Smith proposal (social dividend) and the Senate committee's proposal, using the following graph (which has a 45 degree line that represents equal dollar amounts on both axes). The net redistribution of the Smith plan is represented by the area bounded by the Smith program line, the 45 degree line, and the vertical axis; the net redistribution of the Senate plan is represented by the area bounded by the Senate program line, the 45 degree line, and the vertical axis. These areas are determined by the break-even values and the implied tax rates – these latter values are represented by one minus the value of the slopes of the program lines. The

---

21. The role of the break-even point and that of the guaranteed income level are interchangeable. Either one, together with the value of t, determines the third. We choose the break-even point because it illustrates more clearly the relationship between the mechanisms of taxation, negative income tax and the social dividend. Hereafter the letter t is used to designate the rate of implied taxation on income and the letter B to designate the break-even point.

22. D. B. Smith, "A Simplified Approach to Social Welfare," *Canadian Tax Journal,* XIII, 3 (May–June, 1965), 260–65.

23. James Cutt, "A Guaranteed Income – Next Step in the Evolution of Welfare Policy?" *Social Service Review,* XLII, 2 (June, 1966), 216–31 (hereafter referred to as "Guaranteed Income").

24. Special Committee on Poverty, *Poverty in Canada.*

25. There are at least seven proposals for Canada, including those put forward by D. B. Smith, James Cutt and the Senate's Special Committee on Poverty. There are also the Crowley and Dodge proposals, the Deutsch-Green proposal, Colin Hindle's proposal, and that of the Quebec Commission of Inquiry on Health and Social Welfare. (The commission's findings are commonly referred to as the Castonguay-Nepveu report, after the commission's co-chairmen.) Each of these proposals is described in the author's appendix. The Ontario government's proposal is obviously not submitted as a guaranteed income proposal. It was made by W. D. McKeough, Minister of Economics, in "Preliminary Outline of a System of Property and Sales Tax Credits for Ontario" presented at the federal-provincial meeting of finance ministers in Ottawa, November, 1971. Some programs of the same type are also being applied in several states of the U.S.A.

26. For purposes of comparison, these proposals are transposed for the year 1961.

Net Income after Transfer and after Income Tax Resulting from Application of the Smith Proposal (Social Dividend), the Cutt Proposal (Negative Income Tax), the Senate Committee's Proposal (Allowance Tied to Income) and the Tax Credit Proposal Developed by the Ontario Government
(Five-member family, 1961)

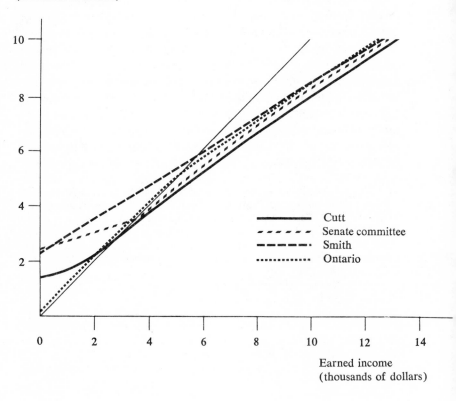

Notes:
1. The break-even points exist where the lines, representing the various programs, intersect the 45 degree line.
2. The point at which a program line intersects the net income scale represents the basic allowance for that particular program.
3. The 45 degree line represents equal dollar amounts on both axes.

Smith proposal makes a much greater distribution than the Senate committee's proposal. Since the combinations $(t = 40, B = 5,812)$ and $(t = 70, B = 3,440)$ produce approximately equivalent guaranteed income levels ($2,325 and $2,408), families with annual incomes of between $250 and $5,800 will benefit more from the Smith proposal.

With Cutt's formula for negative income tax, the net redistribution (represented by the area bounded by the Cutt program line, the 45 degree line, and the vertical axis) is less than in the first two cases.[27] It will be still less with the Ontario proposal where it coincides with the area bounded by the Ontario program line, the 45 degree line and the vertical axis. These relative positions correspond to the general ranking of the guaranteed annual income techniques according to the degree of net redistribution. The fact is that, as they are conceived, the negative income tax and the tax credit assume that strict application of the equity principle can solve the problem of income distribution. It is nonetheless true that any of these techniques is capable of bringing about a particular net redistribution, as this redistribution determines the adjustments to be made in the positive income tax system. In the case of negative income tax, all that is required for a greater redistribution is an increase in tax exemptions; in the case of the tax credit, one only has to increase the credit and obtain the same tax yield in order to raise the taxation rates. Although the allowance tied to income takes little account of adjustments in the positive income tax, the redistribution contemplated will also determine the changes to be made in this case.

This throws some light on an important aspect of the anti-poverty program. For example, the traditional framework of assistance programs leads people to formulate the problem of resource allocation in terms of a choice between welfare and the other public expenditure programs.[28] The guaranteed income formulates it in a different way, because insofar as the income deficiency to be made up determines the amount of net redistribution needed and should lead to corresponding changes in the tax system, one soon finds that it is impossible to go a long way toward a guaranteed annual income

27. The positive income tax is calculated on the basis of the tax reform which became effective in Canada in 1972, except the Smith proposal for a social dividend, in which the proportional rate of 40 per cent suggested by the author is used. However, in all cases, the positive income tax is applied starting from the break-even points.

28. This does not imply that people are unaware of the effect an increase in public expenditures would have on their financial contribution. But people do not regard the acceptance of a medical care plan, which permits a better balance between consumption and ability to pay, in the same way they would regard the sacrifice of part of their standard of living to raise that of other groups in the community.

without affecting the relative positions of the economic classes, either directly or indirectly. This follows logically when one fully accepts a relative notion of poverty. Sooner or later, an income equalization process must necessarily impose sacrifices and pressures on those groups and individuals who hold the purchasing power.[29]

Cost-Benefits of the Guaranteed Annual Income

Defining the general objective of the guaranteed annual income in terms of net redistribution is tantamount to judging it directly in terms of its net financial cost.[30] Therefore, some criteria for evaluating the benefits linked to such redistribution must be added. The impact of the plan on the overall deficiency of income is the most currently used criterion.

Table 1 reproduces the values of the basic variables contained in the Canadian proposals already referred to. By examining these values in relation to that of the poverty lines,[31] we can rank each of these programs as to their effect on low-income families. None of these formulas will entirely resolve the income deficiency but the second will be superior to the first, and so on. Table 2 assesses their cost and total effect on poverty in terms of income distribution in Quebec in 1961.[32]

The immediate goals of the proposals analyzed are not strictly comparable. Some of the proposals merely try to show that, by means of a negative income tax, it is possible to obtain a greater return from the amounts paid in social allowances. This is the case, for instance, with the Deutsch-Green and Cutt proposals.[33] Others consider it essential to materially improve the situation of low-in-

---

29. This takes into account above all the fact that there are greater inequalities in distribution of purchasing power than in distribution of income. Several components of purchasing power – such as the benefits of credit, the value of saving, accessibility to public utilities and work expenses – turn from positive to negative according to the scale of income.
30. In the case of negative income tax or of a system of allowances tied to income, this is the budget cost. In measuring the net redistribution this cost, or the total of the net transfers, is compared to the total income.
31. We use the poverty lines adopted by the Economic Council of Canada, *Challenge of Growth and Change.*
32. Quebec has one-quarter of Canada's population but one-third of the cases of income deficiency as determined on the basis of the Canadian poverty lines. By multiplying the budget cost by three, we get an approximate idea of how much these programs would cost on a national basis.
33. Cutt, however, uses a rate structure that has the effect of reducing the amount of the transfers allowed in relation to the existing system. His system is an extension of the positive income tax which, in spite of everything, is more effective than the existing system in compensating for income deficiency.

Table 1

Basic Variables Describing the Canadian Proposals for Guaranteed Annual Income Transposed to 1961 according to Family Size

Programs	1 adult $S^a = \$1,500$	2 adults $S = \$2,500$	2 adults 1 child $S = \$3,000$	2 adults 2 children $S = \$3,500$	2 adults 3 children $S = \$4,000$	Implied tax rate[b] in %
	Break-even point expressed in per cent of poverty lines					
Cutt	70%	70%	70%	70%	70%	(25–35–40–45–50)
Deutsch-Green	70	70	82	90	96	50
Senate committee	86	86	86	86	86	70
"Adjusted" Senate	100	100	100	100	100	70
Crowley-Dodge	119	143	143	143	143	42
Smith	143	174	161	152	145	40
"Modified" Senate	123	123	123	123	123	70
Castonguay-Nepveu	161	140	132	126	121	(62–71–70–68–67)

a. S represents the poverty line set by the Economic Council of Canada, *Challenge of Growth and Change.*
b. The two values B (break-even point) and t (rate of coverage of the difference between the break-even point and earned income when the latter is nil) have been chosen because they enable us to translate all the proposals in the same form: $P = t (B - R)$. In this equation, P is the benefit and R is the earned income. To obtain the level of guaranteed annual income expressed as a percentage of the poverty line, multiply B by t (implied tax rate).
In the Cutt and Castonguay-Nepveu programs, the value of t is composed of a scale of marginal rates applying to marginal sections of income insufficiency made up. This is why there is a separate rate for each family size.

Family size	One	Two	Three	Four	Five
Cutt	25%	35%	40%	45%	50%
Castonguay-Nepveu	62	71	70	68	67

Table 2

Reduction of Income Deficiency and the Number of Poor Families in Relation to the Amount of the Transfers, according to Various Canadian Proposals for a Guaranteed Annual Income, Quebec, 1961

Programs	Cost of plan in millions of dollars[a]		% of persons emerging from poverty[d]	% of income deficiency absorbed[f]	Income deficiency absorbed per unit budget cost	Additional absorption of income deficiency per additional budget cost	Number of additional families emerging from poverty per additional thousand dollars of cost
	GAI	Total					
1. Cutt	$ 99.7	$ 99.7		14.5%	100.0%		
2. Present system	205.6	378.0	13.4%	26.8	48.7		
3. Deutsch-Green	341.2	314.4b	6.9	38.3	83.6	2.92	
4. Senate committee	341.2	341.2		49.7	100.0	1.00	
5. "Adjusted" Senate	481.7	481.7		70.0	100.0		
6. Crowley-Dodge	637.7	637.7	38.0	72.5	78.1	0.11	0.46
7. Smith	679.9	679.9	38.1	73.6	74.3	0.18	0.012
8. "Modified" Senate	776.4	776.4	55.9	93.9	83.1	1.44	0.88
9. Castonguay-Nepveu	516.6	825.3c	75.8e	96.1	68.7	0.31	1.95

a. This is the total amount of net benefits. Therefore, in the case of the social dividend it is a net financial cost, and in the other cases this amount corresponds to the budget cost.

b. The Deutsch-Green proposal consists of the old age security plan (at that time totalling $108.8 million) and a $205.6 million guaranteed annual income program for the rest of the population.

c. The Castonguay-Nepveu proposal includes a guaranteed income plan of $516.6 million for the non-elderly, the existing old age security program of $108.8 million, and a family allowance plan of $200 million.

d. These are economic units comprising single persons and families. The calculations have been made on the basis of distribution according to both family size and income after transfer and before tax of non-agricultural low-income family units in Quebec in 1961. The number of poor people before transfers was 477,002, or 39.5 per cent of the total number. For the purposes of calculation, we assumed that the families were composed of two adults plus a number of children equal to the family size minus two.

e. This result is overestimated owing to the fact that in the first step of calculations, family allowances were given to more children than were entitled to them.

f. The income deficiency before transfers reached $686.7 million or 42.5 per cent of the total income corresponding to the poverty lines.

come families, and this requires a greater net redistribution. The recommendations of both the Senate's Special Committee on Poverty and the Castonguay-Nepveu commission fall into this last category.[34]

For the purpose of analysis, we have constructed nine programs (table 2, p. 160), two of which are modifications of the Senate committee's proposal. The first variant is the substitution of the Economic Council of Canada's poverty line (Program 5) for that defined by the Senate committee (Program 4). It was necessary because the Senate committee's poverty line defined in relative terms was below that of the Economic Council of Canada, for 1961, whereas when the report of the Senate committee appeared in 1971 it was higher.[35]

The second variant is a new program which retains from the Senate committee's plan an implied income tax rate of 70 per cent but sets the guaranteed income at 100 per cent of the poverty line. Its most attractive feature is that it is midway between the Senate committee's program and that outlined in the Castonguay-Nepveu report.

From the standpoint of cost and impact, programs fall into three groups: those with a budget cost below or equal to that of the existing system; those that would double the total amount allocated for redistribution; and finally, an intermediate group composed of almost equivalent social dividend proposals by Smith and by Crowley and Dodge. By doubling the amount of transfers, 90 per cent of the income deficiency is made up, compared to slightly over one-third.[36] For an equivalent amount of benefits, however, we know that absorption of the income deficiency is directly proportional to the fraction of such benefits paid within the income corresponding to the poverty line. This is what gives the existing system the poorest performance and the Senate committee's proposal the best. Quite a different result will be obtained by using the number of people who have escaped from poverty as a yardstick for measuring the advantages. The concentration of benefits around the pov-

---

34. Their official character also makes them somewhat different from the other proposals.

35. In defining a new poverty line equivalent to 50 per cent of the average income, the Senate committee in its report in November, 1971, tried to correct the deterioration of the Economic Council of Canada's poverty line produced 10 years previously. This correction would not have been necessary in 1961. This is why we consider that Program 4 discredits the Senate committee's proposal somewhat, while Program 5 does it justice.

36. In this regard, the Deutsch and Green plan is a more satisfactory reference basis than the existing system because, having a lower budget cost, it absorbs a higher fraction of the income deficiency.

erty line enables us to obtain better results according to this criterion because, with the income deficiency being small, it is easier to cross the poverty line. The performance of the guaranteed annual income programs is thus divided depending on which of the assessment criteria we use, although these criteria reflect complementary objectives. This is why cost-benefit analysis is still only of limited importance.

In the light of these restrictions, which of these programs would be closest to an optimum solution? Interpreting the cost-benefit ratios is tricky, since the system of programs is discontinuous. To absorb the income deficiency, it seems advantageous in every case to give up the existing system and turn, for example, from the Deutsch-Green proposal to the Senate committee proposal (Programs 3 and 4). Because the rates of implied income taxation drop from 70 per cent (Senate committee) to 40 per cent (Smith and Crowley-Dodge), these programs add little to that of the Senate committee. On the other hand, if we wish to combine the benefits of absorbing income deficiency with those of a decreased number of poor families, a proposal such as Program 8 will have to be considered. Finally, the Castonguay-Nepveu proposal, whch pays a portion of the guaranteed income in the form of a family allowance,[37] is less efficient for absorbing income deficiency but is relatively efficient with regard to the number of persons who escape from poverty.

The brief analysis of these proposals brings out the following points. Whichever technique is used, a better performance of transfer payments can be obtained through a guaranteed annual income program. But, to significantly improve the situation of the low-income families, it would have been necessary in 1961 to double the amount of transfers.

Finally, the study of post-transfer income distribution by quintiles[38] shows that the "modified" Senate committee plan or the Castonguay-Nepveu commission's plan double the share of income in the lowest quintile and slightly increase that of the second quintile. This of course refers to income distribution before tax, but one could think in terms of adjusting an income tax system to the guaranteed income plan instead of vice-versa. This would be more likely to produce an adequate income distribution within the financial limitations.

---

37. The proposed family allowance plan provides for 62 per cent of family allowances, amounting to some $200 million in 1961, to be paid to poor families. See the Quebec (Province) Commission of Inquiry on Health and Social Welfare, *Report,* V, *Income Security* (Quebec: Official Publisher, 1971).

38. See chart 5 in appendix, p. 324.

Economic Effects of the Guaranteed Annual Income

The foregoing analysis would not be complete without some reference to the important place given work incentives in the design of guaranteed annual income formulas. In fact, in this light the notion of the GAI's economic cost is introduced as an extension of the idea of budget cost to which until now we have been restricted. Since the budget cost represents a simple transfer of resources, the true cost of the guaranteed annual income will appear insofar as it results in a loss of production or investment. The first of these effects concerns the incentive to work. As has been noted, the role of the tax rate in the GAI formulas is not clear. Calculating benefits measured by absorption of income deficiency only places the benefits paid above the poverty line in the denominator. The assumption is then that these payments represent a cost: a price to pay to avoid a drop in production or to make sure that the GAI meshes easily with the ground rules underlying the economic system.[39] But taking into account the sometimes doubtful value of the assumptions on which these rules are based, and taking into account the present performances of the economic system, one might well ask whether such a price is reasonable and whether it coincides with the economic cost or with the potential loss of production.[40]

Work Incentives

The theoretical basis for fearing that the guaranteed annual income will have disincentive effects is known.[41] However, it is more difficult to demonstrate the empirical basis of this theory. Often studies are based on a comparison between two situations, one of which is necessarily hypothetical. However, on the basis of the evidence accumulated to date there is no simple correlation between the desire to work on the one hand and net income on the other. This re-

---

39. This cost is equivalent to the economic cost insofar as it coincides with the estimated loss of production. A true cost-benefit ratio would place in the numerator the economic gains corresponding to the elimination of income deficiency, namely the discounted value of the performances resulting from the use of a better human potential and, in the denominator, the value of production losses resulting from reduction in the labor supply.

40. Of course, by experimenting with various GAI formulas having different values of t, we would be able to judge this price. All we would have to do is follow the different values of this budget cost and the production loss with the variations of t.

41. A decrease in the net income from work leads to a work-leisure substitution effect. In the case of positive income tax, the effect of income compensates at least in part for the substitution effect. In the case of negative income tax, the guaranteed income helps to neutralize the effect of income or to reverse its direction.

lationship is upset by several factors. Perhaps the most significant one is the individual's innate drive for self-fulfilment.

Let us consider first the behavior of welfare recipients, among whom it is exceptional to find a person able but not willing to work.[42] Yet eligibility conditions, which are most often incompatible with holding a job, directly encourage people to quit their jobs.[43]

Some empirical research was designed to investigate the disincentive effect of the guaranteed annual income. For example, M. J. Boskin conducted a survey[44] in 1967 among a sample of American workers at least two-thirds of whom had annual incomes below $3,000. It was found that among the lowest income groups the availability of a job is the determining factor in its acceptance. Among the persons interviewed,[45] 53 per cent stated that they would have worked more if they had had an opportunity to do so. With the help of the specific question on guaranteed annual income,[46] the survey also isolated a subgroup of 12 per cent of these workers representing persons in the sample who suffered a disincentive effect. Mr. Boskin estimates this effect to be 8 per cent of the income earned, at most.

Simultaneously, the investigations into the disincentive effects of a progressive income tax revealed certain elements which can be transposed to the negative income tax.[47] Thus, the labor market conditions[48] and financial commitments resulting from the achievement of an adequate standard of living reduce the elasticity of the labor supply. As well, a great diversity of motivations and reactions is found when such a situation is faced.[49]

---

42.   Stephen G. Peitchinis, "Why Should Anyone in Calgary Need Aid?" *Canadian Welfare,* XLV, 3 (May–June, 1969), 6–13. More recently a report on recipients in Ontario confirms this.

43.   Public opinion often confuses cheating with a lack of desire for economic participation by welfare recipients. It is believed that cheaters refuse to work, whereas in fact cheating often consists in not declaring income from work.

44.   Michael J. Boskin, "The Negative Income Tax and the Supply of Work Effort," *National Tax Journal,* XX, 4 (December, 1967), 353–57.

45.   Of whom 38 per cent had worked full time for 40 weeks or more.

46.   For the purposes of the study, the hypothetical benefit from the guaranteed annual income is fixed at an arbitrary amount of $500 compared to a median income of $1,900 earned by the group of workers interviewed.

47.   The study by Break remains a classic: G. F. Break, "Income Taxes and Incentives to Work: an Empirical Study," *The American Economic Review* (September, 1967), pp. 530–49.

48.   This factor may work in both directions, i.e. bring a disincentive effect greater or smaller than that which should be expected.

49.   "Even with certain checks and with a maximum simplicity maintained throughout the questionnaire, however, the evidence yielded by the 306 interviews was a complex of varied reactions open to considerable diversity of interpretation." Break, "Income Taxes and Incentives to Work: an Empirical Study," p. 534.

Whatever concrete results emerge from these motivations,[50] the relationship between the disincentive effects and the decrease in economic growth will be different when considered on the assumption of full employment from what it would be with less than full employment (which is the way the economic system usually works). To begin with, we can take it for granted[51] that the lower a person's salary and the heavier his family responsibilities, the more valid is the guaranteed income as a solution to his resources problem. Whereas in a full employment situation we would expect rising salaries and increased inflation, in the present economic situation we must consider the possibility of shifts in the labor force, provided the GAI does not have too great an effect on labor mobility. Therefore, the relinquishment of certain jobs by older and less qualified workers could make it possible for younger and better qualified workers – a higher percentage of whom are without jobs – to enter the labor force. The former would receive higher benefits but the latter would receive lower wages. Since these effects might in turn produce an artificial scarcity in the low-productivity sectors, a reduction in the labor supply could lead either to the closing down or the modernization of these sectors. Therefore, it is essential that some thought be given to the future of these industries and how they behave in relation to the minimum wage. In fact, it comes back to the problem that is encountered when minimum wage is raised: a choice between a long-term increase in productivity and a short-term decrease in employment in industries already protected and subsidized. In short, insofar as the disincentive consists only of substitution effects in the labor supply and a decrease in the number of jobs in marginal sectors, its cost in terms of economic growth[52] should not normally be high.

Savings

There is also a connection between the economic cost of the guar-

---

50.   Note that management theory is gradually beginning to operate on the assumption of more generous motivations than the motivation attributed to economic man. The traditional bureaucratic system, with its concept of a hierarchy, postulated a minimum return for a given wage. "Management by programs" makes the production effort a variable of responsibility and the instruments of work.

51.   In fact, we simply assume that no worker will want to suffer a decrease in his total income, a belief which is compatible with the basic assumptions of economic theory.

52.   Of course, the same assumptions should be used for assessing costs and benefits. That is to say, if we are on a course of growth predicted on less than full employment rather than geared to a maximum growth potential, the economic costs of the GAI will be lower but so will the benefits ascribed to the elimination of poverty.

anteed annual income and its effect on investment. Opinions are varied on this subject. Savings are a growth factor, but stimulation of demand for durable goods and services also plays a key role. On the other hand, the role of investment as a growth stimulator is not questioned, any more than the role of economic growth in achieving the more general goals of society. In the area of human development, savings could be a means for individuals to participate more directly in economic growth. All these factors provide justification for government intervention in the field of savings – intervention which could be much more significant than it has been. In making procedures for implementing the GAI more flexible, governments may find justification for such intervention. Indeed, the few experiments thus far with negative income tax schemes confirm the existence of a major difficulty, which lies in the short-term[53] fluctuation of incomes. Social insurance plans such as unemployment insurance and income protection against sickness cannot adequately cope with this difficulty, since, to be effective, they require waiting periods. On the other hand, with the help of an institutionalized savings plan, the worker could be encouraged to accumulate capital; a reserve fund could be set for him – for example 10 per cent of his capital – which he would be compelled to use in the event of short-term interruption of his income. This compulsory savings would be proportionate to wages, so that the amount of reserves accumulated by the worker would vary in proportion to his income and his employment background. By introducing in this way a waiting period for negative income tax based on the unexpended amount of the reserve fund,[54] it might be possible to make monthly and weekly payments while minimizing reimbursement on an annual basis.

As most of the individual's savings are held in various forms of investment, this type of plan offers benefits to the workers that are not available with other forms of social insurance. From the point of view of social goals, it might be a worthwhile replacement for

---

53. This difficulty arises when replacing traditional assistance plans by a negative income-type plan is contemplated. To meet the situation of short-term hardship, the eligibility period cannot be defined in annual terms. On the other hand, by establishing it on a monthly or weekly basis there is a risk of abuses or of forced repayments which are diffcult for low-income families to make. For an explanation of a method for reconciling these constraints, see the Quebec (Province) Commission of Inquiry on Health and Social Welfare, *Income Security*, Part 2, p. 46–52.

54. The length of the period is determined by the ratio between the reserve fund and the guaranteed income. If the level of guaranteed income to which a worker is entitled is $120 a month and if his accumulated reserve fund is $60, the period will be two weeks. On the other hand, if he has accumulated $720, the period will be six months.

the income-insurance type of plan, owing to the regressive financing of these plans and the importance of a guaranteed income. In fact, such a savings plan would be fairly well adapted to the present characteristics of individual savings, which are for the most part in the form of compulsory savings.

To the extent that an adequate income is a prerequisite for an individual's economic participation by enabling him to use services capable of improving his ability to work and productivity, the GAI can generate productivity and investment.[55] The importance of effects will depend on how good the guaranteed annual income plan is.

Quality of the Guaranteed Annual Income Plan

In terms of quality, the GAI has a twofold objective: to reform the traditional welfare system (that is, mainly to overcome the alienation of welfare recipients); and to convert a palliative to income inadequacy into an instrument of human development. These goals of justice and development are ambitious. Besides dictating requirements as to the structure of the GAI or the reform it should take when implemented, they demand a consistency in the objectives of social, human and economic development policies which at first sight seem unattainable. Let us deal first with the conditions for implementing the guaranteed annual income.

1 *Justice*

The idea of the guaranteed annual income makes it more closely related to taxation – a universal, indirect mechanism – than to the family of traditional programs based on a needs test.

There is reason to fear, however, that in its practical application, the guaranteed annual income may become a glorified form of welfare, based on a means test and other considerations. This being so, the guaranteed annual income will simplify the administration of welfare programs, while retaining their philosophy. This danger lies in the fact that the standard pattern followed by changes in government programs is most often a combination of the old and the new. Programs are seldom abandoned; they are modified according to a time schedule that makes it possible to minimize both the resistance to change and the losses suffered by the groups who benefited from the old programs.

---

55. For a discussion of these effects, see Boskin, "The Negative Income Tax and the Supply of Work Effort"; also Thomas J. Courchene, "How Canada Practises Economic Discrimination Against the Poor," *Canadian Welfare,* XLVII, 6 (November–December, 1971), 4–6, 30–32.

There are few examples of the application of a guaranteed annual income. But the intentions announced by the U.S. and the Canadian governments seem in harmony with this changing pattern. The Family Assistance Plan proposed in the United States by President Nixon in August, 1969, would be in addition to existing plans. It retains some rigid provisions about eligibility which will help to keep its beneficiaries in the welfare rut.[56] The statements of the Canadian government, although much further from implementation, are perhaps more promising.[57] By selecting the existing family allowances and old age security systems as the area of change, it increases the likelihood of the guaranteed annual income leaning more towards the universal concept of taxation than that of welfare assistance. These remarks apply also to the projects put forward by the Quebec and Ontario governments, the former having chosen to make a breakthrough in the family allowances field[58] and the latter making the tax system the keystone of change.[59] When all is said and done, the first qualitative goal of the guaranteed annual income will only be reached to the extent that we manage to combine its method of distribution with that of the positive income tax. A decentralized service such as the banking system would facilitate dealings between the administration and the clients without the client being stigmatized should he overdraw his account (that is, when he needs a cash benefit).

2 Human Development

Whenever the objectives of human development are considered, we are reminded of the structure of the guaranteed annual income. The "floor" income that is generally used constitutes an economic, not

---

56. This is mainly due to the fact that the program obliges the applicant, whether a man or woman with children of school age, to register for employment or a retraining course. On this subject, see the critique by John S. Morgan and Herman Levin, "The Nixon Stance on Welfare," *Canadian Welfare,* XLVI, 1 (January–February, 1970), 4–11.

57. In its white paper, *Income Security for Canadians,* the Canadian government retains the objective of "converting universal family allowances into a selective guaranteed income program: Family Income Security Plan." Canada, Department of National Health and Welfare, *Income Security for Canadians,* Chart III, p. 30.

58. Bill No. 286, Régime des allocations familiales du Québec, tabled for first reading in the Quebec National Assembly, December, 1971. Under this bill, about 70 per cent of families with children would receive family allowances to an annual maximum of $240 for the first three children ($180 if they are under 12 years old) and $408 for the fourth child and subsequent children.

59. McKeough, "Preliminary Outline of a System of Property and Sales Tax Credits for Ontario."

a sociological, minimum.[60] Families with minimum means, particularly those who remain at this economic level for a long time, are not capable of functioning properly, much less of permitting their members to become integrated in the community.[61] Thus, the objectives of personal development are concerned first with the structure of the guaranteed annual income – that is, a combination of a guaranteed floor income and a rate of negative income tax that will enable a good proportion of the families to raise their resources above the poverty line. Looked at in this way, the payment of benefits above the poverty line should not be regarded exclusively as a cost[62] but, within certain limits, as a benefit attributed to the escape from chronic income deficiency. Thus the Senate committee's program, which seems adequate in terms of the basic allowance, has the weakness of allowing no benefits above the poverty line. On the other hand, if a break-even point equivalent to 125 per cent of the poverty line is set as an objective, a program having a more satisfactory effect on income deficiency will result. The following set of programs, to which our Program 8 or the "modified" Senate committee program belongs (table 3, p. 171), combines the objective of a break-even point higher than the poverty line with that of a guaranteed income level reaching at least 70 per cent of the poverty line. The rate of negative taxation on income fluctuates, then, between 57 and 73 per cent.

Finally, the guaranteed income can only meet an objective of individual development if the economic, social and political structure, supported by government measures, combine to create opportunities. Every anti-poverty policy emphasizes the necessity of reviewing the whole structure of economic and social policies to harmonize objectives. People often talk about the disjointedness of the

---

60. This is true of the "floor" incomes used by the Economic Council of Canada, the Senate's Special Committee on Poverty, and Mollie Orshansky, "Counting the Poor: Another Look at the Poverty Profile," *Social Security Bulletin,* XXVIII, 1 (January, 1965), 3–29. See also Jenny R. Podoluk, *Incomes of Canadians,* 1961 Census Monograph (Ottawa: Queen's Printer, 1968).

61. In this regard, the evidence of persons depending on transfer payments is unanimous and striking. See Quebec (Province), Commission of Inquiry on Health and Social Welfare, *La Voix des Hommes sans Voix,* Appendix 22 of *Report* (Quebec: Official Publisher, 1971). To be convinced, one has only to consult the list of "special needs" set out in legislation on financial assistance: purchases of bedding, furniture, medicines and school supplies; these are occasional expenses which, taken together, constitute current needs that cannot be met by the margin between basic necessities and the income floor.

62. Richard A. Musgrave, Peter Heller and George Peterson, "Cost Effectiveness of Alternative Income Maintenance Schemes," *National Tax Journal,* XXIII, 2 (June, 1940), 143.

Table 3

Estimated Budget Cost of
a Set of Programs with Various Tax Rates

Break-even point in % of poverty line	Basic allowance as % of poverty line	Implied tax rate deducted	Budget cost[a] in millions
123%	90%	73%	$809.7
123	86	70	776.4[b]
123	80	65	721.0
123	70	57	632.2

a. Resulting from its application to Quebec in 1961.
b. Equivalent to Program 8 in table 2, "modified" Senate committee proposal.

system of government programs. This criticism, generally justified, may simply result from the incompatibility of the assumptions underlying the economic programs on the one hand and the social programs on the other. On one hand, by encouraging personal development the social policies assume that man's satisfaction depends on his creativity and participation in the social and economic development of society. On the other hand, economic programs, being oriented towards the major issues of growth, inflation, the presence of foreign capital and unemployment, also recognize the value of human potential as a production factor but consider man a poor agent of economic development. The role of entrepreneur is increasingly played by the big national or international corporations, and hence the individual's participation in development activity is considered marginal.

Until other ways have been found of providing for man's need, economic development will be the focal point of activity aimed at human and social development. Thus, insofar as we deem man to be an outsider in this area of human activity, we make him an outsider in his own development. The logical corollary of this belief is that it is pointless to seek to develop the individual; rather, policies should aim at making him subordinate to production. From this point of view, the guaranteed income would also be meaningless. It loosens the chains that bind man to work by his need to survive. It weakens the need to work in the name of goals which then appear utopian. But are these goals totally unrealistic or are they merely rejected as goals for society? The same society that on one hand seeks for its members the benefits of affluence and leisure – nothing less than liberation from work – on the other hand denies access by the underprivileged to the guaranteed income on the grounds that this would encourage idleness.

These underlying contradictions are reflected in the way government programs work. For example, in an effort to create jobs, the government increases the number of business-oriented programs, the grants for which are geared to the investment-job ratio determined by the firm's type of activity. At the same time, because business response to the need to stimulate jobs is sometimes disappointing, programs have been devised for making grants to ad hoc organizations that are prepared to carry on non-profit ventures.[63] This is an interesting experiment but some questions arise.

---

63. As a result of the experience gained in the Opportunities for Youth Program (initiated in March, 1971), which enabled students to create summer jobs themselves, the Canadian government set up the Local Initiatives Program in October, 1971, to extend a grant to any group showing initiative in the creation of new job opportunities and meeting the eligibility requirements.

For example, why must these groups forego a profit? Why must they create jobs without the help of a substantial physical investment? To the extent that such a design follows the assumption that only business begets development, it may be concluded that these programs are set up as a glorified form of guaranteed income and should not have to be economically viable. On the other hand, if the design of these programs really implies the assumption that an individual or a group can generate economic development, why not let them make a profit and match grant and/or loan assistance programs to investment as is done for a business enterprise?[64]

Indirectly, the guaranteed annual income invites such questions and challenges. It should also encourage the study of a broader range of solutions than may be derived from present theoretical systems. The guaranteed annual income should provide an opportunity for new experiences and testing new theories, because it forces society to look for ways of stimulating human participation in activities that create economic development – ways that are more positive and original than the actual system of "work or die."

---

64. It is abnormal, for example, that in order to form co-operatives and create jobs, organizations to help the unemployed should have to conduct charity drives, while millions of dollars are handed out to business concerns. It is true that the risks are not the same in both cases. But this could very well be taken into account when drawing up profitability requirements, leading the governments to match these grants with technical assistance.

Work Incentives and Welfare Reform in Britain and the United States

by Martin Rein*
*Professor, Department of Urban Studies and Planning,
Massachusetts Institute of Technology, Cambridge*

There is no consensus on the essential features of a negative or reverse income tax. However, four criteria can be identified: benefits are paid in cash; benefits are income conditioned – that is, they are inversely related to income (the higher the income the lower the benefits); income insufficiency alone is the measure of need and the test of eligibility and no work test is imposed; and benefits are closely related to the tax system. As we turn from theory to practice we find that nations have been reluctant to integrate the mechanisms by which taxes are collected and benefits distributed and to reject work requirement tests, but some have accepted the principle of earnings retention and cash payments and the concepts of personal choice and work incentives which they imply. In this paper, the focus is on work incentives.[1]

To encourage employment, policy must avoid penalizing those who earn income by subjecting them to a reduction in benefits equivalent to the amount that their earnings have increased. Some retention of benefits up to an established cutoff point must be permitted as earnings rise. The greater the proportion of earnings retained, the stronger the work incentive. Although disagreement on a precise definition persists, we consider that a negative income tax has been accepted when a benefit or earnings retention principle is supported. However, the use of this principle can serve quite different purposes and yield dramatically different political outcomes. In Britain, negative taxation considered as earnings retention has,

*The author acknowledges with thanks the help of Alan Sager in drafting an earlier version of this paper, and the helpful comments of Leonard Hausman, John Stacpoole, Tony Atkinson and Tony Lynes.
1.   Cavala and Wildavsky identify four characteristics of a guaranteed income: assistance is based on need alone; entitlement is "objectively and uniformly measured . . . in terms of the size and composition of the family unit, its income, and its other economic resources"; assistance is paid in cash; and the tax on additional income is less than 100 per cent. William Cavala and Aaron Wildavsky, "The Political Feasibility of Income by Right," *Public Policy*, XVIII (Spring, 1970), 352.

since August 1971, been applied to extend the buying power of the working poor under a program called Family Income Supplements (FIS); and in the United States, since 1967, the negative income tax has been used to make work attractive to present recipients of welfare. This paper reviews experience in these two countries where the principle of negative taxation has been applied to two different purposes – relieving economic distress and changing work-oriented behavior.

These competing purposes of social policy are themselves of significance to the broader field of public expenditure. To explain the differences, economists distinguish between subsidies and transfers. A subsidy is a transaction designed to change behavior in the private sector. By contrast, a transfer extends consumption for its own sake and does not expect a direct *quid* for *quo*. Some programs, transfer-subsidies, seek both aims. President Nixon's Family Assistance Plan and the 1971 Ways and Means Committee bill (H.R. 1) must be defined as a mixed transfer-subsidy. The British Family Income Supplements program, on the other hand, is a straightforward transfer. This paper reviews and compares policies that demand reciprocity (benefits extended to alter behavior and created to establish a positive incentive for work) with those that are unilateral transactions designed to augment consumption and relieve distress. Some would argue that no policy for the poor may appropriately be viewed entirely or even primarily as a unilateral transfer. Such policies are also designed to encourage social compliance, promote conformity, or facilitate achievement. The relief of distress, in this perspective, always serves some broader purpose of society, such as quelling discontent or maintaining social stability.[2] Hence the distinction between subsidies and transfers can be misleading.

However, I believe that differences in legislative intent are significant for program outcomes. In particular I will try to illustrate that subsidies which purport to change the behavior and attitudes of individuals have different political consequences than transfers to consumers. In the United States, attempts to change personal behavior through subsidies prove too costly to sustain and gradually surrender to administrative and coercive policies. In Britain, on the other hand, the cumulative effect of multiple transfers has led to pressure for fundamental tax reform and to some measure of income equalization between the poor and not-so-poor. At the same time, the relative gap between upper- and middle-income groups may be widening. Thus, debate about the merits of a negative income tax and means-tested benefits must pay attention not only to

2. Frances Fox Piven and Richard Cloward, *Regulating the Poor* (New York: Pantheon Press, 1970).

the details of the program but also to the purposes – transfer or subsidy – for which it is employed.

Development of Welfare Policy in the United States

A review of U.S. welfare policy from 1962 to 1972 suggests that three strategies have been pursued: a service strategy, an income-incentive strategy, and an administrative strategy. Each of these elements can be identified in the major amendments to the Social Security Act in 1962 and 1967, and in the administration's 1970 abortive proposals for the Family Assistance Plan and H.R. 1, which by the summer of 1972 had not yet been implemented. However, over the decade experience has shown services to be of doubtful effectiveness; incentives have proved politically unacceptable because of the high financial costs of implementation. And given the abiding commitment to reduce welfare rolls, policy increasingly, if reluctantly, has turned to administrative solutions.

1   The 1962 Amendments

The 1962 amendments were heralded as the "services" amendments. They emphasized first, problem identification; second, the availability to welfare recipients of information, advice, and referral to other community resources; and finally, some measure of direct help through specific services such as day care. These activities were designed to encourage "prevention and rehabilitation" as a way of reducing the size of the caseloads. While casework (diagnosis, advice and referral) played a prominent role in these services, the emphasis on manpower training was not neglected, as the Community Work and Training Program attests.

The beginnings of an income incentive strategy can be also recognized: Congress required states to allow for work expenses to encourage welfare mothers to seek employment. States were also permitted to disregard income set aside for children's future needs, such as education. The incentive principle was part of a wider income strategy that emphasized broader coverage in less restricted program categories, larger grants, and simplification of eligibility determination. Essentially, it sought a less conditional claim to assistance, emphasized uniformity in the treatment of clients and aimed at an economic improvement by combining employment and welfare.

The administrative strategy took several forms. One was quality control; a new method was devised to review a random sample of the eligibility decisions made by caseworkers, and thus determine the percentage of incorrect decisions. Here it was assumed that rolls could be reduced if the eligibility decisions were more stringently examined. The Senate Appropriations Committee in the spring of 1962 demanded that a survey of the rates of ineligibles on state rolls be completed by the following fiscal year. The federal Department of Health, Education and Welfare (HEW) had simultaneously to make plans for a national eligibility survey while it was drafting the service regulations – illustrating, as Charles Gilbert points out, the "program's basic ambivalence."[3] A second aspect in the administrative approach was to make it more difficult for deserting fathers to avoid supporting their children; this would take the financial reward out of desertions and reduce the number of families eligible for aid. Third, the Community Work and Training Program contained the beginnings of a new type of compulsion; it authorized federal participation in the payments made to those recipients of Aid to Families with Dependent Children (AFDC) whom the states employed on community work and training projects. States were therefore encouraged to institute or expand programs that required recipients to work or accept training.

Congress' interest in work and training requirements was heightened by its five-year extension of the AFDC-Unemployed Parent Program. This program, initially passed in 1961, authorized federal participation in state AFDC programs for families in which the father was unemployed. States were required to cut off payments to an unemployed father who refused to accept work. (This had been a longstanding feature of most, if not all, state unemployment insurance schemes.) In 1962, parents who refused job training were denied aid. The creation of the AFDC-Unemployed Parent Program, designed to reduce family breakup, contributed to a redefinition of AFDC recipients as potentially employable persons, rather than individuals who, by definition, were outside the labor force.

2 The 1967 Amendments

In 1967 much more attention was given to the incentive strategy. The incentives were contained in the $30-one-third rule (which permits recipients to keep the first $30 per month in earnings plus one-third of the balance) and in the expansion of deductions for work-related expenses. Services were not neglected, however, and Congress established a Work Incentives program to help mothers on welfare become self-supporting through job training. The service and incentive strategies reinforced each other. The legislation also contained restrictive features: it required compulsory work-train-

---

3. Charles Gilbert, Swarthmore College, unpublished manuscript on the development of the social service amendments, n.d.

ing programs for AFDC mothers and older children out of school. Those judged able to work or qualified for training were required to accept jobs (if any were available) or placement in the Work Incentives program. Welfare authorities were given power to withhold payments from AFDC heads who refused work or training.

Compulsory work requirements in the Work Incentives program were the result of congressional frustration over the failure of services and the inability of welfare administrators to reduce welfare rolls. However, principles and practice diverged. Voluntary requests for training under the Work Incentives program exceeded the available supply and compulsion was therefore unnecessary. In addition, the law established a freeze on welfare expenditures. The freeze limited federal support for recipients eligible through family break-up to those in the AFDC caseload in the first quarter of 1968. This policy was designed to encourage states to develop manpower and service programs – that is, to take positive action to reduce their AFDC caseloads. But the freeze never went into effect. In addition, the Internal Revenue Service was ordered to give the states information that would help locate fathers who had deserted their families. Congress once again extended the scope of services for which it would match state payments. States were required, for example, to offer voluntary birth control information. The federal government would reimburse states for 80 per cent of their expenditures on training and day care up to a maximum federal contribution of $130 million and $35 million, respectively. Day care funding was increased from $10 million per year to support both the incentive and the administrative strategies: day care, if available, would aid mothers seeking work or training; at the same time, it would enable states to require mothers of preschool children to accept these child care arrangements and find jobs.

3 The Family Assistance Plan

In August 1969, the president proposed the Family Assistance Plan; the bill passed the House but failed to pass the Senate. The incentive strategy was carried still further in this plan by reducing the marginal tax rate from 67 to 50 per cent, providing a $720 disregard for work-related expenses and assuring an income guarantee of $1,600. Daniel P. Moynihan, executive director of the Council on Urban Affairs, insists that no formal work requirements were imposed.[4] He argues that, whatever the rhetoric, employable recipients who refused to accept training or employment lost only the

---

4. Daniel P. Moynihan, "The Politics of a Guaranteed Income: The Nixon Administration and the Family Assistance Plan," forthcoming.

value of their benefits, an amount equal only to $300 in the original proposal but later increased by the House Ways and Means Committee to $500. Moreover, Moynihan asserts that from the start Nixon's advisors and the president himself believed that the Family Assistance Plan would have very little impact on reducing dependency. They came to view it as a straightforward cash transfer. Whatever motives inspired the administration, it is clear the Ways and Means Committee saw the matter differently. "Your committee made a number of modifications in the family assistance provisions of the bill proposed by the administration which are designed to halt the trends that have existed in the growth of the number of families on the AFDC rolls."[5] Work-related training and social services continued to be emphasized. Child care for almost one-half million children in families headed by welfare mothers was requested. Provision was made to limit the cost of services per recipient to $2,000 a year. The Family Assistance Plan also contained an expanded set of administrative regulations in the form of work rules and "suitable work" definitions.

4 *Opportunities for Families*

In 1971 a modified version of the Family Assistance Plan was introduced by the House Ways and Means Committee and placed first on the congressional agenda. H.R. 1, like its predecessor, passed the House; however, a more restrictive bill emerged from the Senate Finance Committee in June, 1972, making it unlikely that the bill would pass at all. The House version increased the guarantee level from $1,600 to $2,400, raised the marginal tax rate from 50 to 67 per cent, established a fixed amount for work-related expenses and eliminated the earlier practice of paying social security and income taxes for welfare recipients who obtained employment. All AFDC recipients were to be divided into two groups. Those able to work or acquire training were to be assigned to the Opportunities for Families Program administered by the Department of Labor. Those unable to work, including families with children under age 6, were to enrol in the Family Assistance Plan administered by the Department of Health, Education and Welfare. The Ways and Means Committee, distrustful of caseworkers' discretion, developed explicit formal criteria of employability in H.R. 1.

The service strategy was of doubtful cost-effectiveness when the cost of child care and work training were taken into account. It was

5. U.S., Congress, House, Committee on Ways and Means, *Family Assistance Act of 1970, Report,* on H.R. 16311, 91st Cong., 2d sess., House Report No. 904, 1970, pp. 9–10.

also of limited effectiveness since it sought to modify skill and motivation without paying attention to the level of unemployment and the structure of wages. It operated one-sidedly on the supply of labor but not on the demand for it. (Recognition of this anomaly led to the creation of some temporary jobs in the public sector, with the requirement that they be held only until permanent employment was located.) In all, 200,000 public employment jobs were to be created.[6]

The legislative outcome of H.R. 1 remains in doubt, but the Congress did graft President Nixon's "workfare" strategy onto existing welfare legislation (the Talmadge Amendments of 1971): during the crowded pre-Christmas schedule it added mandatory registration for Manpower Services Training and employment as a necessary qualification for receiving AFDC.

In June 1972 the Senate Finance Committee abandoned the incentive strategy altogether in favor of a federally guaranteed job program. Only mothers attending school full time or with children under age 6 would be exempt from the "must work" requirements. Thus 1.2 million of the estimated three million female heads of families would automatically be dropped from the welfare rolls and required to work. Three types of benefits would be provided. A federal employment corporation would be created to develop *guaranteed jobs* for those unable to find work in the private sector. The "make work" jobs would pay $1.50 per hour or $2,400 per year for 32 hours of work per week. Those working at the minimum wage would get a wage bonus equal to 10 per cent of the wages covered under social security, with a maximum of $400. Those working below the minimum wages would get a federal wage supplement equal to three-quarters of the difference between the actual wage paid and $2 an hour. In addition to requiring work, the bill penalizes states that fail to set up adequate birth control programs and authorizes $800 million a year for child care and day care centres for children of working mothers.[7]

---

6. These jobs, however, were not intended as permanent and regular. The circumstances of each job holder would be reviewed every six months to determine whether a more appropriate position could be secured for him or her on a regular payroll. This emphasis on the transitional nature of the job must be interpreted, in part, as a safeguard against the displacement of regular public workers from their jobs and a preventive against permanent makework assignments for relief recipients. These jobs, therefore, may be better regarded as social services.

7. U.S., Congress, Senate, Committee on Finance, *Social Security and Welfare Reform,* Summary of the Principal Provisions of H.R. 1 as Determined by the Committee on Finance, Committee Print, 92d Cong., 2d sess., June 13, 1972, p. 67.

Tracing these different legislative efforts to reduce the size and cost of the AFDC caseload over the past decade, a definite shift in emphasis is apparent, most dramatically shown in the Senate's version of H.R. 1. All three strategies of service, incentives and administrative control remain, but more stress now appears to be placed on administrative approaches. Some critics of the House version of H.R. 1 believe that the primary purpose of the bill is "not to improve the well-being and dignity of the beneficiary, but to so control and harass his behavior at every point that he . . . will be either coerced into conformity or driven from the program altogether."[8] But one does not need to accept so sharp a repudiation of the House bill to recognize that the income incentive strategy it proposes is weaker than that already accepted in the 1969 Social Security Amendments. And of course under the new Senate Finance Committee proposals, the individual's freedom to choose between the economic attractiveness of work and welfare is altogether forsaken. "If they're able to work, we're going to put them to work, and that's that," explained Senator Russell Long, chairman of the committee. Faith in services such as day care does continue, but a retreat from incentives is evident, and hence more reliance on administrative control seems certain. States have broadened administrative controls; almost half have permitted the value of welfare payments to erode through inflation and have increased the stigma associated with receiving welfare by raising the rejection rates of new applicants. (In New York City rejection rates increased from 20 per cent in September 1971 to 27 per cent in June 1972, and are expected to level off at 30 per cent.) It is implicitly assumed that the rolls decline as people avoid welfare to preserve their sense of self-dignity. A decline in the caseload for this reason, therefore, offers testimony that those on welfare could indeed have worked but chose not to. An administrative strategy is thus justified not on the grounds of punishing the poor but of weeding out ineligibles.

How can we account for the shifting priorities? Part of the answer is that the service and incentive strategies already adopted have had limited effects during any periods of high unemployment: witness the steady increase in the size of the waiting list of graduates of the Work Incentives program awaiting job placement. Both caseloads and costs have continued to rise. But the more fundamental difficulty is inherent in the pursuit of three related but incompatible aims: reducing poverty (a move that requires a high basic allowance), promoting work incentives (which call for low marginal tax rates), and containing total welfare costs. No one of these aims

8. *Welfare Law News,* I, 4 (November, 1971), Center on Social Welfare Policy and Law, New York.

can be forsaken. In addition, other objectives such as fiscal relief to states must also be taken into account, further compounding the multiplicity of competing and conflicting aims.

5   The Dilemmas of an Incentive Strategy

However persuasive the argument that an incentive strategy can alter the work behavior of recipients and thereby make welfare a self-liquidating program, the strategy leads in practice to intractable dilemmas that compel greater reliance on administrative solutions.

U.S. reformers viewed the negative income tax as an incentive strategy that could alter the work behavior of those on welfare. Their strategy was based on the assumption that people would work if they were economically better off and that this motive alone was sufficient to promote work-oriented behavior. The logic was simple and compelling.[9] Families that had no income would receive an allowance, the value of which would be based on family size alone, not on composition (i.e., children of different ages would not receive different benefits) or economies of scale so that larger families would receive proportionately less. As income from earnings rose, the level of benefits would decline but at a lower rate than the increase in earnings. Thus the family would be economically better off when it worked because it could keep some part of its earnings. The strategy assumed that "economic man" responds to the level of total income rather than the stability of income. The policy did not consider, for example, that lower welfare payments might still be more attractive than higher earnings because welfare income might be dependable and stable. Income from working may be less attractive if it is erratic. If welfare were as easy to get on as to get off, the stability of earnings would play a less important part in the choice between higher earnings and more stable welfare payments. The crucial factor in the strategy has been the rate at which benefits declined while income from other sources (especially income from employment) was augmented. Marginal tax rates are the key to unlock incentives. It was assumed that they could contribute to a higher level of total income, which would in principle be more important in governing work behavior than the stability of income.

The principal difficulty arises because a single goal is seldom pursued in isolation from other equally desirable goals. Public

---

9. Of course, people could not work if there were no jobs, so full employment had to be accepted as a critical assumption as well; nor could they work if they lacked skills, so training seemed important; nor could they work without supportive services to care for their children while they were not at home, so child care had to be provided. By itself the incentive strategy was incomplete. It had to be supplemented with services and jobs.

policy tried to provide strong incentives for the poor to work without discouraging those already on the job but it also hoped to secure a decent basic allowance for those on welfare, without raising total costs to insupportable heights. Coordinating the work-incentive features of the negative income tax with other autonomous means-tested programs in an attempt to avoid "notches" or discouragingly high marginal rates of taxation introduced both political and financial problems.

a   *The provision of strong incentives for the poor to work without discouraging those already on the job is a significant example of these problems.* The incentive strategy for welfare recipients becomes a disincentive for the working poor when the economic position of those who receive both welfare benefits and wages rises above the income of the working poor (after taxes and work-related expenses are taken into account). Many workers may, therefore, be better off leaving the job, waiting whatever transitional period is necessary to secure welfare, and then combining work and welfare. (In 1971, 5.6 per cent of all AFDC mothers worked part time and 8.3 per cent worked full time.) Indeed, the whole strategy of encouraging welfare recipients to work becomes self-defeating if it simultaneously encourages the working poor to seek welfare. It is therefore crucial to include the working poor. "It is the only way to prevent the low-wage worker from dropping into welfare," the secretary of the Department of Health, Education and Welfare explained to the Senate Finance Committee in 1970.[10]

The inclusion of the working poor, however, inflates the numbers of persons eligible for benefits and the total costs of the program. The Family Assistance Plan proposal set forth by the president in August, 1969, would have created a welfare population that included 14 per cent of all families. The more generous basic allowance and lower tax rate combination proposed by Senator Abraham Ribicoff in amending H.R. 1 would extend benefits to some 70 million persons and cost $42 billion when fully in effect by 1976. Such wide coverage was not intended but was the inevitable result of a system that provided both decent minimal benefits and work incentives. This dramatic increase in the scope of the program included many persons who would have received only a very small benefit. Hence, the estimate exaggerates the size of the program somewhat. Because the working poor had to be included in the program, they also benefited from the strong incentives designed for welfare families. The attempt to limit costs by excluding them from

---

10.   U.S., Congress, Senate, Committee on Finance, *Family Assistance Act of 1970, Hearings,* on H.R. 16311, 91st Cong., 2d sess., 1970, Part 1, p. 254.

automatic eligibility for Medicaid – a government shared-cost medical care plan for welfare recipients and the needy – and from other benefits created new inequities, since it left those on welfare better off than those at work. Consequently, the cost of including the working poor under the welfare reform in H.R. 1 constrained the program's ability to serve the twin aims of adequate allowances and incentives to work.

b *The maintenance of a decent basic allowance for those on welfare in combination with a low rate of taxation on earned income, without prohibitively raising the cost of the program is another difficulty.* In addition to the size of the eligible population, two factors drive up total costs of the welfare program:

(1) The level of the basic allowance that permits people with no income to avoid destitution, and

(2) The strength of the work-incentive provisions that enable people to retain a higher fraction of their earnings.

The reasons are straightforward. A higher basic allowance at any given marginal tax rate must increase the income cutoff point at which people are no longer eligible for benefits.[11] Because of the shape of the income distribution curve, each equal increase in the break-even point makes successively larger numbers of families eligible for benefits. Costs can be contained while increasing the basic allowance only if the marginal tax rate is raised. This is, after all, the logic of the present welfare system, which is directed toward relieving distress rather than encouraging work. It is possible to avoid the problem of work incentives by assuming that the program primarily serves those outside the labor force. This is the argument advanced by defenders of established practice. Welfare, they claim, aids those who have no work potential (the blind, disabled, aged, families with dependent children); hence, even a generous system has few work disincentive effects because these people cannot work even if they want to. Critics of the present system reject this argument by declaring that women who have children in school and are supported by AFDC should be at work.

Costs increase as the marginal tax rate is lowered essentially for the reasons just reviewed – more families can receive aid because the break-even point must, by the logic of the scheme, be raised. Costs could be contained if the basic allowance were lowered. The same break-even point of, say, $3,000 could be achieved with a basic allowance of $1,000; $1,500; $2,000 or $3,000. This would

---

11. The formula that expresses the fixed relationship between the basic allowance (A), the break-even level (B), and the tax rate (t), is $A = tB$. The basic allowance is the product of the tax rate and the break-even level.

be possible simply through alterations in the tax rate from one-third to one-half to two-thirds or, finally, to 100 per cent. The cost of each of the schemes would be about the same, but there would be a trade-off between poverty reduction and work incentives. The combination of a low tax rate and a low allowance is more work-oriented than a higher allowance and a higher tax rate. In other words, cost-consciousness may make it attractive to sacrifice the objective of reducing poverty. A much lower basic allowance would be politically unacceptable because it would make many of those currently on welfare worse off. But if one kept the basic allowance high enough to approach present welfare benefit levels, total costs would rise sharply because costs are especially sensitive to changes in the tax rate. The crucial factor is the break-even point, and lower tax rates raise that point. "A plan with a 30 per cent tax rate and a $1,600 basic allowance, for example, is somewhat more costly than a plan with a 70 per cent tax rate and a $2,800 basic allowance."[12] This occurs because, in the first example, the cutoff point is $5,300, and in the latter case it is only $4,000.

Consider a less hypothetical example. From the outset the administration was under great pressure from liberals to raise the basic allowance, always defined as the cash payment with zero income. After all no family can live on $1,600 a year. (Moynihan explains that this situation never exists for the working poor who by definition have earnings; moreover, under the Family Assistance Plan state supplements have been required.[13]) Still the argument was persuasive and in 1971 the basic level was raised to $2,400 a year for a family of four through the combined value of cash payments and food stamp payments. If the original tax rate of 50 per cent were continued, a $2,400 basic allowance combined with a $720 exemption would allow the family to have an income from earnings of $5,520 before becoming ineligible for welfare. This contrasts with the $3,920 cutoff point under the original Family Assistance Plan. Such a scheme would have a striking effect on the scope and cost of the program because over 20 per cent of the 52 million U.S. families have incomes of less than $5,520. An increased allowance of $800 (from $1,600 to $2,400) combined with retention of the 50 per cent tax rate would triple the cost. The work incentive objective had to be diminished, however, in face of political pressure to reduce poverty, and the tax rate was reluctantly raised to 67 per

---

12. Jodie T. Allen, "A Funny Thing Happened on the Way to Reform" (Washington, D.C.: The Urban Institute, October 15, 1971), p. 13.
13. Moynihan, "The Politics of a Guaranteed Income," forthcoming, p. 303.

cent. The perverse effect of this change was to make the work incentive reforms in H.R. 1 less generous than those already law under the 1967 amendments (even with the same 67 per cent tax rate). The disregard and work expenses provisions of the 1967 law accounted for most of the difference: under this earlier legislation, $30 and one-third of the remaining gross monthly salary were disregarded and work expenses reimbursed as incurred. Work incentives and an adequate minimum allowance can be secured only if higher costs and a larger welfare population are accepted.

Many congressmen who do accept the objectives of relieving distress and encouraging work-oriented behavior through economic incentives are reluctant, however, to accept the consequences such policies require. In the Senate Finance Committee debate on H.R. 1, Senator Carl T. Curtis pointed out that if the basic allowance were gradually raised from a $3,000 guarantee level to $4,000, a 60 per cent tax rate applied, recipients exempted from social security contributions and income tax and the basic allowance raised to control inflation, one-third of the United States population would be on welfare by 1977. The Curtis dilemma is inherent in the arithmetic of the negative income tax. It cannot be avoided within that context. It does not appear politically feasible to accept so large a proportion of the total population on "welfare," to forsake the objective of reducing poverty or to abandon the goal of offering quasi-market rewards for work effort. It follows, therefore, that the only other approach available is increased reliance on administrative devices to encourage the poor to work. Bureaucratic solutions are thus substituted for the incentive of a low tax rate.

Some analysts recognize that *compulsory* work incentives have been proposed in H.R. 1 under the rhetoric of strong *voluntary* work incentives. Jodie Allen, a research associate at the Urban Institute who is still reluctant to "return to the old welfare strategy of reliance on bureaucratic compulsion to stimulate work," favors a lowering of the basic allowance. Allen compares three plans at different guarantee levels ranging from $2,800 to $3,200 and concludes that "since the great majority of *working poor families* have more than $2,000 of earned income they will generally be better off with a program with a relatively low basic guarantee and a low marginal tax than under a program with a higher basic guarantee and a high marginal tax."[14] But even the plan with the lowest allowances would cost $20–30 billion, depending on disregards and the treatment of social security and income taxes. Given these cost constraints, it is clear why compulsion becomes a substitute for the incentive of a low tax rate.

---

14. Jodie T. Allen, "Alternatives to H.R. 1" (Washington, D.C.: Urban Institute, n.d.), p. 3.

c *The coordination of work incentive features of the negative income tax with other means-tested programs is a third difficulty.* This problem has its origin in administrative arrangements that treat welfare in isolation from the cluster of means-tested programs of which it is a part. The difficulty of integrating all means-tested programs creates two stubborn dilemmas: a "notch" problem and a high cumulative marginal tax rate. These difficulties undermine the work-incentive approach. A notch occurs when a family becomes economically worse off as its earnings increase (a situation which arises when the family is subjected to more than a 100 per cent tax rate). Means-tested benefits are equivalent to a tax on income and the loss of these benefits affects a person's net resources. High cumulative tax rates that fall short of a 100 per cent tax result from a similar process – the imposition of taxes from several different social programs as earned income rises. A welfare family might in principle receive, in addition to welfare payments, a variety of goods and services that can be converted to a cash equivalent value. These include housing, child care, medical care and food. Moreover, under the present legislation, welfare recipients are reimbursed for the social security and income taxes they contribute. In addition, families that are not at work do not incur expenses for such items as transportation to the job, eating meals away from home and extra clothing.

The Senate Finance Committee, in its 1971 review of the proposal for welfare reform submitted by the president, was severely critical of the serious notch problem created by the program. The Family Assistance Plan called for a $1,600 guarantee and 50 per cent tax rate but it still left situations in which people were actually worse off economically if they went out to work.

In the revised version of the plan (which the Senate Finance Committee rejected) and in the most recent version of H.R. 1, the administration tried to reduce the notch problem by cashing out the value of food stamps – increasing the basic allowance from $1,600 to $2,400 – and altering Medicaid eligibility and benefits. However, it could not at the same time lower the marginal tax rate sufficiently to make it economically worthwhile for welfare recipients to seek employment. Secretary Elliot Richardson of HEW made the choice explicit in his testimony before the House Ways and Means Committee:

The Committee will have to decide whether it places the higher premium on the elimination of any cutoff point at which an individual's income drops, in order to have a steeper incentive line before that, or, to do what we have recommended, which is to flatten the incentive line in order to eliminate the notches.[15]

---

15. U.S., Congress, Senate, Committee on Finance, *Family Assistance Act of 1970, Hearings,* on H.R. 16311, 91st Cong., 2d sess., 1970, Part 2, p. 301.

The revisions created new problems. If the basic allowance were raised to $2,400, a 50 per cent tax rate would yield a break-even point of $5,520, and this would be very costly, because so many more families earn incomes at or below this level than the initially proposed break-even point of $3,700. Efforts to solve the notch problem created cost difficulties. H.R. 1 tried to resolve this by raising the tax rate from 50 per cent to 67 per cent, setting a firm maximum on work-related expenses and excluding social security and income taxes from reimbursable work expenses. The changes lowered costs and decreased incentives.

The proposed new medical deduction scheme would present a second difficulty. Recipients with some other income would receive less than the full Medicaid subsidy, although no one would suddenly lose full medical benefits. However, this scheme would leave welfare recipients less well off than they are under the current Medicaid program, which provides full medical care until family earnings make them ineligible for welfare. One-third of any earnings a family retained above $720 would become the amount deductible for Medicaid, i.e., the amount of medical costs per year a family would have to cover before the federal government paid the rest. Assume a family had a medical bill of $600. Such a family would not be entitled to any subsidized medical care until its earnings equaled or exceeded $2,520. Thus the proposed scheme would have the unintended effect of lowering the economic well-being of families with common medical care costs.

The various efforts to resolve the notch problem, therefore, did not transform welfare into a work incentive system. If anything, the new proposals in H.R. 1 have even fewer work incentives than the 1967 legislation. Hausman shows that, when work-related expenses are taken into account and combined with the value of other means-tested programs, under existing legislation the marginal tax rates for a family headed by a woman range from 30 to 66 per cent in selected cities such as Washington and Chicago.[16]

6 Summary

The argument I have set out interprets the development of welfare policy during the past decade as a series of trade-offs among conflicting aims. There were three such aims: to contain the growth of costs and eventually reduce them; to relieve economic distress by providing a basic guarantee that approached the poverty line; and to promote work-oriented behavior among welfare recipients. Given

---

16. Leonard Hausman, "Cumulative Tax Rates and the Process of Welfare Reform," an unpublished paper prepared for the U.S. Congress, Joint Economic Committee, 92d Cong., 2d sess., June 1972.

the unflagging commitment to make economically dependent family heads financially self-sufficient and thereby reduce the cost and scope of welfare, given the ineffectiveness of services, and given the high cost of economic incentives, it became necessary to place greater reliance on administrative approaches to induce people to work.

Still, this interpretation of events may be vulnerable. The legislative history of welfare reform requires a more complicated analysis. It can be argued that it is somewhat arbitrary to isolate three competing objectives and then assign priority to one. A close reading of legislative hearings makes it clear that Congress has also been concerned with fiscal relief to the states and cities; with raising incomes of the poorest Southern families and the working poor, with reducing family breakup, which a system of payments to female heads is presumed to encourage; and with decreasing regional migration, which may be promoted by sharp differentials in benefit levels. Even this list of inequities, inadequacies, disincentives and inefficiencies is incomplete. There has also been on the one hand anxiety about ineligibility as a result of fraud and deception and, on the other, dismay over discourtesies to welfare claimants and a profound distrust of the size, complexity, and cost of the welfare bureaucracy. Which of these multiple aims merit emphasis?

The task of sorting out objectives is made more difficult because of the lack of candor in discussions of welfare reform. The emphasis on work-oriented behavior is regarded as disingenuous by at least some individuals in the administration, in Congress and among those doing the staff work for both. In private discussions they recognize the difficulties of achieving so ambitious an aim at a low cost and in a short time-period, especially during a period of rising unemployment. The insistence on this objective can be better understood as originating in political rather than rational considerations and, therefore, to isolate this aim and assign it priority over other purposes is misleading. Finally, the same legislative provision could appeal to quite different constituencies and to very different purposes.

Why was inclusion of the working poor regarded as crucial? I have argued the case on the grounds of inequities and the associated work-disincentive effects but other motives can readily be discerned. It was assumed that a program excluding male heads might affect family structure because it offered an incentive for family breakup. In addition, the working poor were primarily white and the welfare poor largely black; thus, for tactical reasons the acceptability of the program to the public might change if the composition of its recipients was modified. However, it was feared that if the working poor were included as welfare recipients, they might forsake the demeaning work they now accepted in favor of benefits without work unless a severe work test were introduced. The "no suitable work" clause in the Family Assistance Plan prevents any recipient from rejecting a "suitable" job but suitability was not defined in terms of past labor-force attachment. It was a restrictive provision that arose less from anxiety over costs than from fear that a "handout" program would threaten the work ethic. Thus, the turn to a more administrative approach can be interpreted not only as the outcome of the dilemma posed by the high costs of low tax rates, adequate grants and extensive coverage but also as the result of more diffuse public attitudes toward both the poor and the work ethic.

An alternative approach to welfare reform was proposed (but since withdrawn) by Senator George McGovern. He redefined the issue not as welfare reform but as tax reform and income redistribution and called for a per capita tax credit of $1,000 a year for every man, woman and child living in the United States regardless of his income or wealth. (This might also be age-graded.) The scheme was not designed as a strategy to reduce welfare or promote work incentives but rather to redistribute income. McGovern's proposal also aimed at combatting poverty and it avoided work disincentives since the tax rate would be set at about 33 per cent. The take-up problem would also be by-passed since receipt of benefits would be automatic. A large visible welfare population would be avoided because the annual grant would be paid to everyone and then recovered through the tax system from those above the tax threshold. Most citizens would still experience some income gain. For example, "if the break-even income for a family of four were set at $12,000, about 20 per cent of federal taxpayers would experience a [net] tax increase while about 80 per cent would keep all or part of the grant."[17]

A family of four that earned $8,500 would keep half its grant. Basically the plan would shift $14 billion from those with incomes above $4,000 to those below that level and $29 billion from those with incomes of $12,000 or more to those with incomes ranging from $4,000 to $12,000.

The scheme would also fold the present $750 personal exemption and the standard deduction of $2,000 into the tax credit reform. A larger tax base would reduce the average tax rate required to cover the costs of the program. Actual cost would depend on whether the break-even point were set at $12,000 or $8,500. These details had not been worked out. The McGovern proposals are strikingly similar in principle to those of the Heath government in

---

17. George McGovern, "How the Economy Should Be Changed," *New York Review of Books*, XVIII (May 4, 1972), 10.

Britain. They were inspired not by anxiety about work incentives and welfare costs but by the diffuse and very American suspicion that money interests are running the country and working counter to the best interests of the average man. Populism is thus the source of the reawakened interest in income redistribution and tax reform in the United States.[18]

The British Experience

The British interest in a reverse income tax, in common with the U.S. interest, has been inspired by many motives. It does not appear, however, to have involved any primary concern for altering work behavior among recipients of supplementary benefits (public assistance) by using income-conditioned benefits as an incentive strategy. Rather, a new principle for distributing public funds has been sought. The hope has been that tax burdens and total government expenditures could in the long run be restrained through increased reliance on selective policies. Those who could afford to pay more for the use of social services should accept higher user charges, while the poor, selectively, should receive benefits based on a test of income. The underlying rationale has been that scarce resources should be concentrated on those in greatest need.

The strategy has therefore called for the gradual reduction of universal and general subsidies. With the exception of the Family Income Supplements program, all the income-conditional benefits existed under the Labour government. The present Conservative government has, in general, like its predecessor, improved the benefits while increasing charges. For example, the cost of school meals, which had been subsidized as part of a broader food subsidy, has increased. Similarly, in a major pending reform of housing finances, the Conservative government plans to increase rents in public housing to a level approaching their market value. Charges in National Health Service programs for prescriptions, dental and optical costs have also been increased. This has produced a strain on the budgets of lower income families. Therefore, special means-tested benefits in the form of free school meals, rent rebates or National Health Service exemptions became necessary to relieve the hardships accompanying price increases in school meals, rent and medical care.

In addition to its strategy of reducing general subsidies and relying on more differentiated means tests for in-kind programs, the government has sought a general cash supplement to aid the working poor, a group that public policy had neglected – but not altogether. The Labour government introduced a way to aid the work-

---

18. Leonard Silk, "An Analysis of McGovern's Populism," *New York Times,* May 10, 1965, p. 65.

ing poor by integrating more closely the new increases in direct expenditures for family allowances with a reduction in the value of tax exemptions for children. This system was known as *claw-back*.

1 From Claw-Back to Family Income Supplements

It may be useful to review briefly the operation of claw-back, because the means-tested Family Income Supplements bill emerged as a result of its limitations. Claw-back was introduced in 1968 as a way to concentrate additional benefits in family allowances selectively among the poor. It operated so that the standard-rate taxpayer, that is, a family paying 32 per cent of its taxable income in taxes, received virtually no benefit from the increases. This included most of the British tax-paying public. This object was accomplished by offsetting the 50 pence increase in family allowances with an equivalent reduction in the total personal tax allowance. In this way the increase benefited in full those below the tax threshold and also, at least in part, those paying taxes below the 32 per cent level. The 1968 increase of £183 million in gross expenditures concentrated only £47 million on those families paying below the standard tax rate. Much of the rest was recouped through taxation; in addition, raising the benefit levels of families also lowered the threshold at which income was taxed, since family allowances were subject to income taxes.

By 1970 when the Conservatives took office, the changes introduced in the tax structure virtually eliminated the range within which the claw-back could concentrate additional resources among the poor. The old standard rate was 8 shillings and 3 pence in the pound, or 41.25 per cent on unearned income. However, with two-ninths earned income relief, the rate became 6 shillings and 5 pence or roughly 32 per cent. The reduced rates of taxation (taxes below 32 per cent) were abolished in 1970 when Labour was still responsible for the budget. In 1971 the Tories reduced the standard rate to 38.75 per cent, or an effective rate of 30 per cent on earned income. (In 1973–74 there will be a single rate of 30 per cent on both earned and unearned income and a surcharge on unearned income over a certain level.) At the same time, the value of personal tax allowances was increased, but by an amount smaller than the income level over which the reduced tax rate had been payable. As a result of abolishing the reduced standard tax rate and increasing personal tax allowances, the income level at which the standard rate of tax became payable was lowered.

Claw-back also created a double reduction in the tax threshold: it increased taxable income (family allowances are taxable) and reduced tax allowances, further lowering the point at which families started to pay tax. The effect of these changes and the net impact of claw-back dramatically limited its further use as a means of selectively concentrating further increases in family allowances among the poor. Consider this example: "A man with two children was, in 1970, paying the standard rate of tax with earnings of just over 16 pounds a week compared with nearly 20 pounds two years earlier, and yet, under claw-back, neither would benefit from a family allowance increase."[19]

Inflation, wage expansion and a rapid rise in the value of supplementary benefits, which exceeded net average wage levels, led British tax policies to move inadvertently from a progressive tax system to a regressive one. Above a certain threshold most of the population, including the poor, pay 30 per cent of their income in taxes. A surtax is only imposed on earnings above £5,000, affecting just a small proportion of the population.

These characteristics of the British tax system had fateful consequences for the further use of claw-back and for increased reliance on means testing. When the Conservatives came into power, the anomalies of the British tax system became evident. Inflation and the general rise in incomes, the treatment of family allowances as taxable income and the introduction of claw-back had all contributed to a substantial reduction in the tax threshold. Furthermore, the government found it politically difficult to avoid the problem of poverty among children. Reform on the left favors universal programs or, more precisely, benefits that are automatically distributed and do not isolate the poor, subjecting them to differential treatment because of their income status. Specifically, the Child Poverty Action Group supported a tax-free family allowance with substantially higher benefits and the elimination of child tax exemptions to cover part of the costs. A modified version of the action group proposal was accepted by the Conservatives before the 1970 election. However, once in office the government rejected this route because it would not work. The only other viable alternative considered was a negative income tax; and this was essentially the course the Conservative government followed, at least on a small scale, when it developed a family income supplements approach to child poverty.

2 *The Family Income Supplements Program*

The program is designed for families with (eligible) children where the head of the family works full time (30 hours or more per week) and the family has an income below the supplementary benefit line. Unlike a positive tax system under which registration is compul-

---

19. David Barker, "The Family Income Supplement," *New Society*, No. 462 (August 5, 1971), p. 241.

sory,[20] the negative tax system is voluntary: a family must apply if it is to receive benefits. The Family Income Supplements program is based on the principle that benefits be paid only to the fully employed and thus departs from most insurance and welfare programs which typically pay benefits only when work is interrupted. In Britain, since the end of the Speenhamland system of 1795, full-time employees have been unable to receive welfare benefits (Supplementary Benefits).

The Family Income Supplements program is a form of negative income taxation. The critical issue was to set the cutoff point for the receipt of benefits. Viewed as a negative income tax, the logical choice was that point where, as the prime minister explained, an individual starts "to stand on his own two feet," i.e., paying taxes rather than receiving subsidies.

If the Family Income Supplements program was seen as public assistance for the poor, the logical cutoff point would be the same as for supplementary benefits. As it happened, the two points were roughly the same and it is uncertain on which principle the figure was chosen.

Once the cutoff point was decided, the other important question was to establish a tax rate at which benefits decline as incomes rise. Possibly because an issue had already been raised about implicit marginal tax rates and their disincentive effects, a 50 per cent tax rate was agreed on. A maximum benefit was also set to limit costs. However, with the imposition of a maximum benefit, a 50 per cent tax rate and a cutoff point at the tax threshold, it was no longer possible to meet the whole income deficit families required. Clearly the only way to meet full need while retaining the income threshold would have been to accept a 100 per cent tax rate. Because of the potential effect on work incentives, this approach was rejected.

In the Family Income Supplements Act (December, 1970) the "prescribed amount" for a one-child family was set at £15, with £2 for each additional child. The rates set by the legislation were never put into effect: by amending regulations the amounts were increased in April, 1971, to £18 and raised again in March, 1972, to £20 for a one-child family. Throughout all these changes all additional children have received an added £2. Those whose earnings fall below this figure have half the difference made up by the state to a maximum initially set at £3 but raised to £4 per week

---

20. To introduce compulsion requires a much closer integration between the tax and benefit systems. For example, FIS requires a statement and a signature of both husband and wife on their combined income. The tax system on the other hand deals separately with husband and wife: if both are earning, they normally submit one tax statement but can be assessed separately if they wish. These returns could not easily be brought together, at least in the short run.

in 1971 and £5 in 1972. The minimum benefit was set at 20 pence. Since benefits go only to families in which the head is employed full time, those receiving supplementary benefits are ineligible. Families headed by single parents and by couples are treated alike.

The system is nationally administered and designed to simplify the process of eligibility review. Earnings are assessed on the basis of the five weeks preceeding the claim. Once an award is made, it continues for six months regardless of any changes in the composition of the family or any variation in income during this period. In determining eligibility, the income of children, capital assets and in-kind benefits can be taken into account but in the early stages, at least, these sources of income have not been scrutinized. The procedure for obtaining a grant has been described by a chief civil servant. The claimant:

must first get a claim form from a post office or a local social security office, unless . . . some . . . agency has supplied it unasked. With it he gets a franked envelope. He fills in the form, attaches – ideally – five weekly pay slips and posts it to Blackpool. (Couples are asked to fill in the forms together and both are asked to sign.) If he has not claimed before and if the family is not drawing family allowance [as in the case of a 1-child family] he should also enclose his children's birth certificates. If he has no pay slips he need not wait to send in his claim. In such cases the Department of Health and Social Security will send him a form to pass on to his employer – all correspondence with employers is conducted via the claimant – and if the claim succeeds he will be paid benefits from the date of his claim. A family in receipt of FIS also acquires a passport which entitles him to other means-tested benefits such as free prescription charges, free dental services, free school meals, etc.[21]

3 Problems of Take-Up and Work Disincentives

The Family Income Supplements program faces two intractable problems: take-up and work disincentives. We shall briefly consider each problem, the kinds of administrative action taken to reduce them, and the new problems and opportunities created by these efforts.

a The problem of take-up

Whereas U.S. public policy seems almost obsessed with the problem of how to reduce the size of the welfare caseload, British policy is preoccupied with how to reach the universe of eligible recipients. A serious indictment of a means-tested program designed to aug-

---

21. John Stacpoole, "Running FIS," *New Society*, No. 485 (January 13, 1972), p. 65.

ment the income of the poor is that it fails to reach those for whom it was designed. Most critics of the Family Income Supplements program have argued that there is something inherent in the means-test process (whereby a potential recipient must apply for an individual means test for benefits) which generates low take-up. These critics have argued that at best a means-tested program is able to reach only half of those for whom it is intended and it is possible that the remaining half includes those in greatest need. The criticism is taken seriously by the government. The secretary of state for social services had estimated the cost of the program on the assumption that it would reach 85 per cent of its eligible population, or an estimated 100,000 claimants among working families. This declaration made the issue of take-up a sensitive political concern. The success of the program seemed to depend on the government's ability to reach the goal of 85 per cent participation.

What, in fact, happened? At the early stages the take-up was discouragingly low. Between May 3 and June 22, 1972, there were only 12,284 successful claims. With a revised estimate of about 165,000 families (140,000 working families and 25,000 wage-stopped[22] families) as the potential universe of eligible beneficiaries, the results were discouraging. The prime minister himself was involved in the issue of low take-up through questions raised in the House, and the civil servants were informed that the campaign must not fail. £60,000 had already been spent during the first weeks of the campaign to publicize FIS. With backing from the prime minister, an additional £250,000 was made available in the weeks before the program became operational on August 3. By December 1971, £310,000 had been spent on the campaign, an amount equal to about 5 per cent of total yearly money payments for supplementary benefits. By the end of 1971, only 93,000 claimants were receiving benefits and only 68,000 of these represented successful applications. The other 25,000 were wage-stopped families, who do not have to apply but automatically benefit indirectly from Family Income Supplements, since a "national FIS" reduced or eliminated the wage-stopped reduction of those on supplementary benefits. This number was still well short of the estimated 165,000 eligible families.[23] However, take-up varied with the value of the benefits. The average weekly payment was £1.72. About 75 per cent of eligible families with claims of £2 or more per week took their benefits. The government claimed that most of

---

22. See J. I. Clark, *Recent Trends and Developments in Guaranteed Income*, footnote 2, p. 283.
23. Great Britain, Parliament, *Parliamentary Debates* (House of Commons), 5th ser., Vol. 828 (21 Dec., 1971), col. 1293-94.

those who failed to apply were marginal cases who could hope to receive only a small amount.

Why did so few families come forward in the early stages of the campaign? Several speculations can be advanced. First, it is always difficult to make the public aware of a new product – cigarette commercials spend substantially more on advertising a new product – and it seems unreasonable to expect quick results. Low-income families will learn about these benefits essentially through word of mouth. If individuals judge the value of benefits to be substantial and fairly easy to secure and do not attach any stigma to the application process, in time this informal system will take hold and applications rise. Of course, quite different interpretations might be placed on the eligibility procedures by the clients themselves. For example, both the husband and wife have to sign the form and declare their income. In a period of wage inflation, husbands may receive salary increases and not inform their wives; hence they may be reluctant to reveal the increases if the value of the benefits they are to receive is only modest.

A second possibility is that the low take-up is largely an artifact based on a mistaken estimate of the universe of eligibles. Government statisticians may have overestimated the number of families eligible for FIS. A period of rapid wage inflation will also help erode the size of the eligible group. Many low-income families hold several jobs and enjoy overtime pay and would thus not qualify for benefits. Estimates of moonlighting and overtime work are not readily available. Moreover, in an era when most people pay income taxes, it is to be expected that there will be some tax dodging by those with low incomes to complement the more subtle forms of tax evasion at the upper-income level. Means tests for benefits might thus be construed as a way to trap tax evaders. In any case, the primary beneficiaries of FIS would appear to be households headed by women who work full time. According to this interpretation FIS will fizzle, a victim of miscalculation.

Third, the low take-up figures may suggest intrinsic limitations to income-tested programs where benefits are not automatically distributed but require some special application. According to this argument, even the most efficient means-tested program for the poor will reach at best only two-thirds of its eligible population. The low take-up figures can be interpreted as evidence of the failure of a non-automatic, selective system (where recipients must apply for grants) as a general strategy for improving the economic well-being of the low-wage population.

The evaluation of take-up in means-tested programs is bedeviled by technical problems – there is no firm way of knowing precisely the universe of eligible persons. Thus the debate remains inconclusive. It is worth noting also that small increases in the definition of income eligibility can significantly alter the universe of eligibles. Conversely, in a period of inflation the failure to maintain the income levels of eligibility must lead to a gradual decline in the number of eligibles. This suggests that means testing may be an acceptable form of distribution when public attention is riveted on it as a critical issue of the day. But when attention shifts to other areas of public concern, the level of eligibility may drift downward and the universe of eligibles automatically decrease. An assessment of the merits of means testing must also take account of these political factors which raise or lower eligibility levels.

The government remained anxious about the take-up levels. It was concerned about both the size of the eligible group and the level of benefits. As we have seen, between the time FIS was announced (October, 1970) and the time it was introduced in August, 1971, the prescribed amount was raised; shortly after the program went into effect, the government decided again to raise the prescribed amount and increase the maximum grant. These increases expanded the number of eligibles and raised the average value of the grant. Under the most recent regulations, the prescribed amount for a family with three children would be £24. A family with a total income of £16 could therefore receive a payment of £4 per week – that is, half the difference between its income and the prescribed amount. This is a substantial amount, equal to 25 per cent of the original family income. But the move to reduce the take-up problem created yet another anomaly. Some families cross the income tax threshold before they stop receiving FIS payments, although the numbers who suffer this double misfortune are not known. The government was giving benefits on the one hand and extracting taxes on the other.

b *The problems of work disincentives: notches and the high rate of taxation*

An overlap between the positive taxation system and the social benefits system posed awkward problems. Before April, 1972, the tax threshold for a family with three children was just over £21. When a family begins to pay taxes, it is faced with an initial marginal tax rate of 30 per cent on its additional earnings. Moreover, the benefits from certain other means-tested programs fall or vanish entirely as incomes continue to rise. As the income of a family with three children rises from £21 per week to £24 (an amount equal to about three-fourths that of average male industrial earnings), it passes through bands of income within which the sum of the new tax liabilities and the foregone benefits exceeds its increased income (see table 2, p. 206). The family is thus economically worse off despite its larger earnings. This is the "notch" problem. A less drastic but more general difficulty is posed by the very high rate at which families are initially taxed as earnings increase.

Tony Lynes, the first secretary of the Child Poverty Action Group, set out to demonstrate the effect that taxes and the loss of selected benefits had on families with income below average earnings. He selected Birmingham for his example – a city that has already put into effect an extensive and unique rent rebate scheme for private tenants.[24] As a family in Birmingham increases its earnings from £13 to £14, total money income rises by only 28 pence. Thus, 72 per cent of the increase has been "taxed" away through the combination of taxes paid out and benefits lost. Subsequent £1 increases in earnings are taxed at rates of 73, 73, 84, 84, 184, and then 121 per cent. (A notch occurs when the percentage exceeds 100 per cent.) The high marginal tax rate in Birmingham is in part due to the structure of the new rent rebate scheme. Tenants are eligible for rebates only within a narrow income range and benefits are therefore withdrawn rapidly as income increases.[25]

Lynes' point was well taken even if the example was somewhat atypical for Britain. A family at work who received only the family income supplement was subject to an 85 per cent tax rate – 30 per cent from income taxes, about 5 per cent from national insurance contributions and 50 per cent from the Family Income Supplements program. If the family received other means-tested programs, the marginal tax rates were further increased. Although not generally perceived as such, means-tested benefits created a tax on added earnings; when added to income and social security taxes this yielded disturbingly high tax rates for the poor.

Of course, the government was aware of the tax inequities and the presumed work disincentives presented by the combination of income taxation and means testing. Efforts were made to lower the marginal tax in several ways by: setting a low 17 per cent rate for new means tests such as rent rebates; staggering the income cutoff points among different existing programs;[26] making families above

---

24. Tony Lynes, "Family Income Super Tax," *New Society,* No. 449 (May 6, 1971), pp. 770–71; and Barker, "The Family Income Supplement," pp. 240–42.

25. The rent rebate scheme was based on an income "allowance" of £17 a week for a couple with two or more children. The rent payable is one-ninth of income below the level of the "allowances" plus two-thirds of any income above that level minus 12½ pence for each child. This is subject to a maximum rebate of the full rent minus 50 pence. This scheme alone generated a withdrawal rate of 66.6 per cent above the income level of £18 a week. This family would have needed earnings of about £19 a week to provide them with the same purchasing power that they would have had if they had been drawing supplementary benefits, i.e., about £16.60 a week including rent.

26. There appears to be pressure among several specialized bureaucracies

the tax threshold ineligible for benefits; and, above all, raising the tax threshold (by raising the child tax allowance and then the personal tax allowance for single persons and married couples). Table 1 shows that the tax threshold has been raised quite considerably since April, 1972, substantially reducing the marginal tax rate for families eligible for income supplements and eliminating it for families with three or more children.

The rate at which several benefits are lost and increased taxes paid is presumed to affect work behavior. But how serious, in reality, are the work disincentive effects of the high tax rates? The answer must depend on how many families receive more than one means-tested program, on whether families know about the level of the cumulative marginal tax and on whether this knowledge affects their work behavior. Little is known about each of these questions. Only a *prima facie* argument can therefore be developed.[27] It is, however, widely presumed that if people were economically worse off after an increase in earnings (notch) or no better off (high marginal tax rates), they would act as rational men choosing benefits over wage increases. In effect, they would, if free to choose, select the level of earnings that maximized total money income (after taxes and benefits).

The political left has not hesitated to include this issue as part of their broader attack on means-tested programs. For example, Michael Meacher, Labour backbencher, criticized the government white paper proposing a national rent rebate scheme to provide an income-conditioned housing allowance on the grounds that it had inherent disincentive effects. He argued that "if the Tories are right, and incentives matter, how can they justify measures that sharply reduce the incentives for the poor to work harder and earn more?"[28] A *Times* report comments: "It is . . . quaint to find the radical left complaining of state aid draining the poor of an incentive to help themselves."[29] It is doubtful that the Child Poverty Action Group is seriously worried that work behavior might be altered. But the trade unions are anxious in view of the possible effect on wage claims. The unions recognize the effect higher benefits have on marginal tax rates and oppose these rates on grounds of equity. On the

to raise the cutoff points and widen eligibility to include middle-income groups. Thus, the staggering of the cutoff points may be a logical solution to notches and high cumulative tax rates but is politically difficult to achieve.
27. New studies are already under way. See C. U. Brown, "Negative Income Tax and the Incentive to Work," *New Society*, No. 505 (June 1, 1972), pp. 461–63.
28. Nigel Lawson, "An Achilles Heel about the Poor," *The Times* (London), July 29, 1971, p. 25.
29. Lawson, "An Achilles Heel about the Poor," p. 25.

Table 1

Family Income Supplements and Taxation – The Overlap

Household	Approximate tax threshold (assumed equal weekly household income)		Income cutoff level under FIS		Weekly FIS benefits	
	Before April 1972	After April 1972	Before April 1972	After April 1972	Before April 1972	After April 1972
Married couple and						
1 child	£15.70	£18.50	£18	£20	£1.15	£0.80
2 children	18.79	21.50	20	22	0.60	0.30
3 children	21.88	24.50	22	24		
4 children	24.79	27.50	24	26		

Source: An adaptation of a table prepared by A. J. Harrison, "Low Pay and Child Poverty," Discussion Paper (London: Child Poverty Action Group, 1972), p. 9.

other hand, it may be argued that the average worker in Britain works long hours, and if these social benefits could bring him the same income while working fewer hours, overall utility would be improved. Shorter hours might also be offset by lower unemployment, so that overall production would not decline. When a worker has the opportunity to change his occupational status rather than the number of hours worked, one might expect him to prefer the better job since it offers status, improved working conditions and other factors that accompany upward mobility, even if high marginal tax rates leave him without added earning power. Moreover, continued eligibility for family income supplements depends on the recipient maintaining full-time employment (defined as 30 hours a week). Since benefits go only to the working poor this makes work more, not less, attractive. Thus FIS benefits create a positive incentive for a family head to continue to work. The head of a working family who receives a quarter of his earnings from FIS may have an economic motive for working fewer hours but not one for quitting work altogether. In other ways the Family Income Supplements program has a neutral effect on the decision to hold a job. The wage-stop rule under the Supplementary Benefits program requires benefits from welfare not to exceed potential income from earnings. But income from earnings now includes benefits added through FIS whether or not these were actually acquired. Thus the working poor receive the value of family income supplements whether they are at work or on welfare.

While it is, in principle, possible for low-skilled workers with large families to be as well off on welfare as in full-time employment, stringent administrative devices encourage the work-shy to seek jobs. These administrative rules were in effect long before the Family Income Supplements program was introduced.

Consider the administrative devices long established by the Supplementary Benefits Commission to discourage voluntary unemployment and to encourage or coerce those on welfare to seek work. For example, if the Supplementary Benefits Commission feels that a man has left his job without a good reason, the commission disallows part of his benefit for six weeks. With growing unemployment, use of this procedure has increased. In addition, the unemployed on welfare are required to register weekly as available for work, are subjected to the wage-stop, interviewed periodically by employment counsellors to determine the reasons for their failure to work, and liable to imprisonment for being work-shy. The motives that inspired these restrictive rules in the Supplementary Benefits program are varied. It is not necessary to view all work tests as punitive. Consideration of equity, for example, may have played some role; but regardless of motive, the four-week and three-month rules were introduced in 1966 under the Labour government.[30] Under these rules unskilled, physically and mentally fit single men under age 45, living in areas with low rates of unemployment, are advised when they receive benefits that they will have to reapply if they do not secure work at the end of four weeks. Skilled men and those with dependents are given three months, at which time they receive a four-week warning. If a man renews his request, the Supplementary Benefits Commission will review his efforts to get work as part of the procedure for rewarding benefits. The claimant must prove he has met the "genuinely seeking work" requirements. Perhaps these rules serve as a trade-off between restriction and adequacy when adequacy is defined as a narrow gap between net earnings and maximum benefits, but this would not apply to single men who are subject to the four-week rule.

4   Inequities and Radical Reform

It is difficult to assess the cumulative impact of various tax rates from income and social benefits on the incentives of low-wage earners. There is little evidence on the multiple usage of services; the linkage between knowledge of high taxation and actual work behavior is uncertain; and the effectiveness of established work-test policies to discourage workers from dropping out of the labor force is untested. Perhaps uncertainty leads to cautious policies.

While the severity of the problem of work disincentives is uncertain, it is clear that hypothetical high taxes and notches offend public policy on grounds of equity regardless of the actual impact such procedures have on work behavior. Inequity arises because the multiplicity of means-tested programs lead, as critics have caustically noted, to the poor paying surtaxes while living on the dole. The irony of this is made more vivid since the government has lowered marginal tax rates for the top income-tax brackets from 91 to 75 per cent in an attempt to revitalize the economy through incentives. Perversely, positive incentives for high-income groups yield

---

30.   Prior to the introduction of the four-week and three-month rules in 1966, local Unemployment Review Officers were given discretion to determine at what point a man was required to declare himself available to accept work that departed from his usual and customary job. After this time, a man was required to accept whatever job was available. Thus the timing of when to exert pressure on a man to lower his sights for work was inequitably administered. Richard Titmuss asserts that the motive for introducing these new rules was to ensure equity, i.e., to replace arbitrary discretion with an administrative rule. For example, 300 young men in Kensington (a middle-class residential area) had applied for work as mass media visual activators (TV work). These middle-class youths were, and still are, treated more leniently than their working-class counterparts.

lower tax rates, whereas improvements in the economic position of the poor produce in many cases even higher tax rates than the rich are expected to pay.

Even so perverse a system is not without its compensating features. It may contribute powerfully to income redistribution, a goal shared by both those who favor selective and those who prefer universal welfare programs. The debate about the high tax rate and work incentives has obscured this point. Some observers have reluctantly noted that "from an extreme egalitarian point of view, there may be something to be said for this situation."[31]

The system in Britain apparently leads to some income equalization among those earning less than the national average, if we assume that families at each income level do indeed take advantage of the social benefits of rent and rates (property taxes) rebates and family income supplements to which they are entitled. These means tests combined with positive taxes can augment by as much as one-fourth the earnings of low-wage families (earnings between £13 and £17 a week) while they can take away between 1 and 20 per cent of the earnings of those in the £18–22 income bracket. This produces income equalization by compressing the total income spread of the low-income and low-middle income workers. Such a system does nothing, however, to equalize the income of the top- and middle-income earners.

Table 2 sets out the evidence on which these conclusions are based, drawing on Tony Lynes' data for Birmingham.

For earnings between £13 and £23 per week, the dispersion of total net money income narrows dramatically once social benefits and taxes are taken into account. Not only have incomes been equalized but the initial rank ordering of families has even been altered. Income equalization is purchased at the cost of high tax rates across the entire income band and notches at a specific earning level.

The trend toward income equalization went largely unrecognized politically. Inequities of the system became the focus of discontent and led to radical proposals for reform. These inequities and anomalies arise from the existence of two parallel systems: "a taxation system which embodies a set of reliefs and allowances based on one set of principles, and a social security system which embodies a different set of benefits and allowances based on a different set of principles."[32] Almost two decades ago Richard Titmuss

31. Lynes, "Family Income Super Tax," p. 771; David Donnison, Director of the Centre for Environmental Studies, London, has in personal conversation noted the same point.
32. Great Britain, Parliament, *Parliamentary Debates* (House of Commons), 5th ser., Vol. 833 (17 March–23 March, 1972), p. 1383.

Table 2

Social Benefits, Taxation, and Income Equalization
(For a family with two children, ages 4 and 6, in Birmingham)

Weekly earnings	Family allowance	Other social benefits*	Earnings plus benefits (Cols. 1+2+3)	National insurance	Income tax	Total income (Cols. 4−5−6)
£13.00	£0.90	£6.52	£20.42	£1.08		£19.34
14.00	0.90	5.85	20.75	1.13		19.62
15.00	0.90	5.16	21.06	1.18		19.88
16.00	0.90	4.48	21.38	1.22		20.16
17.00	0.90	3.79	21.69	1.27		20.42
18.00	0.90	2.96	21.86	1.33	£0.23	20.30
19.00	0.90	2.09	21.99	1.37	0.53	20.09
20.00	0.90	1.42	22.32	1.42	0.83	20.07
21.00	0.90	0.75	22.65	1.46	1.13	20.06
22.00	0.90		22.90	1.50	1.43	19.97
23.00	0.90		23.90	1.55	1.73	20.62

*FIS, rent allowance and rent rebate.

Source: Adapted from a table in Tony Lynes, "Family Income Super Tax," *New Society*, No. 449 (May 6, 1971), p. 771.

criticized the inequities arising from this form of dualism, yet the quote just cited comes not from disciples of Titmuss or the political left but from the Conservative chancellor of the exchequer in his 1972 budget speech. And his proposal for reform is as far reaching as is his assessment of the problem. The new scheme would provide a single assessment of income, to be taxed at a flat 30 per cent rate. This would then serve to calculate both the outstanding taxes above a specific tax threshold and certain social benefits to be paid out to those with incomes below that level. It would be a comprehensive negative income tax, with some benefits integrated into the tax system.

The scheme was defined in more positive terms as a system of credits, but only a few details were presented in the budget message. All forms of personal tax allowances – single, married, and child allowances – would disappear and many forms of social benefits would also be abolished, including family allowances with clawback and the family income supplement. Even so, a broad spectrum of the means-tested programs would remain unintegrated into the new scheme: these would include free school meals, exemption from health service charges, and rent and rate rebates. Credits would be extended whether or not the recipient was a taxpayer, since they are "set off against tax payable but where the credit was greater than the tax the difference would be paid as an addition to the wage or other income."[33] The scheme would be selective – the value of benefits would remain constant as incomes rose; the benefit would be provided automatically without an individual means test. These credits against taxes would continue to be paid during periods of illness and unemployment. In other words, everyone would get a flat-rate credit which would be set off against income tax. Those who pay taxes would treat the credit as income exempted from taxation, while those whose income is lower than the credit amount would receive it in the form of cash transfers.

As *The Economist* points out,[34] the credit proposal will divide the critics of the government's social policy. Now the crucial question is how selective the credit system will be. The new tax threshold will be set by the value of the basic credits and the 30 per cent tax rate. The threshold cannot, presumably, be lower than the existing personal and child allowances combined with the value of family

---

33. Great Britain, Parliament, *Parliamentary Debates* (House of Commons), Vol. 833, p. 1383.
34. "Giving Credit," *The Economist*, CCXLII (March 25, 1972), 14. Full details of the scheme will be published in a green paper (one intended for public debate rather than immediate parliamentary action) and a bipartisan select committee will be formed to study the proposal and submit a report.

allowances. But this value is still much lower than the value of supplementary benefits. To replace FIS, it will need to be higher. The maximum negative tax benefits are likely to fall short of the established poverty line. A 30 per cent negative tax rate must lead to either a low basic allowance or a very high break-even point. The new tax threshold will have to be very high if the credit system is to be as generous as the present welfare system is for low-income people. Such a system will be costly: hence no serious proposals have been made to have the tax credit scheme replace the supplementary benefits scheme.

It seems certain that the "poverty trap" (the work disincentive effect which income-related benefits produce at the borderline between the receipt of benefits and the payment of taxes) cannot altogether be avoided. This is partly because other means tests, especially the national rent rebate scheme, will still be available in addition to tax credits.

However, the government is unwilling for the present to integrate rent rebates and tax credits into a single, comprehensive, graduated negative income tax, and favors a more incremental approach. But more fundamentally, because tax credits cannot avoid the central dilemma of all negative income tax programs (the avoidance of work disincentive effects), a significant portion of benefits must spill over to families well above the poverty line. The lower the tax rate and the benefit levels are, the more severe the problem is. There is in the end, as Samuel Brittan observes,[35] no way to resolve the conflicting aims "to maximize help to the poor, minimize the disincentive effects of high marginal tax rates, and keep down the load on the general taxpayer."

Conclusion

Are there any lessons to be learned from this comparative review of British and United States experience? The task of drawing lessons from patterns is fraught with danger. If policies cannot be understood in isolation from the political, cultural and economic contexts in which they arise, then comparative studies have limited value, for ideas cannot be readily uprooted from one country and implanted in foreign soil. If, however, policy develops at least in a fair measure by accident and by administrative requirements that are likely to be similar everywhere, then the scope for studying patterns in order to draw conclusions is considerably broadened. I proceed on this latter assumption.

Perhaps the most striking conclusion to be reached from this

---

35. Samuel Brittan, "Green Paper Soon on Plans for Negative Income Tax," *Financial Times* (London), September 27, 1972.

comparative review is that irrespective of purpose each system has its limitations; each new intervention creates new problems that need to be resolved. There are no ultimate solutions.

Consider the development of policy in Britain. When the principle of expanding the consumption of the working poor was applied, two intractable questions were posed – those of take-up and incentives. Attempts to encourage take-up by raising benefits and expanding the number of eligibles exacerbated the problem of incentives by creating more overlap between the tax and benefit systems. While some income equalization emerged as take-up expanded, new anomalies erupted because a compressed income distribution altered the rank ordering of families and the poverty surtax led to new inequities. While the political acceptability of means tests may be increased when they reach middle-income groups, the inequities and anomalies inherent in them cannot be avoided.

Specifically, high cumulative tax levels result from means testing and pose awkward anomalies even though they augment the net income of low-wage workers and contribute to income equalization between the bottom and the middle-wage earner. Reliance on means testing to augment the income of the working poor could lead one to ask whether these benefits are a substitute for higher wages (as in the case of family allowances in France). Since benefits are not paid directly out of employer taxes but rather from general taxes, this question has been avoided. At the moment, labor unions seem more troubled about the high marginal taxes than the threat to wage levels. However, when economic improvements occur through transfers rather than from earned income, wage levels may lag. The difficulties created by the compression of the income distribution have not been a matter of political concern. The Conservative government did respond, however, to the problem of marginal tax rates by raising the tax threshold. It has gone still further in its proposal for a major redefinition of the borderline between taxation and social benefits: the proposed system of tax credits represents the most radical reform of social policy in Britain for a quarter of a century.

The most interesting aspect of the tax credit scheme is that it is being developed as a tax reform. This proposal is strikingly dissimilar to U.S. discussions of the negative income tax: it does not attempt to reduce supplementary benefit rolls, guarantee a minimum income or encourage work; instead, this is a tax reform that will also have a partial, although important, effect on these social questions. It is not a cure but it will do some good and thus be less open to attack for not being "the" answer. In short, it is a deliberate effort at pluralist planning where the same policy is directed at multiple aims.

If the most glaring anomalies of poverty surtaxes are eliminated through an increase in the tax threshold and the integration of the tax and benefits system, a new dilemma must shortly emerge. A generous credit system that can significantly reduce the size and cost of the Supplementary Benefits program must precipitously raise the tax threshold; and such a scheme will be as costly as it is redistributive. It would cost about £1 billion to raise the income level of poor families with children through a tax credit scheme, and the level of income they commanded would be that of a pensioned couple on supplementary benefits. The costs would, of course, be much larger if the present welfare level of families with children were accepted as the goal. In a period of inflation, when government realizes in taxes an amount proportionately higher than its increased expenditures, such higher outlays are economically feasible. But in periods of rising unemployment, the pressure for tax reduction as a means to stimulate the economy is difficult to resist. The 1972 budget cuts in Britain were inspired by these and other motives. The fate of the tax credit proposal is unclear but it seems certain that compromises will emerge and create new inequities as policy continues to evolve from one set of contradictions to another.

In the United States, government proposals for reform have been more modest. Except for the 1969 Tax Reform Act which exempted "the poor"[36] from income tax, the structure of the present income tax system has been accepted as the basic constraint; and as a result the pure negative income tax approach (which relates all forms of income to benefits) is trapped in a dilemma from which it cannot escape. If the marginal tax rate is to be kept sufficiently low to avoid glaring work disincentives, the poverty level, or basic allowance level, must also be kept low. But if allowances are set at or near the poverty levels (an allowance level enjoyed by welfare recipients living in high-benefit states, where nearly two-thirds of all recipients live), politically imposed cost constraints are accepted, and means-tested in-kind benefits expand, high marginal tax rates are inescapable. Thus it is illusory to hope that economic incentives alone can encourage work. Stronger work tests as a condition for eligibility have followed. Congress, while accepting the many purposes of welfare reform, has viewed the negative income tax primarily as a means to induce certain AFDC recipients to work.

The process leading to this outcome may be recapitulated briefly. It was politically unacceptable to have a low, minimum basic allowance. In 1969, the president proposed $1,600 for a family of

---

36. For 1972, the level at which United States income tax returns had to be filed was more than $2,050 for individuals and $2,800 for married couples.

four under the Family Assistance Plan. In 1970, H.R. 1 established a $2,400 poverty level by "cashing out" the $800 value of food stamps. Such a scheme seemed to offer fiscal relief to the states through the federal takeover of a greater share of welfare costs and also to represent a visible step in the direction of reducing poverty. But at this high guarantee level it was not thought possible to retain the 50 per cent marginal tax rate initially proposed by the Family Assistance Plan. The arithmetic of negative taxation is the villain. The original Family Assistance Plan yielded a break-even point of $3,920 (a $1,600 guarantee, a 50 per cent tax, and a $720 work expenses disregard). Under this scheme 14 per cent of all families would be covered by the plan. If the guarantee is raised by $800 and the same level of disregards and tax rates maintained, the break-even point is increased to $5,520 and 22.4 per cent of all U.S. families are covered. A 50 per cent increase in the value of the basic allowance triples the cost of the original proposal and expands the eligible population by 57 per cent. Given both the cost constraint and the self-evident political difficulty of a reform that would place nearly one American in four on welfare, it seemed necessary to raise the marginal tax to 67 per cent. The dilemma is illustrated by Senator Ribicoff's 1971 proposal, which calls for an even more generous minimum benefit of $3,000, to be raised gradually to the poverty line; a lower tax rate of 60 per cent; full payment of income and social security taxes and work-related expenses as incurred; and which allows for periodic increases in the basic allowance to take account of inflation. As Senator Curtis observed, such a scheme would, by 1977, make one-third of the population eligible for some welfare benefits. Thus, adequacy threatened the political acceptability of the reform.

The attempts at welfare reform have tried to avoid the Curtis dilemma. In an effort to save money, H.R. 1 not only lowers the proportion of benefits retained as earnings are raised but, in common with the British FIS, does not reimburse welfare recipients for the income and social security taxes they pay. Consequently, as soon as a family's income passes the threshold for paying taxes, additional earnings are reduced at a rate of 86.2 per cent. Even this high marginal tax rate fails to take account of the implicit loss of income suffered when a family becomes ineligible for other means-tested goods and services, especially Medicaid, but including as well the more limited availability of public housing.

For these reasons, the negative income tax has limited potential as a work-incentive strategy. Because congressional policy assigns high priority to the reduction of AFDC rolls and costs – or, at the least, to an abatement in their rise – the limited effectiveness of services and the failure to implement a strong approach have led to increased reliance upon administrative devices that compel recipients to work. This means more coercion. In the Senate version the logic of this position is explained, and entitlement to cash benefits of families with no preschool children is abolished to be replaced by job guarantees for those who cannot find work, and wage supplements for those who can. The demand by liberal economists for a lower negative income tax rate as the single most important, and urgently needed, welfare reform is ignored as the political agenda is shifted.

The only way to avoid the dilemma is to redefine the issue not as welfare reform but as tax reform and income redistribution, as proposed by Senator George McGovern, and discussed earlier in this paper. It has been said that the redistribution of income is emerging as the dominant issue for the closing quarter of this century. The cost of Senator McGovern's proposed program was to be met by substituting a flat 33 1/3 per cent tax for the present individual income tax system and broadening the taxable income base (possibly doubling it).

Yet new problems emerge. Obviously there is the matter of cost, which will largely depend on the political compromises made in the effort to expand the total amount of income to be subjected to the tax, that is, the elimination of tax loopholes and deductions. The lower the taxable base, the higher the tax rate. Aside from costs, new issues arise. The $1,000-per-person grant is less than the poverty line for families under four persons and exceeds it for families of more than four persons.[37] High transfers per person may not promote fertility but encourage creating new households. High-income families at the 50 per cent or larger tax rate would benefit. These difficulties create pressure to have age-graded benefits and surtaxes, which in turn raise problems of administration and incentives.

But even if solutions are intractable, the aims of public policy are important. The same principle of negative taxation when applied to different objectives yields different outcomes. It does make a difference whether a country sets about to relieve distress or alter work behavior, even if the pursuit of each objective poses its own special difficulties. Here the contrasting experience of the two countries is vivid. Negative taxation reform in the United States succumbed to restriction and coercion, while in Britain it surrendered to inequities. If coercion is to be avoided in the United States, the issue must be reformulated and the objectives redefined.

---

37. Russell Lidman, *Cost and Distributional Implications of McGovern's Minimum Income Grant Proposal,* Institute for Research on Poverty, Discussion Papers (Madison, Wis.: University of Wisconsin, Institute for Research on Poverty, 1972).

A lesson from Britain's experience seems useful. It is possible that the British may find a way to erode the scope and cost of welfare by defining the issue as tax reform and income redistribution.

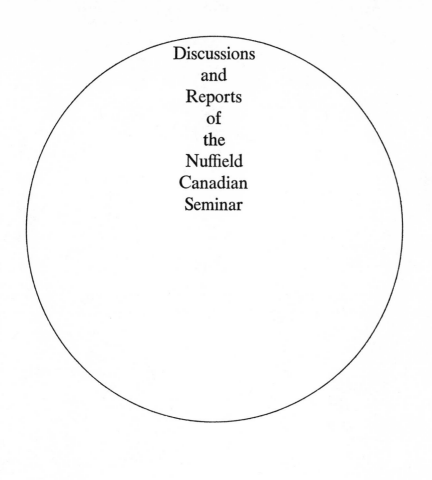

Discussions
and
Reports
of
the
Nuffield
Canadian
Seminar

Plenary Session, Wednesday, April 12, 1972

Chairman: Gérald Fortin
Director, Centre for Urban and Regional Research,
National Institute for Scientific Research,
University of Quebec

Co-chairman of the seminar

In opening the discussion, Dr. Fortin explained that the seminar planners had envisaged an approach which did not limit discussion to the technical aspects of guaranteed income but rather examined the whole concept of guaranteed income in the broad context of political, economic and social systems and of human needs.

The background papers, which all participants had received in advance, were intended to provide a basis for the discussions; they had been grouped in what the planning committee believed to be an appropriate order for presentation at the plenary sessions. Dr. Fortin said the authors would comment briefly on them, highlighting the main points for consideration, and general discussion would then follow.

Why a Guaranteed Annual Income?[1]

Author's Comments[2] by Israel Katz
Director General,
National Insurance Institute, Jerusalem, Israel

1 We must first clarify the aims of guaranteed income. Do we deal with the "welfare poor" only? with the poverty of all lower income groups? with inequalities of income distribution?

2 To decrease income inequality should be a major goal even if it is questionable whether substantial increases in income redistribution

---

1. Background paper, p. 43.
2. These comments, and subsequent reports of seminar discussions, were prepared from taped transcripts. To allow for freer discussion, it was agreed in advance that no participants would be identified in the plenary or group discussion reports except the authors when speaking direct to their papers.

can and will receive political and public support in the immediate years to come.

3   In any event, instruments of income security must be thoroughly examined, or even done away with to be replaced by relatively new inventions such as the various forms of negative income tax.[3]

4   This examination must be in the light of the objectives of existing policies. Following are examples of such policies.

a   *Sweden.* Full employment has been the paramount social policy concern of the past two decades. This reflects the interests of the working class in a capitalistic economy – a class whose position in society is measured by the country's unemployment rate. Raising the level of education, providing decent housing and better health services for all are the next priorities for this generation. Equalization of income and equality of opportunity are not the priority, though there are "quaint hopes" that equalization will somehow automatically be part of achieving the main objective. But in fact, there has not been any impressive change in Swedish income distribution since 1950.

b   *Israel.* Redistribution of education has had much higher priority than redistribution of income. This is because of the need to integrate the enormous mixed immigrant population. But it is being found that as education expectations rise, so do a family's income demands. Israel's great investments in education have not paid off, as the country hasn't grappled with the problem of income equalization.

5   The concept of guaranteed income is closely related to guaranteeing "command over resources over time" (Richard Titmuss' phrase). To reach a real guaranteed income, we must expand not only income but also other forms of resources (such as education, housing, health services), improve their distribution, and integrate the taxation and benefits systems.

6   In Israel, the approach (considered by many) to achieve greater redistribution toward income equality, with integration and not division between the poor and the non-poor, is through "a kind of selectivity of positive discrimination" within universal programs for vital services (including income maintenance). This could be achieved by identifying groups of dependents, types of social needs and particular geographic regions which must be blanketed into universal schemes of economic and social development. Of course there will also remain the necessity for a "humanized assistance scheme" to meet special needs.

---

3.   For a description of negative income tax see J. I. Clark, pp. 274–275.

Discussion on the Katz Paper

1   The major issue for the seminar, Dr. Katz stated, was how do we force and bring about greater income equality? He believed guaranteed annual income (GAI) could not be considered as the primary vehicle, a separate entity, for income redistribution, but as part of a whole complex of economic and social policies and programs.

2   A participant suggested that redistribution was not a political and economic goal at present in Western countries (for example, in Australia), it is usually just a dirty word. You must talk instead about "helping the poor." However, others thought it *was* a goal in some of these countries, implicit when politicians talk to high-income people, explicit when talking to the others. Quite apart from income security programs or tax measures, Canada's equalization grants and regional economic expansion programs for poor provinces and areas were cited as examples.

3   Challenged about how the poor could be given special help without being "distinguished" from others, Dr. Katz replied that people should be distinguished by their category of need, not just because they are poor. For example, there are various groups of "dependencies" – the aging, one-parent families, large families. "Positive discrimination" within universal programs could direct resources to the poor in such groups, including the working poor. Defining the poor as poor and helping them as poor would do little for the redistribution of resources over time. Universality also supports community solidarity which is essential to a country. It is important to decide these principles for the long term, to judge whether programs that are politically feasible to implement now are geared to these goals or are short term only, to be replaced when possible.

4   It was suggested that there would always be "givers" and "receivers" in any GAI or other form of income security program and thus, according to Dr. Katz, redistribution would be hindered. Dr. Katz said he believed there is a limit to redistribution, but this would be defined by the kind of instrument used. He has found the type of approach through programs for groups of people who are not necessarily *all poor* is more popular and politically acceptable, and thus gets further with redistribution.

5   A massive study of the needs of one-parent families in Britain, not yet completed, was cited; about one million parents and children fall into this group. It is becoming clear that solutions for the problems of such groups cannot be developed without taking into con-

sideration the tax structure (at all levels), rents, housing costs and many other variables, including *from* whom income is to be redistributed. Are we talking about redistribution from the take-home pay of the average worker or from those in the top 10 per cent of the income range?

6 It was suggested that the discussion indicated the necessity of defining what is meant by "equality" in discussing better distribution of resources. Obviously, *income* equality is only part of it. Perhaps we should be talking of more equal ways of meeting enormously varied needs.

7 The question of the relationship between the problem of GAI and the problem of industrialization was raised. Even in Eastern European countries, which politically stress equality as a goal, industrialization brings strong pressures for inequality in the distribution of resources. It drains the strongest and most capable people into cities, thus leading to cumulative poverty in the rural areas. It also leads to a wider differential in income and spending power in the industrialized centres.

8 One participant observed that while Canada and the United States do have the creation and equalization of opportunity as a political goal, they are trying to reach it mainly through methods "that have been around since the First World War" (even though they are still considered "radical") and have not proved notably successful. For example, establishing industries in poor regions might give some slight regional growth in productivity but doesn't really help many *people,* and indeed could destroy local communities which have had a viable lifestyle, as in the outports of Newfoundland. The cost-benefits of industrialization are measured in terms of its own output and of urbanization, this participant continued. Highways, electrification, cable TV, etc., are important to the lifestyle of people living in, say, Toronto, but not necessarily so to people in the country; yet, by the above criteria, the rural lifestyle is judged underdeveloped and poor. In short, we are talking about GAI in the context of an industrial society and the question is whether such a society can any longer effect income redistribution, equalization of opportunity, and so on. In this speaker's view, it could not; changes in the entire organization of production, along with changes in the whole series of essentially social programs, must be considered.

Public Policies for Creating Gainful Employment[4]

Author's Comments by David C. Smith
*Professor and Head, Department of Economics,
Queen's University, Kingston, Ontario*

1   Full employment and an equitable distribution of income are usually considered separate and distinct national economic goals. But
there are three areas of overlap.

2   *First,* the level of employment opportunities affects not only employment opportunities for low-income groups directly, but also
average incomes and the level of income available for various redistribution policies. Policies that reduce both are not a sensible
way to alleviate poverty. But what should the full employment goal
be? It may be different (for economic, social, etc., factors) among
countries and within a country. Further, the goal is a multi-dimen-
sional one which takes into account the incidence and specific hardships caused by unemployment. But policies to improve employment levels conflict with other policies (for example, to maintain a
reasonable degree of price stability), and also the trade-off between
them is not a stable fixed relationship. But though better ways of
dealing with the problem may be found, the use of monetary and
fiscal policies for this purpose is unlikely to disappear entirely.

3   *Second,* how does the choice between higher unemployment or
higher inflation affect the *quality* of the distribution of income?
There has been little hard research on this, but recent North American experience indicates that, on balance, low-income groups do
not suffer and probably gain relatively when the economy is at high
employment levels, despite the inflationary consequences. It appears that the cost of goods purchased by lower income groups does
not tend to rise more quickly than average prices, that inflation has
not shifted income from wages to profits, and that, in general, transfer payments have been adjusted (though unpredictably) in line
with inflation. The inequities of inflation are more horizontal: that
is, within given income ranges for people on pensions or on transfer
payments that are adjusted incompletely or too slowly. If society
really wants to ensure income support for the poor or other vulnerable groups, these kinds of income should be linked to a price index to provide a full automatic offset to inflation, despite the fear
that this would increase inflationary tendencies. In addition, discriminatory barriers to employment, especially at non-poverty

---

4. Background paper, p. 51.

wages, must be removed; unemployment tends to increase such restrictions and also to retard learning on the job, which is necessary if the low-paid worker is to increase his wages. To try to reduce unemployment through fiscal and monetary policies alone invites sharp inflation without significant benefits and possibly with adverse consequences to the unemployment rate. For example, because of the time lag in adjustment to the policies they may be out of date and not reflect what the situation would be if policies were stabilized for a time.

4   *Third,* there is a need for special policies to affect the composition of demand for and supply of labor, and to facilitate and promote adjustment processes in the labor market and broaden the scope for full employment policies beyond aggregate demand policies. These policies may, for example, aim at reducing unemployment with fewer inflationary consequences, and at increasing efficiency and real income levels. They may try to achieve a more equitable distribution of employment and income not only through affecting the composition of demand for labor, but also through mobility and manpower retraining programs that adjust the supply of labor, through improving information on job opportunities, reducing restrictive and discriminatory practices and correcting abuses of economic power on both the demand and supply side of the labor market. The problems have not been in shortage of ideas but in developing, coordinating and implementing an effective long-run strategy.

A New Approach to Work and the Problem of Income Instability[5]

Author's Comments by Melville J. Ulmer
Professor, College of Business and Public Administration,
Department of Economics,
University of Maryland

1   This paper deals essentially with the potential role of public employment in improving the working conditions of the poor and combatting poverty, and in providing full employment without inflation.

2   An important factor in inflation in North America is that there is an economically submerged group which is unemployed a large part of the time. The people in it are mostly the unskilled or semi-skilled, with a sprinkling of those whose skills have become obsolete because of technological change. It is possible to get these people

---

5.   Background paper, p. 65.

into private industry by expanding the economy through monetary and fiscal measures. But this creates an excess of demand over labor supply for skilled jobs and a brisk inflation becomes inevitable, which then calls forth efforts to reduce it. Thus there is a stop-go economy, intolerable inflation alternating with intolerable unemployment (intolerable in the political sense).

3   Inflation could probably be beaten with a maintained unemployment level of 5 1/2 per cent or 6 per cent. The irreducible minimum of U.S. unemployment, representing "full" employment, is probably 2 per cent (it was 1 per cent even in the Second World War). Thus a jobless rate of 5 1/2 per cent would leave about 3 1/2 per cent excess of unemployment, really the submerged group who are, in any case, idle a good deal. These should be absorbed into public service jobs, and taxes should be raised enough to keep the private sector at a non-inflationary level.

4   Such a policy would also help to readjust social imbalance. It is becoming clear that, from the national point of view, the need for public goods and services generally is more urgent than for further supplies of goods and services in the private sector – that is, the need for pollution control, conservation of resources, education, paramedical services, nursing homes, urban renewal, day care centres, recreation facilities, and so on.

5   The concept of work in our economy should also be examined. There are two contrasting views in popular thinking: (1) that work is a moral good and also an end in itself, whatever you do (the puritan-Keynesian ethic); and (2) that work is just a means to an end, a necessary ordeal to acquire the material necessities of life. Both views make an artificial distinction between means and ends. Rather, work is in itself important to life and can have direct satisfactions or dissatisfactions for us, not necessarily related to monetary gain. There are three important consequences for a public employment program if this last view is followed.

6   *First,* moral considerations apart, it would in general pay government to employ people whose marginal product is too low for employment in private industry since government would in any case have to support the family if the head were unemployed. The true cost of hiring someone at $8,000 a year would perhaps be only $4,000–5,000, whereas private industry would count it a saving of $8,000 if such a person were fired.

7   *Second,* government can include in its calculations of social costs and social benefits, as private industry cannot, the nature of work

per se. Thus there are benefits in deliberately arranging working conditions and the techniques of production to be more attractive to workers.

8 *Third,* work activity yields psychic returns, positive or negative, depending on the nature of its contribution to society. Properly organized public employment can, far more readily than private employment, direct the activity to needs that are clearly real and urgent.

9 An extensive public employment program would also prevent huge and irretrievable output losses from lack of production through unemployment: for example, an estimated annual U.S. average of $50 billion since 1948.

Discussion on the Smith and Ulmer Papers

1 In answer to a question, Dr. Smith stated that the table in his paper on annual unemployment rates in six Western countries related to the *total* labor force, not just to men. The questioner considered the involvement of women to be most important; he suggested that the great increase in their numbers in the British labor force in the 1950s and 1960s (a period of relatively full employment, only 1 per cent to 2 per cent unemployed) had been mainly responsible for the demand inflation and stop-go economy. The major income gains for skilled and semi-skilled workers had been "because mom went out to work." He pointed out that the GAI (which is what, in his view, the present British welfare system amounts to) has risen in the past 10 years in relation to the take-home pay of the lowest group of wage-earners. If we consider male workers only, we should add to the GAI the other marginal costs of unemployment, such as the cost of means-testing when unemployment benefits are exhausted (about $30 per test). The total income for the unskilled unemployed man might then place a greater demand on the economy than the income he could earn. Thus government "creation" of unemployment in itself could lead, ironically, to further inflation. But when the additional income for the family from women in the labor force is taken into account, there is clearly a greater demand stimulated by the unemployment policy, and a further tendency toward a stop-go economy. The questioner was not suggesting that all women should be sent back to the home, but the implications, for the economy, of women in the labor force have to be faced in considering the rate of unemployment that is "tolerable" in relation to the "tolerable" level of inflation. However, the questioner did not think stop-go was an evil: the procedure had long been used in social security programs, why not elsewhere? He thought Dr. Ulmer's point was that if his public employment (or social manpower) policy were implemented, less demand on the economy (inflation) might be created than by unemployment when all social welfare benefits for the unemployed were totalled.

2   Dr. Ulmer reiterated his view that a stop-go economy *is* an evil; through its violent swings, it can throw millions of families, as in the U.S., "into utter disarray, demoralization and idleness, which they accept unwillingly, of course." He said that with regard to "working" women, the labor force statistics in his paper included them, but this was misleading in relation to unemployment. People who can't find jobs get discouraged and stop trying so that when a count is taken, based on "actively looking for work," they are not included. Many of these are women.

3   A participant stressed that the relationship between income distribution and employment rates is most important. Statistical analyses in Sweden have shown that about 50 per cent of all income differentials in the adult population under pension age are due to differentials in the per annum employment rates of individuals. Differences because of occupation levels, sex, age groups, type of industry were also taken into consideration in the analyses, but the controlling factor in one half of the cases was the employment rate. It was also found that the only real source of more household income equalization in the past few decades was from the additional income provided through the participation of women in the labor force.

4   The same speaker considered that the old fashioned (1920s) concept of unemployment (which is very misleading) needs changing in line with the earlier comments, particularly with regard to women. If a man claims he can't get a job, this is accepted as unemployment; if a married woman wants a job but can't get it, she is not always considered unemployed. This is the main difference between the sexes in the unemployment count. The new concept of measuring unemployment should include this and other forms of "hidden" unemployment. In Sweden, calculations have been made including both open and hidden unemployment and the average annual rate has been estimated at 20 per cent. A similar estimate on U.S. figures shows an annual unemployment rate of about 30 per cent. (The same sort of calculation in Quebec indicates an annual unemployment rate of 30 per cent in Montreal and 50 per cent in the rural, non-farm areas.) It is also important to base the count on a year's observation, rather than on a day or on two weeks (normally used in labor force sample surveys), to learn how many

"discouraged" workers have completely dropped out of the labor force.

5   Dr. Smith agreed that, as stated in his paper, present national employment rate measurements are very crude. He mentioned an area of current confusing evidence – the relationship of labor force participation rates to the state of economic activity. In the U.S., the relationship is positive, rising when opportunities are good and falling when unemployment increases, which suggests some underemployment ("hidden" unemployment). Inclusion of underemployment in the statistics would give a better measure of unemployment and would certainly show an increase above what is now indicated in a period of high unemployment. On the other hand, information for the Canadian economy neither indicates nor confirms the above relationship. Why should the same tests come out differently in the two countries? More work is needed on this.

6   Another speaker questioned the conventional wisdom about employment, which assumes that there is a rational labor market, that the employers' views of educational requirements are appropriate, and that people are unemployed because of lack of individual skills rather than lack of jobs. This view is irrational, a pure derivative of technology and profit motivation. The perspective should be that of Dr. Ulmer: providing jobs for *people*. Rather than government being the employer of last resort, it should be trying to change the composition of output instead of taking the current composition as a fixed goal and result of what is done, and should consider the consequences of such change for the people in different positions in our society. We must look at our goals in employment. This would raise issues of the environment, of "class" unemployment (as in the case of blacks in the U.S.), of "mal-employment" (the official, plus the "hidden" unemployment, which in slum areas in the U.S. can be as high as a 50 per cent rate), of how a "desirable" job is defined (which should not only be by income but also by "satisfactions," the character of the work itself), and of how employers make decisions about unemployment. The goal is not just the elimination of unemployment but also the development of new concepts of employment.

7   An example given to underline the artificiality of current notions about "skills" was the present unemployment among highly trained people (Ph.D.s, etc.). Although the number of such people is small, their unemployment rate is very high. This speaker considered that, in a certain sense, no one is "unskilled" or "unemployed": they are "doing things" even if unpaid. Clearly, the reality is that industry classifies people as skilled or unskilled and that higher unemploy-

ment lowers the efficiency of experienced workers, prevents the young from learning on the job, discourages people from improving skills that could not be used and encourages discrimination against certain groups. Measures to meet these problems are required, but this should not be the only approach. "We tend to see the problems in the people and the potential solutions in the institutions, whereas the potential solutions are in the people and the problems in the institutions." We may, he suggested, have to change the nature of industrial structure substantially.

8 It was stated that, in Canada, organized labor has long questioned the validity of the unemployment figures. There are many forms of hidden unemployment. Following are the principal individual views expressed in the discussion on labor in Canada.

a Although Canadian productivity is increasing, the government has artificially developed a situation of scarcity so industry has tightened its operations. Lay-offs include relatively skilled or semi-skilled workers, also supernumerary workers (to take care of situations such as absenteeism through illness, etc.) who are normally employed in many industries, representing as high as 5 or 6 per cent of their labor force.

b There are false standards in Canada about *taught* skills (through formal education) which are reaching absurd heights – for example, requiring Grade 12 for janitorial work. Yet much of Canadian industry depends on workers with *learned* skills, on-the-job training (loggers, etc.). On a GAI, people would receive income without reference to their education or skills.

c Income is not the only goal of workers: they take pride in their work and would rather work than be unemployed. We are wasting their skills if we don't gainfully employ them. Workers are unemployed because of government policies on the economic *operations* of the country rather than the stop-go economic *program*.

d The problem of the working poor is of particular interest to labor. In the Economic Council of Canada's 1968 statement, it was estimated that, based on 1961 data, 66 per cent of families in the poverty group worked (about 30 per cent full time), and there is very little change when the data are calculated for 1967. There are great variations and problems, not only between industries but also within an industry in different parts of the country. Similar disparities have to be taken into account in considering a GAI because of variations in *costs* of living, though not necessarily in living *standards* or quality of life (which may be better in, for example, small towns than in large cities). GAI might have to be $5,800 in Toronto but only half that amount in some small towns. Canada has unique problems because of its size, type of growth and various regional structures.

e GAI (as a cash payment) is not a panacea, as some people would like it to be. We must think not only of income maintenance but also of equal opportunity for other things – for jobs, participation in community activities, and so on.

9 A participant made reference to Dr. Ulmer's "triangle" of employment, inflation and taxation – to provide public employment for large numbers of people and hold down inflation through taxation. A problem in giving priority to employment in socioeconomic policy is that we are blocked by a 19th century view of work, of what is productive and non-productive, based mainly on the concept of organized industrial labor. We simply cannot accept that there are different types of work activity. This falsifies our measurement of GNP which is very arbitrarily computed. The most obvious omission is the housewife looking after her home and children; even beautifying her garden, and thus the neighborhood, is a contribution to our resources. In this speaker's view, we need to be less rigid in defining work and measuring productivity, but we must also try to solve the problem of stabilizing society and controlling inflation through various approaches, not just employment. Dr. Ulmer's "triangle" would be more acceptable if it included employment *or* GAI.

10 A speaker commented on the current situation of "full" employment in West Germany. There are actually more jobs than people to fill them and foreign workers have been brought in for unskilled labor that native workers do not want to do. This has led to problems (and could again) in times of recession. Perhaps West Germany should be thinking much more about a new structure of employment and of adjusting this to the supply of workers. An example given was the use of disabled people in industry, which was at first resisted but had then been found to work well in a number of instances.

11 Other speakers stated that in countries with full employment (for example, Australia and New Zealand) GAI is not an issue. In such countries, there are no working poor; in a full employment situation, the workers can push up the wages, and the country can afford a decent level of family allowances which takes care of the problem of varying family responsibilities. In addition, in a situation of high demand for labor, employers are willing to train people on the job, thus eliminating a good deal of government manpower training expenditures. In this view, employment is the first priority whereas the guaranteed income argument seems to revolve about unemployment.

Plenary Session, Thursday, April 13, 1972

Chairman: J. Harvey Perry
Executive Director,
The Canadian Bankers' Association, Toronto

Co-chairman of the seminar

Poverty and Direct Forms of Income Security in Canada[6]

Author's Comments by Tom Philbrook
Professor, Faculty of Environmental Studies,
York University, Toronto

1 The central conclusion of this paper is that the structure of income distribution in Canada has not changed at all in the past two decades, nor probably in the previous decades. Income distribution in Canada reflects our social class structure and the structure of organization, the hierarchical character, of our large-scale institutions.

2 These structures are the reality and are quite unlike our vaunted democratic social and political objectives. Of course there is some mobility between social classes, but we don't know whether it is greater upward than downward. Certainly we cannot continue to assume there are good opportunities for people to move upward; the probability of doing so is actually quite low. We must start politically from the fact of the relatively unchanging character of Canadian society (indeed, of most Western societies). Otherwise, we simply create misery and misunderstanding when expectations are raised and not fulfilled.

3 Since changes in the income distribution structure haven't come about automatically, we are faced with a choice: to accept the present pattern, or to reject it and make deliberate efforts to alter the fundamental structures. The latter could not be accomplished in a matter of years; it would take decades.

4 Within Canadian society there appears to be a great willingness to accept the present situation. This would mean that we continue in

---

6. Background paper, p. 79.

the present policy framework of tuning up slightly our present income security and social services policies. The concept of a GAI is almost an automatic development in this process: it is neater and can have less stigma than many of our present transfer payments. From this point of view, GAI can be considered a necessary, almost inevitable adjustment to sustain the status quo and the political role of income security measures. It has been argued that this role is essentially a way of dealing with the possibilities for serious political unrest in the context of a cyclical economy in which people will be troublesome if they don't have something to live on. Thus the objective of the "welfare system" is not humanitarian but to maintain the security and peacefulness of the society. It has been found in the United States that the increases and decreases in welfare benefits, etc., correlate quite closely with changes in the economy. This should be studied more thoroughly in Canada.

5   Personally, the author would prefer to reject the present social class and income distribution structure. But although we have gone some way in conceptualizing change (for example, in defining national growth as social progress rather than in purely economic terms) we haven't done much thinking through of meaningful alternatives and their implications. Any kinds of policies (for incomes, employment, wage and price controls, etc.) that would affect income distribution imply changing areas that we now regard as sacrosanct. These would include internal industrial and corporate management and the whole question of ownership (for example, private versus common ownership). It is clear that academics and professionals must also talk more to other individuals and groups, such as various types of citizens organizations, to exchange knowledge and gain insight into the relevance of their own ideas.

6   Western societies are moving toward what has been called a system of friendly fascism in which the individual loses control and the institution tends to take over. If we accept the present society because we are familiar with it and can live with it, we may be accepting something for the future that none of us wants.

Discussion on the Philbrook Paper

1   Dr. Philbrook was asked whether he implied that the wage and salary differentials in the Canadian "hierarchy" should be diminished, and whether, to control the elites and future income distribution, no one, for example, should be allowed to own more than one house. Dr. Philbrook replied that he was really talking about unnecessary income. Families who are above a decent wage or salary

level (which he thought should normally not be less than $10,000 a year in Canada at present, except for people who prefer to take less in return for more interesting jobs) should receive only cost-of-living increases; people really don't need an income of $100,000 a year. There is evidence to show that people work imaginatively, intelligently and hard without the incentive of money; the whole notion of money incentives is based on old-fashioned liberalism that was perhaps necessary for 19th century industrialization but is now outdated. He had no strong views on the question of one house per person.

2   One participant suggested the distinction was in the profit motive: no one should own more than one house for *profit* although he might have a summer cottage for *enjoyment*. Also, more should be done in Canada by the Central Mortgage and Housing Corporation for cooperative housing (which has less support than do private entrepreneurs) so that the cost of cooperative housing could be within the reach even of people below an $8,000 annual income. (Several Europeans commented that they would like to move to Canada if a $10,000 minimum income were accepted!)

3   In reply to a question about how immigration (which the participant saw as a great pressure on Canada) fits into Canadian social stratification, Dr. Philbrook said that it undoubtedly causes a variety of tensions, in addition to those created by the French-English ethnic situation, both at the top and bottom of the income distribution scale. Canada does not have a consistent immigration policy; latterly, immigrating into Canada has become very difficult. Another participant suggested that if there were to be redistribution of income from the top to give everyone not less than $10,000 a year, there would be a real impact on migration. For the last 40 years or more, Canada has had an excess of emigration to the United States over immigration from that country, and this increases when the normal gap of 20 per cent in real per capita income (in favor of the U.S.) widens by even as much as 1 to 3 per cent. Moreover, the people who tend to migrate are mostly from the better educated, professional and thus more mobile categories. Dr. Philbrook replied that this is certainly a difficult area, but one could not go entirely by historical patterns. There are, or may be, cultural and political changes in the minds of Canadians vis-à-vis the U.S. that could alter the trends.

Social Services and the Guaranteed Annual Income[7]

Author's Comments, by Nicolas Zay
Director, School of Social Work,
Laval University, Quebec

1 The assumptions of this paper are as follows.

a GAI is a mechanism the purpose of which is to provide benefits to people whose income is under the poverty line, defined in dollars and cents, regardless of the status of the applicant on the labor market.

b The social services are conceived as "public utilities" (universal).

c A new relationship between the GAI and the social services should be looked for.

2 The relationship of the social services to the social assistance system in North America is to support the efficiency of that system. The purpose of the social services program is to help people become self-sufficient; the less it costs to do this the more efficient it is considered.

3 The social services have three roles in relation to GAI.

a *Supplementary*: to bridge the gap between the provided income and poverty as measured by criteria related to the effective level of living of the individual rather than by income criteria.

b *Supportive*: activities to help people make the best use of the benefits by handling their income efficiently.

c *Substitutive*: for people who cannot make use of cash income – such as children and the mentally handicapped.

(It must be remembered that social services are not restricted to GAI recipients; as public utilities they should be provided to everyone who feels the need for them, especially low-income groups.)

4 The basic questions about the social services for discussion in the seminar come under four headings.

a *What services should be provided and how can priorities among them be established?* This is important since the social services affect, directly or indirectly, the level of living and are therefore related to the amount of GAI benefits. We probably can never afford all the social "public utilities" that are required, so we shall have to develop better mechanisms than now exist for deciding priorities according to the needs and wishes of people.

b *To whom should the services be provided?* Do GAI beneficiaries require special services? If so, what are they? What is the rationale

---

7. Background paper, p. 97.

for restricting accessibility? If GAI beneficiaries do not require special services, how can they make use of the available universal social services?

c *Who should provide the services?* If social services are to be universal, could they be offered on a competitive basis by the public and private sectors? Can or should we develop further a system in which government pays and sets standards for services without administering them (as now obtains in children's aid societies in several Canadian provinces)?

d *Who should pay for the social services provided to GAI beneficiaries?* Should the financing be different from that used for universal social services? If social services are "public utilities," then society must provide and pay for them. However, if alternatives are to be offered (public and private), money must be channeled (for example, on a fee-for-service basis) to make the private sector really competitive.

Discussion on the Zay Paper

1 A participant suggested that many of the problems of financing, management and responsibility for the social services are already with us in Canada and perhaps institution of a GAI would not much change their nature. He expressed doubt that complete separation of the provision of cash benefits and of social services (discussed in Dr. Zay's paper) would be a good solution. The idea of choice in the other social services (as there now is in medical services) is worth considering. Indeed, freedom of choice is perhaps the key problem in the association of cash benefits with the social services; the latter could be imposed on people whereas their use should be voluntary.

2 It was pointed out that the separation of cash benefits programs from the social services has already taken place in the United Kingdom. All the public social services (outside the fields of education, health and income security) – that is, the "social care" or "social work" services – are now under single departments and budgets. Despite this extreme of "administrative functionalism" there is still the problem of coordination, both among these services, particularly at the local level of delivery to individuals, and between them and the services for education, health, etc. This problem exists in every country but differs in relation to the way services are organized. New Zealand was cited as an example of the reverse situation to Britain's; there, the services and income security measures are integrated into a single program. The services are for everyone which helps reduce the problem of stigma. The speaker thought it unnecessary to replace such a program by a GAI.

3 A participant observed that some people in Quebec view differently from Dr. Zay the relationship of income maintenance (including GAI) programs and social services. This view considers them fundamentally distinct, with different objectives, and aimed at different groups in the population in the sense that social services may be provided to people receiving income benefits but also to people not requiring this income. If the social services had to carry out the three functions suggested by Dr. Zay in relation to GAI, we could end up with objectives that contradict and even neutralize each other.

4 It was suggested that Dr. Zay had not really defined "social services" and that such a definition was urgently needed if the debate about them was to go forward. How do we know what a social service is? What criteria should we use in defining what is and is not a social service? What do we mean by the social service team?

5 A participant raised the question of whether we are talking about GAI as a broad concept, an objective for the future, or as an income-test technique approach to income security. In the short run, it is the latter we should be discussing, for the following reasons.

a In most Western countries, long-standing income security programs are operating, many of them based on direct contributions, and the possibility of making a clean sweep and substituting a GAI for them is not great. In these circumstances, use of the GAI, the income-test technique, will tend to be supplemental.

b Estimates of the costs of a complete GAI program are so vast that they could not be borne in the near future. Thus we will tend to get a GAI proposal, perhaps below the level of health and decency, but maybe as a supplemental program. This means that social assistance will still have to carry a heavy load in the foreseeable future, and social services are more likely to be related to it than to the GAI proposal. (For example, Canada now has an income-test supplement to the flat-rate universal old age security payment, and social services are not related to this; old people needing services go to the social assistance system.) So in the short run, Canada will have to sort out whether social services should continue to be related administratively and operationally to social assistance benefits or to be separated from them.

6 The same participant also commented on policy development in the use of the income-test technique in relation to services as well as to income security. If we cannot have universality in some of these areas because of insufficient overall resources, how do we "ration" the resources to people receiving the services? Eligibility for low-income housing is now decided on an income-test basis. If we can't get a total day care program, should the same approach be used for public funds for day care, or should eligibility be decided on a *needs*-test basis? The same question would arise over homemaker services, and over drugs (not now covered by the Canadian overall health care system). If we decide that the test can apply to the working poor as well as to those on social assistance, an income test rather than a needs-test approach seems logical. However, how do we then coordinate all these various income tests (for the aging, for example, income tests for housing, drugs, homemaker services and the income supplement)? This problem must be faced soon if we are to follow the income-test approach.

7 A participant expressed optimism about the potential of existing social security programs (for example, in Britain) to achieve the *concept* of a GAI. There is danger, in considering a GAI or negative income tax, of throwing out the baby with the bath water, of producing (as has been mentioned) a below-subsistence income level. The possibility should be explored of further exploiting present programs in order to meet needs (on a universal or universal-selective basis), and to provide higher incomes and more redistribution of income. On the question of coordination, we must not forget that the people in greatest need have a tradition of *oral* communication; they can express themselves and their needs in speech but not necessarily in the middle-class way of filling out forms. Personal face-to-face contacts are required to identify needs, and to inform, advise and help about choices of services. This is the job of social services staff, but the first need people usually have is cash. Currently the staff of the U.K. supplementary benefits program, with a caseload of some 3 million, has about 16 million face-to-face contacts a year. How you educate and train the cash-delivery system staff so that they are an efficient part of the welfare referral system for identification of needs is an essential factor, whether for social assistance or for GAI.

8 For the definition of social services, a grouping into five categories was suggested by a participant, not as being exhaustive but as a "first orientation." These are services for economic assistance, treatment, institutional care, giving information, and social action. The relationship of the economic assistance services to income security generally is clear, but the other four have been developed, historically, as substitutes for income security measures. If basic income security is provided, then the other measures can be used effectively for people when the problem really is one of treatment, institutional care, information or social action. We must also distinguish between social services *direct* to people and what might be called community social services. The latter, to a certain extent, are

independent of the beneficiary – for example, control of drugs, of many forms of deviance, of population and pollution, and services with an arbitration element in them (such as for racial or other socially mixed groups). The different relationships of these two categories of social services to a general social security system should be considered.

9 A participant stated that this two-category grouping is important since much of the debate on social services is about whether they are or should be community oriented or concerned with individuals, their circumstances and needs. And part of the debate is about whether the state of receiving economic aid is itself a form of deviancy which needs to be corrected. Most thoughtful students have come to the conclusion that it should not be so regarded and that social services should not be used as though they are "correcting" delinquents or the mentally ill; thus they should be separated from the income security programs. However, in spite of the rhetoric on this, public policy, at least in the U.S., has moved toward treating the economically dependent as a class of deviants who must be treated through social services. Over and above this debate is the whole question of how effective these kinds of "treatment" services are in overcoming deviancy (such as drug addiction, or economic dependency if it is considered a deviant condition). The evidence suggests that they contribute little.

10 In responding to the discussion, Dr. Zay made the following points.
a There is a difficult choice to make in the organization of social services: whether the emphasis should be on certain groups of people (immigrants, unmarried mothers, dependent families, the mentally retarded, aged, etc.) as in the past, or whether it should be on providing services to be used by all according to *whatever* need is present. As of now, we have a mixture which is an overlapping mess. The first choice might seem the more humane, said Dr. Zay, but he personally would choose the second. Once there is concentration on selected groups, they become "problem groups" that have to be treated like sick people; he doesn't consider that immigrants, unmarried mothers, etc., are "sick." People should have services because of their actual needs, including supplementary services for *special* needs, not because of their "group classification." This is true even in the "war against poverty": the poor might use services more than others because their need is greater, but the services should not be designed specifically for the poor.
b Dr. Zay underlined that he does *not* consider GAI a substitute for other economic security programs such as the social insurances. He sees it as a residual program, in this sense somewhat allied to social assistance but differentiated by the method of computing eligibility

for payment and the guarantee of it "as a right."

c   Dr. Zay heartily agreed with the other Quebec view mentioned,[8] insofar as the administrative and operational relationships of the social services and GAI programs are concerned: that is, the programs should be entirely separate, perhaps not even in the same provincial department. However, there is still the problem of coordination, mentioned earlier, which includes consideration of the three roles he had outlined for the social services in relation to GAI. For example, a universal health services system, such as we now have in Canada, undoubtedly would affect the amount of the benefit payment in a GAI.

The Possibilities of Income Transformation[9]

Authors' Comments by S. M. Miller
Director, Urban Center,
New York University, New York

and Martin Rein
Professor, Department of Urban Studies and Planning,
Massachusetts Institute of Technology, Cambridge

Presented to the seminar by Dr. Miller

1   There has been disillusionment in the 1960s, in many Western countries, with the widely accepted theory that Keynesian economics could produce growth *without* inflation and *with* income redistribution. In the search for alternatives, social policies became "economic policies for the poor," expected to mop up after economic policies failed. Social policies cannot achieve this; basic economic policies and structures must also be directed at income redistribution. But our taxation and transfer payments policies have had limited impact on the reduction of income inequalities. And we must now not just try to solve the old problems but raise questions of broader new kinds of goals, of social relationships as well as income inequality. In this context, there are several major questions to consider in relation to GAI.

2   *Assuming GAI as a transfer policy, what are its prerequisites and corequisites?* It is clear from the discussions here that GAI cannot be a panacea for all needs, so what should accompany it to ensure a powerful impact? This includes, as already mentioned, considering

---

8. See paragraph 3, "Discussion on the Zay Paper," p. 234.
9. Background paper, p. 117.

expansion of existing programs in more useful ways.

a　Much more thought must be given not only to "deepening" the transfer system but also to making the taxation system more redistributive and progressive in reality, not just in formal structure, than it now is in many countries.

b　To have an effective GAI there must be fuller and quality employment; with high unemployment, the cost burden of any *adequate* transfer system would be politically unacceptable. And the new jobs created must also offer work satisfaction to individuals.

c　The major thrust of this paper is, as already indicated, that social policies cannot take the place of basic economic policies. So we must look at the kind of aggregate economic policies that a country is developing and at who benefits from them: that is, not only at the overall impact on the rate of growth but also at the effect on redistribution. There is no economic policy that is neutral on the question of redistribution.

d　We must consider the *composition* of the gross national product, not just its level and growth. Its composition can affect redistribution since what is included in it can cause different kinds of industrial development, of demands for occupations. This leads to questions about what kind of society we want, what are the desirable directions for economic growth – through increased military expenditure? or expenditures on pollution control? We must be concerned with the rate and nature of changes taking place in society.

e　Inequality reduction is the goal, not just bringing people up to a certain level of income, but reduction of inequalities in income and other social relationships. This aims not just at reducing poverty but at changing the social stratification of society. In this, if the factors indicated are taken into consideration, GAI can play a useful role, but not necessarily the major sustaining role.

3　*What kind of GAI will have the greatest redistribution effect?* This is an extremely difficult matter to come to grips with: it is easy generally to agree in principle, but there are violent disagreements on details. Some of the questions involved are:

a　the level of benefits of a GAI, their adequacy; how these are calculated and decided upon;

b　how a GAI can be kept dynamic, constantly related to changes in the society;

c　how GAI should be organized and administered;

d　"political" questions such as the legal rights and protection of individuals, the decision-making mechanisms and the participation of claimants in them, how political support for a GAI can be won and how GAI links up with other urgent matters, such as environment and income policies.

4 *How can the GAI be used to contribute to the development of long-run structural change in society?* As usual, we are struggling with problems of the past that should have been solved long ago, and we are being overtaken by new issues such as those raised by Dr. Philbrook. A major point is the long-run possibility of making new choices possible for individuals in how they live (for example, in communal settlements if they wish), in how they allocate their income, and so on. We should discuss how GAI can be productive toward long-run visions about what a better society would be like.

5 In summary, there are two main issues.

a What is the appropriate role for GAI? It is not a panacea; it can play a useful, not a "grand" role. It cannot substitute for basic economic policies, but can build on them in useful, positive ways.

b What is the content of GAI? how should it be planned, organized, regulated and supported? In the modest recognition of what *cannot* be accomplished lies the possibility of beginning to talk constructively about what the GAI might be able to do.

Objectives and Economic Repercussions of Guaranteed Annual Income[10]

Author's Comments, by Nicole V. Martin
Professor, National School of Public Administration,
University of Quebec

1 Many GAI proposals have been submitted as a device to increase the efficiency of transfer programs. More of the money spent should go to the poor.

2 But if, as often happens, these proposals are bound by the two constraints of no more money and no tax rate higher than 50 per cent, they are not going to do much to alleviate poverty. For these constraints are the same as those which have served in the past to restrain the impact of income security measures.

3 The result might be better allocation of public money or more equity of access to transfer money, but we would run the risk of carrying out redistribution through the transfer of money from people without employment to low-wage earners. This is a novel but scarcely desirable policy.

4 If it is going to be tried, GAI should be carefully examined to find

---

10. Background paper, p. 149.

ways of redistributing more money. That means getting away from the constraints that come from our system (in general) of defining economic agents and allocating income among them.

5 Thus GAI should be examined for qualitative objectives. It should play a significant part in improving the quality of life. In the first place, this quality could be measured for what is achieved in income redistribution both through a negative income tax (or other technique) and through the operation of the positive income tax. The quality of a GAI should also be judged by how far it improves the condition of underprivileged groups. In particular, its quality should be measured by the effect on the *relative* socioeconomic position of groups according to criteria concerned with access to consumer resources, savings, leisure and work – in short, all those things that make up the actual or potential quality of life.

6 In this context, the chief attraction of GAI is that it could be a turning point in income security policies. It could mean we would face up to the real cause of poverty: deprivation of economic resources. This deprivation is often camouflaged as illness, physical or mental handicap, or old age which, in the last analysis, are associated with poverty only because of our system of income distribution.

7 Insofar as GAI is perceived as an instrument capable of effecting a real change in income distribution, the kind of constraints it must face will depend on the capacity for change – or better still for transformation – in our socioeconomic system. The seminar papers and discussions have underlined the many factors emphasizing the need for such transformation. There are new types of problems that demand new types of solutions. We are beginning to face the need for new approaches to economic and social problems, and GAI can be but part of one of these.

8 In examining the well-known problem of unemployment/inflation, Professor Ulmer opts squarely for full employment through public services or employment in the public sector. He remarks that work should be considered as a direct "output" for social well-being, rather than just an "input" to obtain productivity. We can add also that work should not be considered as the only means of *development* and of man's command over resources.

9 Leisure and investment are and should also be considered as outputs for social well-being. Leisure, if it is sufficient to permit man to be productive for himself and his community, is a source of the development of well-being. Equally, the individual's capacity to save

– to be an investor, perhaps even an entrepreneur – is not just a source of command over resources but also a contribution to the development of well-being.

10 Thus, what might be needed is a model that makes possible the redistribution of the opportunities for work and savings – and also the *amount* of work and leisure – among individuals. We should look for a balance between the effects on productivity of a new allocation of opportunities for work and of opportunities to save and invest.

11 It may well be that such an approach would help to solve the famous unemployment/inflation enigma. In North America, it is possible that this approach should be in some way related to regional economic disparities. It has often been urged in Canada that there should be a regionalization of fiscal policies, which is only a first step toward a more selective approach to employment and development problems.

12 In this kind of approach a GAI can facilitate the more radical changes that are necessary both to solve the present acute problems and to bring about greater equality.

Discussion on the Miller/Rein and Martin Papers

1 A participant pointed out that so far the seminar had concentrated on broad questions, important in themselves but not necessarily relevant to the immediate question of GAI. Problems of income redistribution, of equality and inequality, full employment, the tolerance level of inflation, universal social services – all are desirable goals, involving the middle class as well as the poor. But the need for "GAI is a crisis of the poor by definition" and first things should come first. The speaker stated that there are immediate specific issues such as: what kind of a tax rate (recovery rate) on earned income is desirable or reasonable with an income guarantee? what rules should govern benefit payments, reporting, definition of family units? Is it reasonable to distinguish in any way between the chronic dependent (the "deserving" poor) and the people reluctant to work (the "non-deserving" poor)?

2 Three broad points were emphasized by another speaker.
a The income test technique (applied in the negative income tax form of GAI and proposed for Canadian family allowances) would give a new dimension to the question of income redistribution. Under

social insurance or present demogrant[11] programs this has largely been horizontal, but vertical redistribution would be increased with the new technique: "we would be reaching up to the working poor in the population." This is a fundamental change, based on the argument that the economic system is not providing adequately for these people through the normal wage system and that, for example, raising the minimum wage is not enough since it takes no account of family responsibilities.

b The question of whether GAI should be a main support or residual program would depend on the particular circumstances in a country – for instance, whether social insurance programs are deeply entrenched or whether there is a strong puritan work ethic. It is possible that such programs might be held constant or even phased out and the GAI take on greater importance. However, these are political conditions, depending on people's attitudes.

c The regional problem is vital in countries such as Canada. How do you compensate through income security programs for the great variation in wages not only between regions but also within a region? Automatic mechanisms, as in the social insurance programs, cannot deal with variations in the standards of living. Some form of social assistance will always be necessary as a back-up to any GAI approach for emergencies and special needs and for variations in standards of living.

3 It was suggested by one participant that Dr. Miller's phrase "social integration," as used in his paper, might mean reducing the autonomy of the individual. However, it *ought* to mean including a greater number of people in society-wide programs and that therefore the regulations should be less restrictive and more adaptable. Defining people as some kind of social assistance recipients should not be part of a GAI program. The speaker added that "the social division of labor" is also a problem in achieving integration; the GAI approach, which is *not* based on this division should help broaden the definition of what is considered "socially acceptable" and useful work.

4 Consumer credit, a participant argued, is a form of guaranteed income, supplied through private enterprise, in that it enables people to buy the minimum of goods that society (not the bureaucrats) has defined as socially necessary. The most use of it, in proportion to family responsibilities and income, is made by the poor at a great cost to them and profit to the rich. The cumulative debt for a family over a number of years could mean the commitment in advance of 50 to 60 per cent of regular annual income and sometimes up to two or three years' income at one time. This is redistribution in re-

---

11. For an explanation of the demogrant, see J. I. Clark, pp. 273–274.

verse, from the poor to the rich. Perhaps, with a program of GAI, government should take over the operation of consumer credit but at low interest rates.

5 Another participant made the following comments.

a As well as *inter-personal* (through transfer payments, etc.) and *inter-regional* redistribution of income, there is a third kind which might be called *inter-temporal* – the way individuals choose to distribute their income over their life span. But this is not a free choice because people are told how to do it and forced to do it through contributions for sickness, old age, etc. – the middle generation paying for the young and the old. Can GAI help to give more freedom of choice in this?

b It is not surprising that the various measures, through taxes, for *inter-personal* redistribution do not achieve their full goals. People will always try to evade such measures, and this must be recognized and stricter controls applied.

c "Relative" poverty should be considered. But what then are the implications of using "poverty lines" for programs since they are so rigid and give room for so few alternatives for action?

d In discussing equality we should perhaps think of a suggestion advanced in the 1930s: if all people were given the same income there would be a problem of allocating work among them; perhaps they should pay for the right to work, to have a special profession or job!

6 It was agreed that there were two major lines of approach in the seminar discussions: some people wanted to concentrate on the social consequences of a GAI (for example, its impact on social and economic structures, on the pattern of work); others were more interested in actual implementation, the mechanics of organizing and administering a GAI. On the latter point, it was thought that the current U.S. experiments with GAI, briefly outlined in J. I. Clark's paper,[12] should be more closely examined to help the group reach some specific and practical conclusions. It was stated that governments and politicians in a number of countries (certainly in Canada) are looking for advice and ideas, in the context of present not future society, which this seminar should try to give.

7 A participant presented four concrete problems in implementing GAI.

a *The marginal tax rate in relation to the benefit level, and the relationship of that level to the bottom decile of earnings in a society.* For example, should the benefit level be set at the tax threshold of

---

12. Pp. 289–291.

the bottom decile or below it (the principle of "less eligibility")? How far should it cover the working poor? How should it be "tapered"? If earnings are allowed, should the GAI be taxable, and, if so, at what rate? (If it is not taxable in these circumstances, it is potentially regressive rather than progressive in its distribution effects.)

b *The relationship between GAI and housing costs.* The British experience is exploitation of the welfare system by both public and private housing; when minimum income levels for the poor are raised, rents go up proportionately so there is no net benefit. Thus rent controls become a corollary to GAI.

c *A "work test" as part of the eligibility regulations for GAI.* This is usually viewed as necessary if the benefit level is above the bottom decile income line. (It is applied in Britain in the family income supplements (FIS) program for the working poor.) Should people be required to take any job or only jobs similar to those for which they have been trained? (An extreme example of this problem was cited: in London at one time 150 unemployed were registered as shepherds.) How far should choice and individual freedom be curtailed as the benefit level becomes higher? Without a work test, middle-class young people (mainly) will take advantage of a GAI scheme, thus tending to make it regressive in nature; they are more ingenious in avoiding work than are the poor who do not register for jobs for which there is no demand. This mainly middle-class action is not solely to "milk the system" because of laziness, it is also a question of rising job expectations. Thus a trained visual media technician, say, expects to work at this job and may go "on welfare" until a similar job opens up, even though laborers' jobs may be available.

d *The data bank problem associated with the information necessary to make a GAI successful.* The problem of equity and equalization, etc., must be faced to ensure that the programs as implemented are primarily helping the poor. The consequences of any course of action must be spelled out.

8 It was pointed out that in most United States GAI proposals, benefits are set well below the poverty lines. This is considered incentive enough to take employment; a work test is not needed. Senator Abraham Ribicoff's plan, for example (in amendments to H.R. 1),[13] is set at three-quarters of the poverty lines, with gradual escalation, say, from $3,000 to $4,000 a year. But unless there is integration with the regular tax system, such a plan would effect no more income transfer than social assistance and one-third of the U.S. population would be on the scheme by 1977. The integration could take

---

13. See Rein, p. 180.

various forms – such as a taxing-back or a tax credit system. A participant stated that if the principle is applied that a negative income should vary with earnings, a work incentive should be included. This is the only concept so far actually used – as in the British FIS and proposed in the U.S. Family Assistance Plan. However, neither of these plans meets the requirement, urged by some, of integration into the regular tax system. Are they transfers or subsidies?

9 It was noted that the Ribicoff type of plan would produce, for many people, a very inadequate income, below that of the working poor. Moreover, as the plan is on a year-to-year basis, a normally well-off person might get a benefit which really would lead to regressive distribution – for example, someone who worked for only eight months a year but earned $8,000 in that period.

10 Following are comments made in the discussion about the preliminary results of current U.S. experiments with the negative income tax.

a In the New Jersey projects,[14] it appears that this form of GAI has little disincentive for *primary* workers (chief family earners) to work, and that *secondary* workers tend not to drop out of the labor force but to search for higher paying jobs and work at them for shorter hours. However, other experiments seem to indicate that there *are* disincentives. The question remains: if income is guaranteed, will people stop working?

b A real problem has been found in getting the right kind of reporting from beneficiaries, in interpreting to them what is required so that they understand, for example, what kinds of income are to be included or excluded. In implementing such plans, some form of "intermediary" group is necessary to give information and reassurance so that there won't be "unhappy beneficiaries."

c Negative income tax was conceived as a benefit to employed people. Since the experiments were launched, more generous social assistance benefits have been established. This has led to an issue of "political overlap," especially in establishing eligibility and in monitoring the projects.

d A serious limitation in these experiments is that the beneficiaries know they are being observed and may not behave normally. Differences in behavior have been noted, and assessment of the results must therefore be qualified. However, if experiments go on long enough, this problem may disappear.

e The receipt of a "windfall" or of a permanent form of personal income is another complication in the experiments; this includes the way in which the recipient views the effects on his situation of any resulting official action.

---

14. See J. I. Clark, p. 290.

11 Support was expressed for the view that an intermediary group "to interpret and help" is necessary, and it is part of the social services. However, this participant had found that people chiefly complain not about lack of services but about the social assistance program which treats the poor as different and stigmatizes them. It should be replaced, as a *main* support program, by other forms of income security, and GAI is the most "universal" way of distributing money. GAI should not be considered residual and should be linked with the universal social services. Another participant doubted whether GAI *should* be a major instrument of public policy. In any case, no definitive conclusion has yet been reached about its significance and usefulness as such an instrument; the options are still open.

12 Reverting to the work test as applied in Britain, the question was asked whether benefits were at all near the going wage in industry. In reply, it was stated that people could get by on FIS for some time, including students who are eligible for FIS at 16 but also often have family help. It is more a question of rising expectations about satisfying jobs. This is not confined to the middle class, but having the middle class involved helps "destigmatize" the welfare system. How long should people be allowed to wait for the "right" job if their expectations are unrealistic? The work test involves interviews at intervals up to a certain time, but how do you define and test the criterion of "genuinely seeking work," which is an attitude of mind? The speaker stated that the work test should not be a punitive measure, although it could be so if operated by staff without adequate training, with racial prejudices, and so on. Instead, it should be positive in its effects, applied by constructive, tolerant staff to help people find satisfactory alternatives through the cooperation of other agencies, such as rehabilitation retraining services.

13 Referring to earlier suggestions that we should develop the potential of existing income security measures rather than instituting a new program, a participant made the following comments on the Canadian situation.

a The Canada Assistance Plan has only been in force from 1966 and is certainly not fully developed in most provinces. There is a heavy commitment to it "in a societal sense," and it is perhaps an open question whether we should be moving to a GAI at this time.

b A new administration would have to be built up for GAI, with staff having quite different capacities and training from those in present programs, and this could not be done in a few months. It is unlikely one could get the kind of dedicated skilled staff that are used in experimental projects and who would give a different performance from that in routine administration.

c On the *method* of a GAI, Canada (and perhaps Britain, too) with the tradition of universal programs should consider a demogrant form of GAI, with tax-back procedures, as an alternative to a negative income tax system. There are pros and cons, of course: many consider the demogrant method too costly, though estimates made for the Senate Committee on Poverty have neither proved nor disproved this view. The reduction of stigma is urged in favor of the demogrant, but the poor are stigmatized in many ways besides that of being "on welfare" (by dress, housing, behavior, school performance). It could be argued either that "welfare" is the last back-breaking straw or that it is just one more stigma people have to live with.

d The federal-provincial cost-sharing system in Canada, and the continuous pressures for change or alternatives to it, complicate the development of new income security programs.

e Also because of cost-sharing, there is great provincial variety in these programs; certainly not all the provinces would agree to a federally determined GAI program.

f There is need for constructive staff work in direct contacts with clients (for example, in relation to the work test), but the kind of hierarchy of organization and salaries that exists in the public services means that the most suitable staff are likely to be two or three levels above direct client contact. These hierarchies will have to be reduced, the organization made more horizontal, which is difficult for government agencies to achieve. The most feasible approach might be upgrading the responsibilities, training and salaries of staff "who are dealing with human beings and not just with paper."

14 A problem was raised that must be considered in *any* plan that depends on individuals taking the initiative in applying for benefits: how can the most needy, the most shy people be reached? Perhaps a check on those registered for the *compulsory* schemes would help find them. For example, in Sweden it was found that a great number of the needy who were registered for the compulsory health insurance plan were not registered for income security schemes, often for fantastic reasons.

15 Returning to the question of GAI as a major or residual program, a participant suggested that negative income tax, though seemingly objective, is extremely inefficient financially. For example, assuming a GAI of $4,000 a year (the poverty line for a certain sized family, all of which would receive this payment) and an "internal" tax rate of 30 per cent, benefits would result for families up to earnings of $12,000 a year. The people above this level would be paying for the plan and would be the only ones paying positive taxes. As a major scheme, this would be very expensive and, from that

standpoint, impractical. A negative income tax plan could, however, have a role as a modest supplement to other income.

16 Another speaker argued that this view erected "the usual straw man – the very generous GAI that completely eliminates poverty." Serious supporters of a negative income tax do not believe there could be a single-schedule approach to the problem. For example, the Castonguay-Nepveu commission proposed two schedules: one for people who can work and the other for unemployables.[15] According to this view, the intent of a GAI is to provide a supplement to earnings; the total income should then take people out of poverty. But GAI should not, by itself, be expected completely to eliminate poverty for those *unable* to work.

---

15. See J. I. Clark, pp. 277–278.

Plenary Session, Friday, April 14, 1972

Chairman: J. Harvey Perry
Executive Director, The Canadian Bankers' Association, Toronto

Group Chairmen's Reports[16]

1 John C. Spencer
Professor and Head, Department of Social Administration,
Faculty of Social Sciences, University of Edinburgh

I should like first to indicate the themes that seemed to run through the two group sessions that I chaired.

First was the problem of defining guaranteed annual income, and particularly the question of whether it should be a "topping-up" process or a basic program. I think it is fair to say that in our discussions virtually no one (especially Canadians) wanted to make the GAI a basic program that would subsume most other programs. The second theme was work and work opportunities; the third was the definition of minimum income and needs; the fourth was the relation between full employment and GAI, and the fifth was the links between GAI and the social services.

Following are some of the main points that emerged in the discussions.

a Under the first theme there was much discussion about fitting GAI into the individual cultural, economic and social structure conditions of particular countries and of keeping in mind their varying approaches to other income security programs. For instance, one participant thought that the GAI concept does not apply to developing or socialist countries, nor to countries in Western Europe where

---

16. Seminar participants met in three groups, or working parties, for more detailed discussions in which the observers also took part. The composition of the groups was changed for the first two sessions; the groups decided to combine for the third and final session. The three group chairmen were assisted, respectively, by rapporteurs Michael Audain, David Ross and Novia Carter, who are program directors in the Canadian Council on Social Development.

there is a clear distinction between social insurance and social assistance – as in West Germany, France and Switzerland. He suggested that one of the main motivations behind GAI appears to be income redistribution which is not the concern of social insurance systems except on a horizontal basis (risk-sharing among working people). Still others pointed out the effects of social and economic structure on the use of GAI as a redistributive and anti-poverty measure. In Quebec, for example, it might be necessary, because of high unemployment, to bias the program heavily toward the very poor (non-working people), whereas in the United States such a bias which would largely help black people might become a racial issue.

The point was also made that in an agrarian society such as Yugoslavia, different techniques must be employed to reduce poverty from those appropriate to a more industrial society. When a high proportion of a country's population is in the process of industrialization, the selective migration to urban areas that this produces forces the issue of industrialization of agrarian production; this poses an economic question of a different order.

A speaker suggested that most Western countries seemed to be facing three common problems:

(1) a social assistance level that is believed to be inadequate;
(2) the working poor who cannot get their income problems (such as those related to family responsibilities) resolved by minimum wage legislation;
(3) the fact that if governments measurably increase social assistance payments (to those unable to work or unemployed) they appear to "compete" with the too low level of minimum wages.
He saw GAI as an "extra technique" that should enable the entire population to enjoy certain standards of health and decency by obviating the need for social assistance and providing a supplement to the wages of the working poor.

Another participant considered GAI with two objectives in mind: as a means of extending and rationalizing existing social welfare measures; and as a technique for guaranteeing the right to assistance, thereby supporting the notion that work is not the be all and end all in our society. Still another speaker said that social programs generally appear to be "a patchwork on the labor market"; perhaps we need to question the concept and validity of the labor market as it currently exists.

Incidentally, one participant questioned the use of "annual" in GAI. Why not just guaranteed income? It was suggested that the word "annual" was simply for convenience as standards of living are usually measured on an annual basis.

As already mentioned, the discussion did produce a consensus that GAI alone cannot be a panacea for our income security problems. But it also showed that there is a good deal more disagreement or at the least confusion about the meaning of GAI than we had perhaps at first anticipated.

b The second theme was work and work opportunities, and current Canadian approaches to this – particularly through Opportunities for Youth and the Local Initiatives Program – were presented and discussed. These have unique features that are of international significance, and it was interesting for those of us from other countries to compare them with our own efforts: for example, the British Urban Aid Program and the 1930s Work Projects Administration program in the U.S. which, it appears, the Nixon administration is thinking of reviving. It was noted that the Canadian projects are labor intensive which is the kind of work Melville Ulmer had in mind (in his background paper for this seminar) when defining his public employment concepts. It was suggested that a public employment policy would be one way to overcome the problems that low minimum wages create in achieving progressive income security programs. The temporary and haphazard nature of the Canadian programs (OFY and LIP) at this time was a cause for concern; on the other hand, if they become permanent they run the danger of adopting the standard public service format and becoming highly bureaucratized.

A massive homemaker service on a permanent basis with full- or part-time staff was cited as an example of means of providing work opportunities. One danger seen here by some was that this kind of service might develop standards and training skills that would cut out the use of autonomous groups and indigenous leaders which is such a key and desirable part of OFY and the LIP: in short, create the kind of artificial skill requirements that are sometimes a barrier to the provision of other types of social services. On the other hand, it was suggested that the development of paraprofessionals could be very positive; for example, a group of cleaning women in Holland have achieved high status by organizing their own union, achieving good pay, having their own uniforms and equipment.

c We then moved to the third theme: defining minimum income and needs. If one of the aims of GAI is to provide a minimum level of income, what should this be, and who should decide what it is and therefore what needs it is supposed to meet?

A participant suggested that definition of need is extremely complex as people have different views about it, varying with regions, social class, etc. Probably it is impossible to find any one notion of need. Another view given was that you *could* define need in "grocery-basket" terms and raise income accordingly, but people might be poorer still in relation to current social and psychological definitions of need. Perhaps we should have to consider "quality of life" in setting a GAI level. It was also pointed out that providing additional goods or services leads to the creation of new needs, of dissatisfactions, aggravated by the suggestions, through advertising, of immense needs. This means that the process of evolving a better society is continuous and we must not become complacent if, for example, a GAI concept is implemented. Another point made was that once a GAI is set it must be guaranteed as a right and that the system must be uniform, automatic and systematic. Since any foreseeable GAI level is bound to be on the low side, other programs would be needed to back it up, particularly help on housing costs (usually the biggest variable in the expenditures of the poor) and assistance for exceptional needs and emergencies.

This led back to the basic objectives of GAI. Is it, asked one participant, just supposed to meet minimum needs? If so, he considered this a most inadequate objective. Another speaker said that social justice – equity – should be the main objective of a GAI. A third agreed that meeting minimum needs did little to lift people out of poverty; if GAI were pegged to this level it would simply mean guaranteed annual poverty.

As you see we did not come to any firm conclusions on this topic either. But we did identify the very real problem that exists in defining needs and the relation of a GAI level to them, and the necessity for research and study in order to make better judgments on this.

d In the discussion on the fourth theme, full employment and GAI, it was suggested that David Smith, in his paper, had been too optimistic about the possibilities of creating full employment without inflation and that he should have dealt with the problem of wage and price control. Dr. Smith commented that he was, in fact, not very optimistic about achieving a high level of employment with price stability although this situation had obtained in 1950–55 and in earlier periods in Canada. He saw the unemployment – inflation problem now as being caused by what he called "policy induced cycles": that is, cycles more related to political activity than to economic demands. In his opinion, if Canada wanted a little more equality and a little more employment, perhaps it would be wise to opt for a little more inflation. As to wage and price controls, current U.S. experience suggested that these are very difficult to hold for any length of time although they might make some contribution in the short run.

On the relationship between transfer payments and inflation, Dr. Smith expressed some concern about the effect of increased social security payments on existing expenditure patterns: for example, would the level of savings be affected? However, he felt this was not a serious problem as the government could always, through the tax system, adjust the level of demand and generate more savings if it wanted to. But there was the problem of how much you could tax the middle-income group in Canada without increasing emigration to the United States.

Some interesting differences of opinion emerged on the relative importance of full employment and GAI. Dr. Miller was asked why his paper had stressed that full employment was a prerequisite to income redistribution in the U.S. He stated that a massive program of cash transfers at a level that would lift people out of poverty would simply cost too much; the benefits would have to be reduced to real inadequacy unless there was full employment. Another speaker did not consider full employment necessary for the introduction of the GAI concept, stating that with a different approach to work, as in the public employment program suggested in Dr. Ulmer's paper, the problem of level of benefits could be solved.

A participant asked why countries such as Canada and the U.S. put up with less than full employment, citing Australia and New Zealand as countries with full employment and, he maintained, a decent level of living. Others asserted that full employment did not necessarily solve the intractable problem of low wages, especially in a country such as Canada with particular problems. Among these were climatic conditions resulting in seasonal industries, and a large number of self-employed with fairly low incomes – such as farmers, shopkeepers, insurance salesmen – for whom full employment would do little. It was also suggested that the age and labor force structure in Canada almost defied the possibility of producing full employment; at a time when we are not enjoying a very high rate of economic development we are going through the highest rate of labor force growth in the world. We might possibly be facing another labor shortage by 1980, but it was suggested that, with advancing technology, Canada and the U.S. might never again have full employment in the traditional sense.

An interesting argument also arose about the role of the economic system. On the one hand, it was asserted that the function of the economy is to produce goods and services to meet our many and differing needs, not to provide jobs. The opposing view was that the economy fails when it does not provide full employment; there is no more realistic political goal than full employment.

To sum up, I think what I might call the "flavor" of this part of our discussion might best be expressed in the words of one participant: "It is time we dragged the economy back into society."

e   Finally, under the fifth theme, the linkage between social services and the GAI, a participant who found the term "social services" a rather fuzzy concept asked: "Is there a body of the social services that is inextricably intertwined with the notion of income maintenance, or are social services intended to deal with another general set of problems?"

One view expressed was that social services are linked in part to the incapacity of certain individuals to achieve income self-sufficiency; they should therefore be coordinated with measures for income redistribution. But it was a moot point whether they should be "inextricably linked." However, another speaker thought that, though the tendency in countries now adopting the GAI concept is to separate other social services from the cash transfer operation, certain of such service functions should be an integral part of any income security program. These should, in his view, include provision of information about other social services, referral and linkage to them, and advocacy (identifying problems for which no service currently exists). He believed that these functions could be undertaken by non-professional workers within the income security system.

This view in turn was challenged on the ground that these services should be available on a universal basis to all citizens. It was pointed out, however, that the problem with universal services was that they seemed generally to provide the most benefits to middle class people who are skilful in using them; thus we also need to have a service component in income security schemes. This is particularly important as the income security system is likely to be in touch with such a large proportion of the population.

At the close of the session a participant summed up his impression of our discussion of the fifth theme. It appeared, he thought, that in the judgment of the professional social welfare people present, the administration of a GAI would not require the development of a highly specialized professional class. There is a social service component in such programs; this could, however, be staffed by indigenous non-professionals, who might perhaps do a better job than more highly trained workers (particularly in the area of "outreach" to the clients). However, this seemed to assume that the GAI would not embody a work test. He suggested that if a work test is necessary, a range of discretionary authority would be involved that could not be properly discharged by untrained people. He added the general observation that it was obvious that the question of a social service component would have different connotations for varying types of GAI programs.

Naturally, not everyone present agreed with all of this interpretation and the personal views expressed. However, there was full endorsement of the final statement by a participant: "some staff will always be necessary to help the computer deal with the problem of the lady whose dog ate her monthly cheque!"

2 Reuben C. Baetz
Executive Director,
The Canadian Council on Social Development, Ottawa

In the first session, the group concentrated on the ideas and the proposals in the Smith and Ulmer papers. We discussed at length both the role of full employment in the income distribution process and the feasibility of achieving full employment today through the pursuit of traditional monetary and fiscal policies.

However, it was difficult to restrict discussion of these issues, and it was as if the group had tacitly agreed that traditional approaches through full employment were indeed inadequate. For example, rather early the basic and perplexing question was raised: what is full employment?

Comments in our first plenary session shattered, I think, some of our earlier assumptions about what is employment and unemployment, or what are accurate unemployment statistics. There may be a great deal of hidden unemployment in our data, since, as noted in a plenary session, it is becoming increasingly recognized that when unemployment increases, secondary workers, such as housewives and the aged, tend to become discouraged and drop out of the labor market. Hence the recorded unemployment rate understates the true rate.

But given that we have to work with some data, and we must agree on some definition of full employment, the point was raised that even at full employment there are many people who do not earn incomes sufficient to lift them beyond the poverty level. Recent studies have indicated that about two-thirds of the "poor" population are in fact in the labor force. Market activity alone, therefore, does not seem to provide an adequate answer to this group's problems.

Discussion of full employment followed another important avenue: this was whether, in fact, full employment is a feasible goal in today's circumstances. There seemed to be consensus within the group that in Canada today, and probably in the United States as well, full employment as traditionally measured is virtually impossible to achieve. Therefore, we have the choice of the type of public employment proposals advanced by Dr. Ulmer or certain variants such as the Local Initiatives Program in Canada, or of a guaranteed annual income approach through one or more programs of transfer payments, or (more probably) of some combination of both.

At this point the group moved rather quickly to a discussion of the issues of the guaranteed annual income. The first issue raised was whether or not an employable person has a right to a GAI when gainful employment is available. Or, to rephrase the question, is the GAI available on demand? This immediately divided the participants into two groups. One group claimed that if the GAI is made available on demand, and if no work test is required, a strong work disincentive will be created. The other group considered the GAI on demand as opening up avenues to an entirely new type of lifestyle for most people. In effect, if the GAI is payable as a right, regardless of employment circumstances, people will be free to choose their own lifestyles and reject a role in the traditional market sector if they wish.

The question of work disincentives seemed to become the focal point in the discussion. In defence of the belief that GAI will not provide particularly strong incentives for people to disengage from the traditional labor market and simply loaf around on a GAI, it was pointed out that many working poor do not go on welfare even if the incentives to continue to work seem weak. As an example, it was reported that 20 per cent of Sweden's labor force is regarded as "slum labor," that is, labor which earns poverty wages in undesirable working conditions. Nevertheless, such people do not fall back on Sweden's excellent welfare program: they choose to work rather than live on welfare. It was felt similar experiences could be cited in many countries. Also, the view was again expressed that traditional labor market employment is too narrow a context; when we can offer people a vast variety of interesting jobs, provided by the public sector, we can come back to the question of whether people who opt out have a right to income. Finally, it was suggested we were spending too much time in discussing the smallest group involved – the so-called loafers. Most people who would benefit from a GAI are the unemployables, the working poor (who would go on working) and the unemployed who are genuinely seeking work.

However, while the possible disincentive to work may be of small consequence to social scientists, in reality it looms large as a political issue. And although we agreed in our group that we were spending a lot of time on an academic question, we recognized the importance of the political factor, the people factor, I might call it, in determining social policies and social programs.

Having discussed the relationship between the GAI and the employables, we turned to the GAI and the unemployables. And again, the discussion began with a question: is a guaranteed annual income for unemployables a right? It was recognized that unemployability is defined differently in different countries, which immediately created a problem for comparative discussion. For example, female heads of one-parent families are regarded as employables in some countries and as unemployables in others. Therefore, when we tend to classify our unemployed into these two categories – the unemployable and the employable – we should think more carefully about what we mean by "unemployable." It is not nearly as neat a category as we often believe.

Without attempting to reach consensus on whether either employables or unemployables have a right to GAI, and without trying to define "unemployable," the group went on to consider some of the other problems in a GAI scheme. Even if one accepts the right to a GAI as a goal, the method of implementation can seriously dissipate the planned objectives. This would include the level of payment: a participant observed that the benefits of a well-designed income security program could be so low as to be meaningless, resulting only in guaranteed poverty. The benefits can also be dissipated through a change in the real value of payments over time, or the results can be skewed through the definition of the beneficiary (i.e., whether it is the family unit or individuals), and, finally, through the pattern of administration which can create many barriers to easy access. It was suggested that when decisions are made on these problems of implementation, it would become automatically apparent whether the GAI was simply an extension of public assistance or a new evolutionary concept.

A final observation that I would like to make on this session is that sometimes what groups choose not to discuss is as significant as what they do discuss. What struck me as being significant was the tendency to shy away from serious consideration of income inequality and the redistribution of income – which would undoubtedly be required with the introduction of an effective and adequate GAI.

The papers by Miller and Rein, Martin, Zay, and Philbrook provided the subjects for our second group discussion. Briefly, these papers cover: income inequalities, and the fact that these have not narrowed over time; a description of various GAI schemes along with the costing of such schemes; a description of the present methods of granting direct aid to the poor in Canada; and the role of social services in a GAI program.

It seemed inevitable that in a discussion of GAI interest would turn to the negative income tax (NIT) as the major method for delivering GAI. In fact, throughout the group discussions it almost appeared that GAI and NIT were considered synonymous.

The discussion turned at the outset to some of the specific issues that must be resolved before the implementation of a NIT scheme is possible. We opened with the question: to whom should a negative income tax apply, to both employables and unemployables? It was proposed, for purposes of the discussion, that the negative income tax should apply only to those in, or potentially in, the labor market – that is, the employables. There was a feeling, if not a consensus, that it would be highly undesirable to apply the same guaranteed floor income to those permanently removed from the labor market.

For instance, a strong incentive to work accomplished through a low recovery rate built into a NIT scheme would be cruel to those who are clearly unemployable, such as the aged and disabled. Canada's Special Senate Committee on Poverty in its report *Poverty in Canada* proposed that the NIT scheme apply right across the country to both employables and unemployables, both to those in the labor market and those permanently removed from it. I hope that this seminar will have a powerful influence in challenging this notion.

The question was raised: if we are considering negative income tax as a device for helping the working poor only, why should we not consider a minimum wage policy as a device for helping them? The reply was that a minimum wage cannot realistically adjust income to family size nor to other family income.

It was then suggested that we could combine a minimum wage policy with a more vigorous program of family allowances. The consensus of the group was that family allowances have not had an altogether illustrious history – at least not in Britain, Canada, and some other countries; we were somewhat pessimistic about the use of family allowances as a key program. However, a participant drew our attention to the family allowances program in France which provides large payments and in which benefits for wage earners derive exclusively from employer contributions through a tax on their payrolls. This does contain elements of a minimum wage adjusted to family size, but there was agreement within the group that minimum wages alone were not the solution to the poverty of the working poor.

The group made an attempt to define poverty lines, or an adequate floor under a NIT scheme. However, the discussion ran into problems around the question of how one could establish an objective minimum that would be based on the needs of a family. For example, what are the basic *needs* of a family: is an automobile in today's world a basic need, is a television set a basic need? It was agreed that needs appear to be relative and in a constant state of flux.

Realizing the tremendous amount of subjectivity involved in establishing minimum levels of need, the discussion went on to other issues stemming from negative income taxation. We did not attempt to define the minimum under a NIT scheme in terms of the other definition of poverty – that is, reducing income inequalities by some given degree – where there is not so much subjectivity. If we agree to raise the share going to the bottom fifth from where it is at present (7 per cent) to, say, 12 per cent, then we can work out what the minimum level should be and we can adjust it for family size. However, the group made no attempt to pursue this approach.

A government official cautioned against relying completely on giving poor people cash handouts without building in some form of control over rent. He explained that, following a statutory increase in universal old age pensions, he invariably receives a considerable number of letters complaining that the increase in pensions has been matched by an increase in rent. Therefore an effective NIT scheme must be accompanied by some control over shelter costs.

But the issue of rent control was approached cautiously by the group in light of its rather unsatisfactory history, and it was suggested that we concentrate on increasing the supply of housing, including public housing. It was pointed out that in Britain and Western Europe, public housing represents about 40 per cent of the total housing stock, substantially higher than in North America. However, in Canada the public housing approach is being rejected because of the stigma attached to the poor people who become so visibly identified. There appears to be a basic difference between the approach to public housing here and in Europe.

There was some consensus that providing housing allowances to the poor would have more merit than simply building more and more public housing units. Also, there may be great possibilities in the cooperative housing approach. There seemed to be agreement that when considering a housing policy in cooperation with a NIT scheme, one might have to pursue a multi-faceted approach, since there appears to be no simple answer to providing cheap housing.

The group did not shy away from one of the most difficult issues in the NIT approach – that is, whether a work test should be part of the scheme or not. As in our first session, it appeared that this issue alone was the most important in determining whether a GAI scheme delivered through NIT would provide a new way of life and a new departure for society, or whether it would simply become an extension of the present welfare system. In the discussion of the work test, attention naturally turned to the approach adopted in Britain. There, a work test applies in that a single worker must find suitable work within four weeks and a married worker within three months, or he is required to take whatever work is available. However, it was noted that when the occupational unemployment rate in a region goes above 2 per cent, this rule is waived. (In light of the prevailing rate in North America of 5 per cent and 6 per cent unemployment, it would appear that we could almost permanently waive that rule here!)

The work test was discussed perhaps more vociferously than any other issue in the session. The group seemed to be divided between those who considered GAI as simply an extension or improvement of the present welfare system, and those who considered GAI to be a departure toward a new society.

Finally, under a NIT scheme it was questioned how much information is necessary to make the scheme efficient, and whether the amount of information infringes upon an individual's right to privacy. Through our computer technology we can obtain all types of information on people, but it raises a fundamental question of the invasion of privacy, expressed by one participant as "the right to hide." For example, it was mentioned that in Britain, of the total money spent on one-parent families headed by females, only 9 per cent is recovered from the deserting males, while in Sweden there is a 70 per cent recovery rate. The reason given for the 70 per cent rate is that Sweden has an efficient information network that would probably not be acceptable in Britain or in some other countries.

In conclusion, it should be noted that in neither session did we refer to the important question of the role of the social services in a GAI program, except for a brief discussion of housing. This, I am sure, was not from lack of interest but because, in the time at our disposal, we gave higher priority to other issues in GAI. And while, of course, we did not resolve these issues, we felt we had clarified considerably their pros and cons. We hope these results can be used effectively in the next stages of evolving a sounder social security system in Canada and other countries.

3   Arthur J.R. Smith
President,
The Conference Board in Canada, Ottawa

I suppose one could say that this has been a seminar whose basic concern has been the quality of modern societies. Any grand conception of that subject might well have started with a larger base – with fundamental issues such as the evolution of relationships of individuals to political and legal systems, and the central concepts of freedoms and rights. But I think the organizers of the seminar wisely decided not to start with these large issues, which fall essentially within the realm of philosophers (if not of angels), but instead sought to focus attention on the narrower issue of the guaranteed annual income and the pyramid of issues relevant to it.

I think the concept of organizing the sessions with an introductory, broad paper by Dr. Katz to help set the stage, and then of moving into three sets of twin papers to narrow the focus of attention and discussion was a good design. The first set of papers dealt with income generation from employment; the second set looked at forms of income security and of services falling outside the income-expenditure streams, and the third set looked at income distribution and the GAI (and some of its variants) in a closer way.

The logic of this design was that in the three working parties there would be an opportunity to take up the sets in order. In the first group that I chaired, on employment and unemployment, we followed the procedure fairly closely. There was general agreement with the ideas presented in some of the papers – particularly the Miller/Rein paper – namely, that high employment is a necessary, but by no means a sufficient condition for a healthy society and for adequate attention to the fundamental problems of inequality. In other words, a high quality society cannot coexist with a poorly functioning economy that is not generating an adequate flow of new jobs. Only under high employment conditions is it possible to move forward to better *quality,* and *equality,* within society.

The discussion took two interesting directions. One was whether there might be a tendency today toward more mismatching between job-seekers and job-providers – a failure of markets in some sense, and an inadequacy or a failure of manpower and labor market policies. Certain implications emerged from this. One of them was the possibility of manpower constraints added to traditional treasury constraints on providing more jobs. And on the quality of manpower, there was an interesting focus in the discussion on the importance of *experience* – of learning by doing – as a key aspect of manpower quality, often neglected especially among those who place heavy emphasis on education and skill training in more formal ways and via institutional activities. Along with that, some suggestions were presented implying that, in the last analysis, government might have some role in assisting in the acquisition of experience. This, in effect, raised the question of whether governments may have a similar role to play, because of the externalities and social benefits involved, in providing experience as well as the basis for educational systems.

The second direction in which the discussion moved was to consider giving more attention to what some called the "quality of employment" and others "meaningful activity." I suppose here there is a wider counterpart, in a sense, to the position of university students seeking jobs which, in relation to their training and background, they would find interesting and exciting. At lower levels of education and training there may be an equal and perhaps in some sense an even more compelling need to promote interesting and personally rewarding – not necessarily in a pecuniary sense – employment opportunities. The latter, I think, was merely part of a wider conception of the need to enhance opportunities for choices for individuals, and we had a wide-ranging discussion on that.

At the same time, we had a rather troubled and inconclusive discussion about whether wider choices for some may mean fewer choices for others. In the end, we talked about increasing the quality of employment, and what kind of policy strategies we should be thinking about. Following are several suggestions.

(1) We should consider giving much closer attention to how we can phase out dead-end situations.

(2) In our society, we have a number of jobs that could generally be considered to be lousy jobs. Perhaps in a more "equal society," one of the things we may have to think about is whether we may all have to take our turn at doing lousy jobs some time in our careers.

(3) How do we go about the imaginative creation of the kinds of job opportunities people want? This can pose some major issues and problems. The group wound up thinking that this is not *just* a government responsibility; that you need thought and action across a broad spectrum of society, both private and public.

Finally, this group touched on the problem of people who get into situations, over a lifetime, in which there is no sustained or progressive expansion in their incomes. More thought must be given to how we develop their capacities. Perhaps, in the end, it will be managerial qualities and capacities that will have to be developed to help such people improve their productivity, and hence their income over a lifetime.

In the second group I chaired (which merged into the third where we were joined by members of the other groups), the logical progression would have been to proceed to a more detailed consideration of the second set of twin papers (Philbrook and Zay). But the second working party balked at this. There was, in fact, little discussion about social services – how they could be better delivered, how beneficiaries might be more adequately informed about their availability, what the relationships are between these and income-support programs of various kinds. This left a significant gap, but the group hurdled the subject like a speedskater over a string of barrels.

Interestingly, as in the other work groups, the discussion did not proceed to an explicit consideration of income distribution and redistribution. There was no "hot evangelism" of the kind that frequently surrounds some debates about this subject. At the same time, there was a clear recognition that income distribution has not changed radically in the last decade or two, and a general view was expressed that we have perhaps not yet reached a time when we can visualize a radical shift in income distribution in the near future.

Yet, I think it would be a mistake to leave the impression that there was a great sense of despair about this. One of the points made was that under conditions of rapid growth and change, especially of the kind we've been experiencing over the past quarter century or so, there are many ways in which the advantaged can exploit their advantages, and many ways in which the disadvantaged may be unable to keep pace. In brief, growth is virtually synonymous with change, and change – especially rapid change – favors the advantaged. Thus over the past 25 years, one would normally have expected to see a marked widening of disparities. But what we have been able to do by our social policies is at least to prevent a declining proportion of income in the lower quintiles, as shown in the income distribution tables presented at this seminar.

The discussion then moved to the guaranteed income and its variants in the Canadian context.

First, there was recognition that GAI in some forms could largely encompass (or perhaps partially replace) existing income support programs for low-income groups.

Second, it was recognized that there would be some complex, political, jurisdictional and administrative adjustments involved in steps toward implementation of GAI (perhaps particularly so in a country such as Canada), and there was some discussion both of the constraints upon, and the possible benefits to be derived from, its application. However, it is important to record that there were strong views expressed, possibly a consensus, that in Canada, at this stage, it really is more important to focus on high employment conditions than on any significant expansion of income-support programs. In other words, the development of employment opportunities was considered to be a priority above that of further basic shifts in our social policy framework.

Third, there was also recognition of the limitations of a GAI as a *comprehensive* cure for income deficiencies. Various alternative conceptions were discussed. One was that of using some variant of GAI as the centre piece in a system, with supporting programs that would be needed for those who somehow or other could not be adequately covered by it, and supplemented by other measures to take care of other particular situations of need that might arise. Another conception of the GAI (or one of its variants) was to view it as essentially some kind of income supplement to a number of existing income-support programs so that it would play a "residual" role. I think it is fair to say that the discussion evolved toward more emphasis on this second concept. Nevertheless, it is quite clear that in the last analysis we really need something that no single system will be adequate to provide: we shall need a two- or three-tiered program because of the complexity of the problems.

Considerable attention focused on constraints and possible benefits. On the constraints side, there was a discussion of costs and how they would be financed. There was also a brief discussion about the constraints that might be involved in an international context, from Canada's point of view, with special reference to the implications for Canada-U.S. relationships and, even more particularly, to the possible impact on immigration and emigration.

We similarly had some discussion of housing. It was agreed that under any GAI scheme, special attention would be required to keep down housing costs for low-income people, so that income transfers to such people are not simply siphoned off largely into payments for housing.

Finally, there are the political and practical problems of introducing a plan of this kind in the context of numerous programs of income support. In this country, with its federal system, and with wide regional diversities and a highly decentralized system of decision-making, there are obviously difficult questions about how to proceed in a practical way to undertake any significant and comprehensive GAI plan.

On the benefit side, special attention was drawn to the removal of stigma associated with income tests, and the simplification and improvement of access of low-income people to income support. One step in this direction in Canada – the introduction of the supplement to old age pensions – has perhaps already had more far-reaching effects on individuals than had been fully anticipated or realized. There is also the possibility of some reduction in administrative costs and improved efficiencies in the delivery of assistance, depending on how we proceed to relate the GAI to other programs.

Even those who were prepared to speak positively and encouragingly of guaranteed annual income in the Canadian context were careful to say that there is a tendency among those who have not thought deeply about the subject to expect too much of a GAI. I suppose this was one of the most important conclusions to emerge from the discussions. I should not want to leave the impression that this emerged in a negative way. The tone was merely one of caution about the highly complex matters that must be confronted in approaching any GAI plan. Implementation of any really effective guaranteed income is not going to be easy. What will be needed is objective and careful appraisal of the whole range of problems, such as those which emerged in our discussion as well as others which lie beyond it.

Discussion

1 A participant observed that the seminar had concentrated unduly on employment, when it is doubtful whether even full employment could make a major contribution to solving social ills, including poverty. In continental Western Europe, there is a strong trend toward early retirement, at age 60 or even 55, although jobs are available and the great majority of the retired lived in poverty. For

example, in France, 2.3 million people over 65 have only the equivalent of $60 a month. Yet people apparently prefer this to continuing to work under the conditions they have experienced so far. The major advantage of GAI over straight social assistance is that it could be used with the working poor. But why is North America so set on trying this new technique rather than considering a system of family allowances on the European model? A GAI involves the same kind of problems (of eligibility, of income test, etc.) that have already been met in, say, the well-tried French family allowances program, which might, as one of the group reports has noted, provide a satisfactory form of income security geared to family responsibilities.

2 Another participant made the following points.

a There should be no question about the fact that people must have some minimum income. Whether or not it is called a "right," money is necessary to live in our society and must be provided one way or another. Also, because of the economic interlocking of the public and private sectors, all salaries and wealth are essentially publicly generated; the public-private distinction is ideological rather than real. Moreover, the level of our salaries and wages has little to do with the actual jobs performed in a puritanical conception of work.

b Historically, there are two quite different approaches to GAI: as part of the concern to solve fundamental problems of the economy, or simply as an alternative technique for providing basic assistance. The implications of the two approaches require further exploration.

c The difference between accepting the present social order and trying to build a new one is not just the practical versus the philosophic. Both involve practical and philosophic considerations.

d For a substantial portion of the population, even full employment has never worked well as income security. Also we must realize that equalization is not an element in our economic structure: it has to be imposed by government authority if at all.

e Our system today does not provide meaningful employment for most people, and indeed much of such employment is being phased out through technology. Most of what satisfying work there is goes to the elite and those close to them.

3 A speaker argued that "political constraints," a term generally used in the seminar discussions in a negative sense (for example, barriers preventing the wiping out of existing programs for something "better"), might have constructive implications. If, as it appeared, the seminar participants were approaching a consensus that GAI is not a panacea for the problem of income security but could be a part of the solution (perhaps only residual), it might be just as well if political constraints forced us to look at how to use GAI in working with existing programs. The long-term goal of GAI should not become an alibi for not getting on with current improvements.

4   On employment, a plea was made not to exaggerate the number of people who "voluntarily resign" from the labor force. For example, the swing in the U.S. unemployment rate from 3.3 per cent in 1969 to over 6 per cent in 1970 was due to a sudden lack of jobs, not a sudden decision by people not to work. The speaker considered that society has an obligation to provide jobs for people and this is closely related to GAI because, with a prosperous economy, we can afford to be more generous in income security provisions. Also, we must improve the quality of jobs: people should have an opportunity to fulfill their potential as well as to earn money.

5   A participant supported a family allowance program, at least as one essential element in an income security system, but raised the question of population policy (not heretofore mentioned in the seminar). This growing issue in many countries could be in real conflict (ideological, political and economic) with what we might wish to do in social policies.

6   Another participant, referring to the proposal (in Reuben Baetz' group report) for separate types of GAI for those in and out of the labor force, suggested that this would not constitute a new formula for income security. Such a scheme would be no different from the distinction in social assistance between the employable and unemployable. This had always caused great problems – for example, in definition of eligibility, in petty bureaucratic decisions, and delays in moving from one category to the other. It certainly would not make for justice and equality, or an improved system.

7   The seminar was told they should not be discouraged to recognize there is no simple solution to the problem of income security, nor overwhelmed by the fact that a variety of effort is needed which will take a long time and about which there will be no finality in terms of reaching the ultimate goal. The speaker stated that there is an implicit and changing system of relationships involved: for example, benefit levels, price levels (such as for housing), consumption patterns, and so on. In matters so complex, the tendency is to think technicians alone can handle them. But every technical decision is also a political value decision, and moral values are also involved. The meeting of the technical and the value approaches in a group such as this is a beginning process, not an end. People must learn how to "fight" more constructively with each other, to

communicate, to get a blend of joint concerns that will develop a policy that meets a variety of objectives. There is a need to widen this communication and concern to many "publics," remembering that no one has a single purpose in talking about GAI. It is at the same time a technique and an aspiration.

8 A participant argued that, far from being too broad and philosophical, the seminar had been too concerned with the pragmatic. Of course, practical solutions for social problems must be sought, but they must be within a framework of social or "welfare" theory much more clearly worked out than the seminar had done. This is especially needed for two reasons: to enable us to understand why great social problems exist, and to evaluate the actions taken to combat them. Within this framework, the starting point is the individual human situation, and the discussions in the seminar on GAI had really been about how to fill the gaps between the existing situation and the minimum desirable situation according to certain criteria. Such criteria cannot just be monetary but must include the many other factors (mentioned in the seminar) involved in a *real* standard of living. (Much research on this is going on in Scandinavian countries.) The individual situation must then be given a national orientation because the question of gaps in the individual's welfare is mainly influenced by collective institutions and the role of the state is to influence these institutions on behalf of people's well-being. Family institutions, their effect on people's upbringing (barely touched on in the seminar) also require more study than they have so far received. In short, parallel with actual social programs, we must develop social theories to a much greater extent.

9 It was pointed out that the large increase in one-person families has important implications for a GAI. For example, in West Germany, such households formed only 6.1 per cent of all households in 1871; they made up more than a quarter in 1971. This is partly because social services and benefits enable people (such as the elderly) to live alone, and this is considered a blessing both for them and for their relatives. But many of them still cannot afford to pay for the services they need that were previously supplied free by the family group. One implication of this is that family (children's) allowances cannot be considered an alternative technique if GAI is to be available to all who need it.

Toward a New Concept of Society

Concluding Commentary by Gérald Fortin
Director, Centre for Urban and Regional Research,
National Institute for Scientific Research,
University of Quebec

Rather than attempt to summarize the seminar discussions or draw conclusions from them, I want simply to give you some of my personal impressions. These impressions, even though subjective, are perhaps shared by some other participants.

My first impression is that, unlike many other conferences I have attended, I had here the feeling of being involved in a kind of group dynamics which, as in all group dynamics, was to some degree frustrating. Confrontations, more or less overt, took place between representatives of countries whose history and experience were often poles apart, between professions maintaining their own points of view, between different political systems and ideologies, and between those who had come looking for a discussion concentrated on the ideological and philosophic aspects of GAI and those who were here to exchange ideas on techniques. These differing attitudes sometimes gave one the feeling of listening to a dialogue among the deaf.

My second impression is that, throughout the seminar, people wanted to avoid discussing ideologies. Perhaps *because* we shunned that debate, we remained prisoners of the ideology of charity and of pure economic liberalism. Often I found coming up in our discussions the idea that to help the poor is a charitable duty. Again and again we came back to the ideology of the welfare state, in which some kind of income redistribution would correct the abuses of the economic system. But for some of the seminar organizers and some of the participants, GAI is not only a technique: it is a hope of moving out of the welfare state and entering what we might call the "state of social development." This hope is explicit in the new name chosen by the former Canadian Welfare Council: The Canadian Council on Social Development. However, the concept of social development is still not well defined. It is for this reason that I speak of a hope rather than a reality.

Our discussion of GAI brought us very close to a discussion of social development. We didn't get far because we took the accepted assumptions of the welfare state too much for granted. Among other things, we should have taken more account of the technological context in which we are living, which is not necessarily the same technological context in which both capitalism and socialism, in their classic forms, were born. Inasmuch as we are already living in the post-industrial society (and this is particularly true in North America), we should have defined more closely the characteristics of this society and the effects of these characteristics on the class structure, on the relationships between rich and poor, on the pattern of employment and work, and so forth. Through such considerations, we could no doubt have achieved from the start an approach embracing social development and the new ideology that has still to be evolved.

Incidentally, I got the impression that some of our economist colleagues considered the main objective of the economy to be the creation of employment rather than of goods and services. In my sociologist's naivety, I have always had the impression that the function of the economic system is to produce and distribute goods and services. As I understand it, to work may be an objective but does not constitute, in itself, a "good" or a "service."

Society should guarantee interesting and creative activities for all. But, except in the purest form of economic liberalism, you cannot equate the concept of activity with the concept of employment or work. In our various societies, as represented at this seminar, the concept of work is more associated with the need to have income to purchase goods than with the possibility of creative activity. This view should perhaps be changed. Should GAI (as was almost suggested by Dr. Ulmer) be entirely in the form of jobs and work within which creative activities would be allowed for? Must we, in the post-industrial society, continue to stress so heavily the idea that consumption of goods is dependent on so-called productive work? Already 70 per cent of the labor force is in service jobs which, by general definition, are considered non-productive. Thus, the meaning of work has changed, and this movement is going to continue. It is essential to foresee the consequences.

Turning to another subject, I note that we completely ignored the question of the impact of GAI on those receiving it. In this respect, we were too much the politicians and technicians. The only perception we had of the beneficiaries was that they are poor and so ought to be helped. We should have asked ourselves what being poor really means in the context of the market economy. Among other things, it means (particularly in North America) being subjected to the same advertising as the rich, and therefore being made to feel the same needs. The result for the poor, in practice, means having to turn to credit buying to a proportionately high degree and thus being constantly in danger of bankruptcy because of the uncertainty of sources of income. In this context, GAI offers both stability and predictability of income. Even more than the amount of the payment, stability and predictability of income are important for the poor person because he can then know what he can buy – in other words, what he can borrow. For the poor, the word *guaran-*

teed is perhaps more significant than the actual income. This is an important consideration that should weigh in favor of the establishment of GAI.

I should like to raise a final point: that we have discussed the guaranteed income in too static a context. We have taken it too much for granted that, at bottom, GAI is nothing but a different technique for distributing the funds already being distributed through slightly less orderly social measures. We shut our eyes to (or perhaps are afraid to admit) the fact that GAI is more than a technique: it is a hope for a different kind of society. In the guaranteed annual income concept, the amount of money distributed is less important than the new way it offers for looking at the social realities, and then acting on those realities.

As I stated at the outset, GAI represents the hope that we shall abandon the ideology of the welfare state and move toward the society of social development. It is a hope less for an ideological revolution than for a new concept of society which takes fuller account of man and of the profound significance of his developing technology.

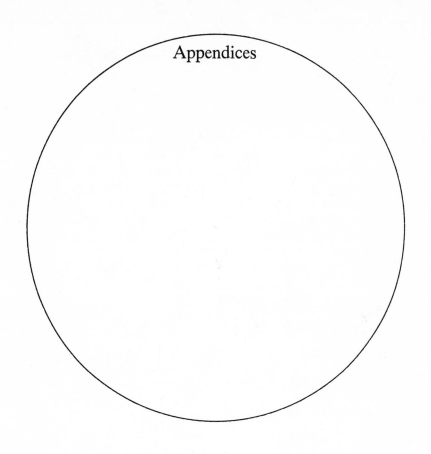

Appendices

Recent Trends and Developments in Guaranteed Income

by J. I. Clark
Principal Research Officer,
Social Security Research Division,
Research, Planning and Evaluation (Welfare) Branch,
Department of National Health and Welfare, Ottawa

This paper examines recent trends and developments in guaranteed income in selected countries – proposals for guaranteed annual income schemes, the evolution of comprehensive income security systems in certain countries toward a form of guaranteed annual income, the trend of social assistance to guaranteed income, and the use of guaranteed income techniques in new income maintenance programs.

The paper is divided into three sections. The first briefly explains the concept of guaranteed income, negative income taxation and social dividends. Explanation of these concepts is offered in support of the general thrust of the paper which is to show how guaranteed income is developing in line with the different meanings of the concept. The second section deals with developments and trends in guaranteed income in selected countries. The final section briefly examines social experimentation using the negative income tax technique in the United States as well as proposals for guaranteed income experiments in Canada.

The Concept of Guaranteed Income

1 *Approaches to guaranteed income*

Guaranteed income is the approach to income maintenance whereby the state guarantees a level of income support to persons and families using procedures which determine eligibility and the amount of the income guarantee by taking a person's or a family's income into account. The approach stresses the guarantee or *right* to income support which is either clearly understood by all or is clearly set out in legislation and guaranteed by right of appeal.

Guaranteed income can be provided using some or all of the following instruments of income security.

a *Demogrants* are payments made on a universal basis to all members of a population group such as children or the elderly. Benefits may be subject to income tax (as for the old age security pension) or not (as for family and youth allowances) – both Canadian programs. The right to benefit is set out in the legislation establishing the universal benefits and is normally subject to appeal.

b *Social assistance* payments are provided to persons or families who are needy, subject to a needs test or means test of their income and resources. Social assistance can be considered as a form of guaranteed income when the right to income support is clearly established by legislation, is guaranteed by rights of appeal, and is administered in the spirit that a needy person has a right to income support. Normally, social assistance is not provided to full-time workers but such an extension would provide a much more comprehensive form of guaranteed income to needy persons. As the traditional social assistance is modified, it approximates the concept of negative income tax. This can come about by specifying income guarantees, by reducing the normally high tax rates, by simplifying the application process, and by improving the procedures for assessment of income and assets.

c *Social insurance* programs are those under which benefits are paid to eligible insured persons and, in certain circumstances, to their dependents. Benefits are provided for specific risks such as retirement, disability, sickness, maternity, unemployment, or death of the insured person. The right to benefit under social insurance flows from the contributions made by the persons insured, by their employers, or by both, and is further assured by rights of appeal.

d *Negative income taxation and social dividends* provide income to persons and to families subject to an income test. Under the income test, the maximum income guarantee is provided in full to a person with no income but is reduced for a person with income using a tax rate applied to this income. The negative income taxation approach involves a prior reduction of the income guarantee before payment is made, while the social dividend approach makes payment of the benefit and subsequently recovers from persons with other income. Both approaches can operate as an integral part of the positive income tax system or externally to this system. The right to income support would be determined by the level of a person's income and this right would be subject to appeal.

While a guaranteed income can be provided by a combination of several or all of the instruments of income security described, it is more usual to consider guaranteed income in relation to the negative income taxation or social dividend approaches.

Negative income taxation and the social dividend approaches have three basic variables, any two of which determine the third.

(1) *The income guarantee,* the payment which a person or family would receive if he had no other income.

(2) *The implicit tax rate,* the rate at which the basic guaranteed income payment is reduced as income from other sources rises.

(3) *The breakeven level of income,* or the level of income at which the income guarantee is reduced to zero.

In addition, these approaches must be concerned with a number of other aspects, namely:

(1) *The definition of income*

(2) *The definition of the family unit*

(3) *The accounting period* to be used to determine eligibility and benefit amount

(4) *The payment period* during which benefits are disbursed.

2 *Evolutionary trends in negative income taxation and social dividends*

There have been several recent developments in the negative income tax and social dividend approaches.

First, the negative income tax approach has emerged as the most favored as it has several practical and financial advantages over social dividends. Negative income tax reduces benefits prior to payment and thereby economizes on resources, eliminates the problem of making recoveries through the tax system, minimizes the problems resulting from overpayments, reduces the level of cash flows, and does not provide interest-free loans to recipients not eligible for benefits. For example, the negative income tax approach is being used for social experiments on the guaranteed income in the United States and is the usual approach adopted in new income maintenance programs which use an income test.

Second, there has been a trend away from absolute association of these approaches with income tax because of the differing and often incompatible objectives of taxation compared to income maintenance objectives. In the development of programs using negative income tax or social dividends, relatively few were tied to the income tax system.

Third, the principles of income testing and the selectivity resulting in these approaches have been used in specific income maintenance programs as a means of providing payments to persons and families with low incomes.

Developments in Selected Countries

Despite all the recent interest in guaranteed income, there has been no significant swing to this approach. No country, for instance, has implemented an overall guaranteed annual income program, although many proponents in several countries have made proposals for implementing such an approach. Many countries, particularly the highly industrialized and economically mature ones, have developed their comprehensive income protection systems to such an extent that a guaranteed annual income is being provided through a combination of programs. Several countries have made sweeping revisions to their basic social assistance programs so that the reformed programs provide a guaranteed income to persons in need but generally these reforms have not been extended to those working full time. Finally, a number of countries have used aspects of the negative income tax and social dividend approaches for new or revised income security programs.

The development of guaranteed income in selected countries is examined below using the framework set out in the preceding paragraph.

1 Overall guaranteed annual income

No country has implemented a single overall guaranteed annual income plan. There have been in the past few years many proposals for implementing such programs, both in Canada and the United States.

In the United States, proposals for a comprehensive guaranteed income have been made by Robert Lampman, Edward Schwartz, Robert Theobald, Milton Friedman and James Tobin, to mention only a few. The U.S. proposals have generally advocated the use of the negative income tax approach as a means of directing income support to persons and families with low incomes.

In Canada, quite recently, proposals relating to a comprehensive guaranteed annual income plan have been discussed in the federal government's white paper *Income Security for Canadians*, in the report of the Special Senate Committee on Poverty, *Poverty in Canada*, and in the report of the Quebec *Commission of Inquiry on Health and Social Welfare* (the Castonguay-Nepveu report). Following is a brief summary of these proposals.

a White paper on income security for Canadians

The white paper on income security took the approach that one overall guaranteed annual income program cannot operate as a single instrument of income security policy in Canada. Several other programs still have important functions to perform and some involve obligations of a contractual nature. Social insurance programs – such as unemployment insurance, workmen's compensation and the Canada Pension Plan – are still needed. These programs were designed only in part as anti-poverty programs, and have the role of providing insurance protection for people generally against certain social risks.

Although the guaranteed income approach was found to have limitations as the sole instrument of income security policy, it was seen to have an important role when combined with other approaches. This approach provides the most direct way of alleviating poverty without loss of dignity and self-respect. It is the one instrument that is available to provide additional income to the working poor who are in poverty.

The white paper suggested that this technique could be employed effectively in those areas where incentive and administrative problems are not serious and where it could be used in combination with and as a supplement to the income security programs.

The major new thrust in the white paper proposals was development of the guaranteed income technique within the income security structure. The first proposal was to improve the guaranteed income technique already being applied in the case of the guaranteed income supplement for the aged and to establish GIS as a permanent rather than a transitional measure in the income security system. The white paper indicated that "this program provides a point of departure for the future extension of the guaranteed income approach to people who are not normally in the labor force but who may, for one reason or another, have had insufficient social insurance protection." The disabled are in this category.

The second proposal in this new thrust was to provide low-income families with higher income benefits. It was proposed that the guaranteed income technique should be applied to the family and youth allowances plans to convert them from universal to a selective program – the Family Income Security Plan. The white paper stated that "this program provides a departure point for the future in the development of the guaranteed income approach for those in the labor force."

The white paper discussed some of the major criticisms of the guaranteed income approach, including the high cost of such a program, the need to strike a balance between the goals of economic growth and greater equity in the distribution of income, the concern about its impact on the incentive to work, and its probable administrative problems. The white paper suggested that more information was needed before a general guaranteed income program could be adopted covering all people in the labor force.

b *Castonguay-Nepveu report*
The report of the Quebec Commission of Inquiry on Health and Social Welfare (the Castonguay-Nepveu report) suggested a three-tiered income security system for Quebec, consisting of a basic negative income tax scheme as the first tier, social insurance programs as the second, and an income-tested family allowances program as the third.

The basic negative income tax scheme, called the General Social Allowances Plan, is designed to replace the Quebec program of social assistance.

Social insurance programs would continue to operate but benefits payable thereunder would be fully integrated with benefits under the General Social Allowances Plan. These programs include workmen's compensation, Quebec Pension Plan, unemployment insurance, old age security pensions and the guaranteed income supplement, and veterans' pensions.

Families with dependent children covered under the General Social Allowances Plan would receive additional income support with respect to these children through an income-tested family allowances program which would use the negative income tax approach.

The General Social Allowances Plan suggests two categories of benefits which vary with family size. The first category is intended for those who work and is designed to provide an incentive to work. The second category is intended for non-employables and persons with limited employment capability.

The first category benefits are not high enough to provide for minimum living needs on the assumption that these will be increased by income from employment. Benefit levels will be 60 per cent of the levels proposed for the second category. The implicit tax rates proposed for first category benefits are: the guarantee will first be reduced by 33 1/3 per cent of assessed income up to $2,000, and then the tax rate will be 55 per cent of assessed income on $2,000 and above.

The income guarantees for the second category are set at the poverty thresholds proposed by the Economic Council of Canada and are to be escalated each year by reference to a cost-of-living index. By relating the income guarantees to the poverty levels, it is intended that the guarantees be high enough to provide for minimum living needs. The income guarantees for persons in this category will be reduced using a tax rate of 100 per cent of assessed income.

An interesting aspect of the GSAP proposal is the dual benefit category – one set at a level deemed to be sufficient for minimum living for persons who are unable to work, and the other set at lower levels in order to supplement earnings.

c *Guaranteed annual income proposals by the Special Senate Committee on Poverty*

The Special Senate Committee on Poverty recommended a uniform national guaranteed annual income program using the negative income tax approach. The proposed plan would cover all Canadians who are in economic need. Initially the plan would exclude non-

Canadians and single unattached Canadian citizens under 40 years of age. The basic income guarantees would be set at 70 per cent of the poverty lines developed by the Senate committee. The plan would use a tax rate of 70 per cent applied against other income. The committee recommended that the plan be financed and administered by the Government of Canada.

Dealing with the problem of interaction of the guaranteed annual income scheme with other social programs, the report recommended that the Canada Assistance Plan be modified to provide social services and assistance on a needs basis to those not covered by the plan; that family allowances, youth allowances and old age security pensions be abolished; and that social insurance programs such as unemployment insurance, Canada Pension Plan, programs for veterans and for Canada's native peoples be continued. The committee further recommended that the guaranteed annual income scheme be integrated with the income tax system by suggesting that the income tax exemption levels be raised to the poverty lines so that no one in receipt of the guaranteed annual income would be liable to pay income tax.

2 A combined approach to guaranteed income

The continuing trend in the industrially advanced countries to development and extension of income support and social services has resulted in the combined approach to guaranteed annual income. The income support patterns will differ for each person or family under the combined approach to guaranteed income. For some, a single program will provide sufficient income which, with savings or pensions from employment, will be adequate for their needs. For others, several public programs will provide the guarantee, e.g., income support under unemployment insurance may be supplemented by assistance payable under a social assistance program. In other situations, programs are designed for specific categories in the population or for specific risks and the income support for these different categories or risks can be supplemented if needed by a basic social assistance plan.

Following are descriptions of the income security systems in New Zealand, Canada, and the United Kingdom to illustrate how a guaranteed income may be provided through a combined program approach.

a The New Zealand social security system[1]

The prime objective of New Zealand social security is to provide a

---

1. "Social Security in New Zealand," *International Social Security Review*, No. 1 (Geneva: ISSA, 1971).

system of benefits to which each person contributes according to his means and from which each derives benefits according to his needs. Hence, the requirement to contribute to social security through general taxation is compulsory and no one can contract out of this responsibility. Also, eligibility for benefits other than emergency benefits is based on residence and not on citizenship or contributions.

Under the New Zealand Social Security Act of 1964, cash benefits without an income test are payable for children in families, for retirement, and to miners who, because of their occupation as miners, may have become permanently and totally incapacitated for work. Cash benefits are payable subject to an income test for old age, widowhood, invalidity, orphanhood, sickness and unemployment. Emergency benefits may be granted at the discretion of the Social Security Commission to a person not qualified to receive any benefit other than the benefit for children, and who can satisfy the commission that he is incapable of earning an adequate living for himself or his family because of age, disability, or any other reason.

Finally, subject to a test of income and assets, supplementary assistance may be provided for those who are unable to help themselves and whose income and resources, including social security benefits, are insufficient to meet needs.

The cash benefits provided are flat rate and standardized and are made available subject to the condition that no one can receive two benefits other than the benefit for children in the family. The benefit levels are set lower than prevailing wages to provide an incentive to those who are able to work as well as an incentive to save for those who retire from employment.

The availability of cash benefits to meet specific conditions, the provision of emergency benefits for those in need who do not qualify for any other benefit, and the provision of supplementary assistance which can be paid in addition to benefits or as a substitute for emergency benefits provide a system which guarantees income sufficient to meet essential needs. The essential nature of guaranteed income under the New Zealand social security system is further strengthened by the fact that rights to benefit are firmly established and that discretionary powers are limited to those situations where these powers must be exercised.

b *Canada*
As mentioned before, the federal government's white paper on income security in its examination of the income security system rejected an overall guaranteed annual income program but recommended the continued development of the system towards a combined program approach to basic income security protection. The

white paper suggested a reordering of priorities and a changed concentration of resources among the four instruments of income security policy: guaranteed income, demogrants (or universal payments), social insurance and social assistance. As recommended, the social insurance and guaranteed income programs were to be improved and strengthened, less emphasis was to be placed on demogrants, and the inadequacies of social assistance were to be overcome.

Since the issue of the white paper late in 1970 certain developments have occurred. The proposals on unemployment insurance have now come into force to extend coverage to all employed persons in the labor force, to improve unemployment benefits, and to add new benefits for sickness and maternity. Benefits for the elderly in Canada have been increased under the guaranteed income supplement to improve the thrust of guaranteed income in the system. Legislation for a Family Income Security Plan was introduced into parliament in 1971, subsequently revised, and then died on the Order Paper when parliament was dissolved on September 1, 1972. This plan would replace family and youth allowances, a scheme of universal payments to all children under age 18, with a new program that would provide benefits to families with children using an income test. Improvements in the Canada Pension Plan are expected to come into force in January 1973. Discussions will be held between the federal government and the provinces to try to resolve and reduce the inadequacies of the social assistance programs operated by provincial and municipal authorities.

Canada has a combined approach to guaranteed income consisting of programs using the social insurance, or guaranteed income, or demogrant, or social assistance techniques. The white paper proposals which are already in force as well as those which are yet to be implemented will greatly improve the structure and scope of the income security system in Canada.

c *United Kingdom*

The United Kingdom has a comprehensive system of income security which is essentially a form of guaranteed income provided through a combined program approach. The income security system consists of a basic social insurance plan called national insurance which provides benefits to insured contributors and their dependents for unemployment, sickness, retirement, injury or disease resulting from work, and in the case of death, to surviving widows and orphans; a family allowance program which pays benefits to families with two or more children; war pensions; and a supplementary benefit scheme which gives income protection to persons aged 16 and over who are not in full-time employment. A new scheme called the family income supplement was established in

1971 to help families with low income who could not qualify under the supplementary benefits scheme because the breadwinner works full time. Family allowances, supplementary benefits, and the family income supplement scheme are discussed in more detail later in the paper in relation to the development of the guaranteed income approach.

3 *Social assistance as an instrument of guaranteed income*

In some countries, the basic social assistance programs have either been altered over time or changed dramatically to provide a form of guaranteed annual income to needy persons and families. Canada and Britain are two countries in which widespread changes have been made to basic social assistance programs, and where programs are tending towards guaranteeing incomes to the most needy persons in the population.

a *Social assistance in Canada*
The enactment of the Canada Assistance Plan in 1966 marked a significant step forward in the evolution of social policy in Canada, and at the same time represented a significant break with the welfare traditions of the past. As a result, Canada now has a comprehensive measure providing federal financial support for social assistance and welfare services. Under this plan, the federal government contributes 50 per cent of the cost of payments of assistance and of improving welfare services. Persons in need and their dependents are eligible for assistance through provincial or municipal departments of welfare. Persons assisted are those who lack the means of support, who do not get sufficient support to meet needs from other government income security programs, and in some provinces employed persons in special circumstances. All provincial legislation provides for appeals. The general grounds for appeal are denial, reduction, suspension or cancellation, or inadequacy of assistance. The comprehensive nature of the plan, the emphasis on the principle that assistance is based on need, and the provision of the right of appeal are essential features of guaranteed income. The white paper *Income Security for Canadians* reviewed the progress of the Canada Assistance Plan and developments under provincial administration of social assistance. The paper identified a number of inadequacies and problem areas which, if resolved, would greatly improve the general thrust of social assistance and the delivery of welfare services in Canada. These areas are: recognition of assistance as a right; reduction of dependency by improving the work incentive dimensions of social assistance in combination with training and rehabilitation; adequacy of assistance payments; the need to clearly establish rights to appeal, and

provision of appeal machinery which will be speedy, impartial, and non-expensive.

If an overall guaranteed annual income program were to be adopted in Canada, the role of the Canada Assistance Plan would be reduced considerably – to providing supplementary income support (where average benefits under guaranteed income were not adequate to meet special needs or to take into account special circumstances) as well as to providing welfare services.

b *Supplementary benefits in the United Kingdom*

The supplementary benefits scheme implemented in 1966 emphasized entitlement to benefits as a right. The act and regulations specify the basic scale rates, the definition of income, and the general conditions of entitlement. The Supplementary Benefits Commission, which administers the scheme, has considerable discretionary powers to meet exceptional needs and circumstances. The scheme combines basic rights to income maintenance to meet average needs with a flexibility exercised through discretionary power to deal with exceptional needs and circumstances. A right of appeal is provided which covers the whole of the assessment process including the use of discretionary powers. The purpose of the scheme is to provide income support to all persons whose resources are less than their requirements. *Resources* include cash income with certain exceptions being permitted, capital excluding owner-occupied homes and personal possessions, and resources which have been deliberately abandoned or transferred to others. *Requirements* consist of a basic scale for normal weekly needs to which is added an amount for rent and, where payable, a long-term addition to provide for extra expenses expected with long-term cases. Supplementary pensions (payable to the aged) and supplementary allowances (payable to all others) may be adjusted for special circumstances such as special diets, extra heating and other unusual expenses.

The scheme covers all persons aged 16 and over except those in full-time work, but excludes persons starting work and certain disabled self-employed people. Work incentives under the scheme operate directly through the requirement that persons capable of work register for work and indirectly through an arrangement called the "wage stop"[2] which is applied to those who have the choice of working or not working. An application for benefit involves a personal assessment. Normally a visit is made to the applicant's home to get information needed to assess a person's re-

2. The "wage stop" limits the benefits received under the scheme to the amount which a person would normally earn in employment and to leave him neither better nor worse off than when he was working. While not designed as an incentive to work, its use has this effect.

sources and requirements. Applicants for the supplementary pension have a choice of being visited in their homes or visiting their nearest social security office.

In summary, the supplementary benefits scheme provides a form of guaranteed income to all persons in need with the exception of those working full time. The guarantee is implicit in the clear specification of entitlement, in the definition of resources and requirements, in the basic rights established under the scheme, and in the right of appeal which extends to all processes of the assessment including the exercise of discretionary power.

4 *Programs using the negative income tax and social dividend approaches*

The negative income tax and social dividend approaches have been used to redesign current programs and to design new programs of income maintenance.

Israel, the United Kingdom, Jersey, Denmark, Canada and the United States have either recently set up programs or are proposing programs using the negative income tax or social dividend approach.

a *Israel*[3]
Israel provides pensions to all persons aged 70 and over regardless of their income or of hours worked. The fixed pension has been set at a relatively low level in order to provide pensions to all elderly persons including those unable to pay contributions. By itself the old age pension proved to be insufficient to provide for basic needs and over the period 1957 to 1965 declined significantly as a percentage of average wage from 18 per cent to 10.5 per cent. Faced with growing need from old age pensioners who had little or no income besides their pensions and with limited financial resources to increase pensions, Israel adopted in 1965 a supplement under which a person receiving an old age or survivor's pension would be eligible for a supplement if he or he and his wife had no income over and above the amount of the old age pension payable to an insured person without dependents. Israel's supplement to the aged is an application of the negative income tax approach.

b *United Kingdom*
(1) *Selective family allowances:* Family allowances are payable to all families with two or more children including families receiving supplementary benefits or the family income supplement. In January

---

3. Based on unpublished discussion paper, "New Instruments in Social Security for the Prevention of Poverty in Israel," by Israel Katz and Arye Nizan presented to the ISSA Conference on Social Security Research, Vienna, 1969.

1968, the principle of selectivity was introduced with respect to the increase in benefits proposed under the family allowances program. Under this approach, benefits continued to be paid universally but income tax allowances for children were reduced so that the increases in benefits were recovered entirely from families paying income tax at the standard rate and above, and partially from families paying income taxes at reduced rates. Families not liable to pay tax received the full amount of the increase. This process involved an application of the social dividend approach whereby benefits are paid to all eligible families and recoveries are subsequently made through income tax.

(2) *Family income supplement:* A new program was implemented in August 1971 under which a new benefit of up to £5 a week is payable to families with at least one child whose head is working full time and whose total income is below a prescribed amount which varies with the number of children in the family. This scheme was designed to provide income support to families who were not eligible to receive supplementary benefits. Income includes gross earnings of the family head, family allowances and the wife's earnings. An eligible child is defined as a child under age 16, or over 16 if still in school. Full-time work means that the family head, and in the case of a couple this means the man, must work 30 hours or more a week. The supplement is one-half of the amount by which a family's income falls below the appropriate prescribed income level. The maximum supplement payable is £5 per week and the supplement is usually awarded for at least 13 weeks and will not be affected if circumstances change in this payment period. The family income supplement uses the negative income tax approach to fill 50 per cent of the gap between a person's income and the guarantee level up to the maximum weekly limit of £5. Benefits are determined before payment and are based on total income received in an accounting period preceding the benefit period.

c *Jersey, Channel Islands*[4]

The current system of family allowances consists of a basic benefit of 42p per week for each child in the family, except the eldest, paid to all families regardless of their income. In addition, supplementary family allowances at the same rate are payable where family income is below a certain level.

The States of Jersey in 1971 proposed a fundamental change in the system. Under the new system, which is closely linked with income tax, the child tax allowance plus the cash family allowances would be £100 per child in families with income up to £667.

---

4. Based on Leaflet T. Form 2, *A Guide to the Proposed New Family Allowance Structure* (States of Jersey, Channel Islands, November, 1971).

Above this level the value of both allowances would decline as income increased up to £1,700 income level, at which level the cash family allowance would be reduced to zero. At income levels of £1,700 and above, only the flat-rate child tax allowance of £30 per child would be payable. Family allowances would be based on income in the year prior to the year in which the benefit is paid. Provision is made for reassessment where a family suffered a substantial reduction in income.

d *Denmark*[5]

In 1967 Denmark enacted a form of "negative tax" to compensate persons with low incomes for the increase in consumption taxes. The scheme provides a small allowance which varies according to taxable income under certain income limits. This scheme is a tax rebate scheme which uses the negative income tax approach to relate the amount of payment to the level of income.

e *Canada*

(1) *Guaranteed income supplement:* In 1967 Canada implemented a new program using the negative income tax approach to provide supplementary benefits to aged persons receiving the old age security pension. The supplement as of May 1972 is a maximum of $67.12 a month for a single person or a person married to a non-pensioner and a monthly maximum of $119.34 for a married couple both of whom are pensioners. This means that, with the $82.88 monthly old age security pension, a single person would be entitled to $150 a month and a married pensioner couple to $285.10 a month. The purpose of the supplement and basic old age security pension is to provide a guaranteed minimum income to elderly persons. Income is as defined under the Income Tax Act. To ensure equitable treatment between single and married pensioners, the income for each married person is taken as one-half of the combined total income of the married couple. The accounting period used is the calendar year preceding the year in which benefits are paid. To provide for the situation in which income declines in or following the accounting period, applicants are permitted to substitute estimates of certain items of their income for corresponding items in the accounting period. The supplement is subject to an income test and the maximum monthly amount of the supplement is reduced by one dollar for each two full dollars of a pensioner's monthly income other than the old age security pension or any supplement. The program provides for appeals on eligibility and the amount of

5. Henning Friis, "Issues in Social Security Policies in Denmark," *Social Security in International Perspective, Essays in Honor of Eveline M. Burns* (New York: Columbia University Press, 1969).

benefit. Legislation following the issue of the white paper on income security improved the guaranteed income technique already being applied in the case of the guaranteed income supplement for the aged by increasing the level of benefits and by making it a permanent program rather than a transitional measure.

(2) *Family income security plan:* The second proposal in the new thrust in the white paper towards using the guaranteed income technique was to provide low-income families with higher benefits by converting the family and youth allowances plans from a universal to a selective program, the Family Income Security Plan. The proposed program would pay benefits of $15 a month for children under age 12 and $20 a month for children aged 12 to 18. The benefits would be subject to a test of income (as defined under the Income Tax Act) received by a family in the calendar year preceding the year in which the benefit would be paid. The benefit year would run from September to August. The plan provides a basic exemption of $4,500 for a family with one child plus an additional $500 for each child in the family in excess of one. Above this basic exemption the monthly benefit would be reduced by 33 cents for each full $100 of income by which the income of the child's family exceeds the basic exemption. Options are provided, where family income may be substantially reduced, to permit families to substitute estimates of income for income in the base calendar year and a new benefit would then be calculated. Anyone exercising such an option must, if his income subsequently increases, submit a new estimate of his revised income which would be substituted for income in the base calendar year and his benefit would again be recalculated. Appeals are provided under the proposed legislation with respect to determination of income and benefits.

(3) *Ontario's tax credit scheme:* In 1971 Ontario proposed a tax credit scheme which would refund to Ontario taxpayers a portion of property and sales taxes paid. The amount of refund would depend on income. Persons not eligible to pay income tax would receive the full amount of the refund while those liable to pay income tax would receive refunds proportionately reduced as their income increased up to the point where refunds would be eliminated. The Ontario proposal is an application of the negative income tax approach which uses an income test to determine the amount of tax refund to be made. An agreement was recently reached between the province of Ontario and the federal government under which the federal government agreed to administer a scheme of property tax rebates for Ontario residents under the federal income tax system beginning with the 1972 tax year.

f *United States Family Assistance Plan*
A significant proposal for the reform of the welfare system in the

United States was made by President Nixon in August 1969 in his proposal to set up a Family Assistance Plan. This plan would use the negative income tax approach to provide federal payments to all needy families with children and would replace the present Aid to Families with Dependent Children (AFDC) program. Unlike AFDC, it would provide federal benefit payments for families headed by men working full time as well as for families headed by a mother or an unemployed father.

Bill H.R.1 introduced and discussed in Congress in 1971 provides for two new totally federal programs for families. The new programs would be adopted for five years to give Congress an opportunity to review their operation before continuing them in subsequent years. The new programs would be established by a new title XXI in the Social Security Act.

Following are the main elements of the proposed United States family programs.

(1) The separation of needy families into two groups, those with an employable adult (including families in which the father is working full time for low wages) and those without an employable adult, with appropriate help tailored for each group.

(2) Incentives and requirements for work, training, and rehabilitation.

(3) A heavy investment in the training, rehabilitation, and job placement of poor families with expanded child care, manpower training, public service employment, and family planning efforts.

(4) Uniform requirements for eligibility for cash assistance and uniform administration with specific limitations and requirements.

(5) As a support for the entire program, an efficient, modern, and national administration mechanism designed to assure that only those who are eligible receive benefits, while avoiding unproductive red tape and delay.

Families in which there is an employable adult (including those in which the father is working full time for low wages) would be enrolled and paid benefits under the Opportunities for Families program administered by the Department of Labor. Every member of a family who is found to be available for work would be required to register for manpower services, training and employment. In addition to the family benefits, an incentive allowance of $30 a month would be paid to each registrant in manpower training (states could also provide up to $30 a month). Necessary costs for transportation and similar expenses would also be paid.

All eligible families in which no member would be available for employment would be enrolled and paid benefits under the Family Assistance Plan administered by the Department of Health, Education and Welfare. The Family Assistance Plan would cover female-headed families with children under age three (under age six until

1974) and families in which the only adult members are incapacitated or otherwise exempt from registering under the Opportunities
for Families program. Those who voluntarily register for work and
training would be placed under the Opportunities for Families program. Incapacitated individuals in families would be referred to the
state vocational rehabilitation services and would be required to
participate in any program of vocational rehabilitation. In addition
to family benefits, an incentive allowance of $30 a month would be
paid to FAP beneficiaries undertaking vocational assistance, plus
allowances for transportation and other expenses. Child care services necessary to enable the recipients to take vocational rehabilitation services would be provided. Family planning services would be
offered to all appropriate family members and must be furnished
when requested.

Benefits payable to eligible families under both the Opportunities
for Families program and the Family Assistance Plan would be
$800 a year for each of the first two family members, $400 each
for the next three members, $300 each for the next two members,
plus $200 a year for the next family member. The maximum
amount a family of eight or more can receive is $3,600.

Benefits would be reduced dollar for dollar by the amount of any
income earned or unearned available to the family from other
sources unless it is specifically excluded. A portion of earnings
(and limited amounts of other income) would not be counted. The
first $720 of earned income each year would not be used to reduce
the family's benefit nor would one-third of any earned income
above $720 or a tax rate of 66 2/3 per cent.

The latest version of the bill does not require the states to supplement the basic federal payment. If the states choose to supplement the payment, they may do so directly or may contract with
the federal government to make the payments.

Guaranteed Income Experiments

1 *Canada*

The federal government has indicated its willingness to collaborate
with provincial governments in carrying out pilot projects to study
the guaranteed income. In the fiscal year 1972–73, $5 million plus
any savings to the federal government under the Canada Assistance Plan will be provided to assist in carrying out such studies on
the basis of 75:25 federal-provincial sharing. These funds would
be used to finance transfer payments and research on experimental
projects testing the guaranteed income approach. Testing may focus
on a number of objectives such as to get information on the question of work incentives, family change and mobility, the economic

and social impact of guaranteed income, and administrative problems related to such a program. This information would be needed before a program could be adopted covering all people in the labor force.

The provinces of Manitoba and Ontario are designing studies at present and a number of other provinces have indicated their interest in the matter.

2   United States

A number of experiments on guaranteed income are now being conducted in the United States.

a   The New Jersey experiment

This experiment focuses on the question of work response of male-headed families of working age to a negative income tax plan. This project concentrates on the urban poor in five communities. The project was initiated in 1968 by the Office of Economic Opportunity. The design and operation of the project has been subcontracted to the Institute of Poverty, University of Wisconsin, assisted by Mathematica Inc. Two progress reports have been issued to date and a final report is expected in 1973. Emphasis in the final months of the experiment is on phase-out and softening the effect of withdrawal.

b   The rural income maintenance experiment

This project is sponsored by the Office of Economic Opportunity and has been designed and is being operated exclusively by the Institute of Poverty, University of Wisconsin. The experiment is being conducted in two rural areas, one in North Carolina and the other in Iowa. It is a controlled type of experiment and is designed to test the work response to negative income tax in predominately rural populations. The population consists primarily of male-headed families of working age. A report is expected in 1973.

c   The Gary (Indiana) experiment

This experiment is designed to test the effects on work effort of negative income tax combined with day care and social services. The population being tested is the black male-headed and female-headed families of working age. The experiment is sponsored by the Department of Health, Education and Welfare and is funded through a HEW contract with the state of Indiana Department of Public Welfare. The design and operation of the project is subcontracted to the University of Indiana. Enrolment of families began in March 1971. A preliminary report is planned for the fall of 1973 with a final report planned for approximately one year later.

d *The Seattle-Denver experiment*

This experiment is designed to test work effort combined with man-power services. The population is male-headed and female-headed families and couples of working age. The project is funded by a Department of Health, Education and Welfare contract with the state of Washington Department of Public Assistance and the state of Colorado Department of Social Services. The design and operation of the project are subcontracted to Stanford Research Institute. Mathematica Inc. operates the project as a subcontractor to Stanford Research Institute. Enrolment of families in Seattle began in November 1970. As a result of a steep increase in the level of un-employment in Seattle, the sample was divided between Seattle and another city with similar characteristics but with a low level of un-employment. The city selected was Denver. Enrolment in Denver began in August 1971.

The Seattle-Denver experiment is designed to run three years but 25 per cent of the sample will continue for two additional years.

The purpose of these experiments is to provide data on the effects of income maintenance programs employing the negative income tax approach that would be useful in formulating income security policy. In addition to assessment of the overall effects on the economy, information is needed on behavioral responses and the effects on people – such as the effect on incentives to work and on incentives when income is provided in combination with manpower services, the effect on family formation, family mobility and family change, and the effect on the demand for social services and on consumption patterns. It is not possible to provide answers to all of these questions but through experiment a start is being made.

Benefits and Costs of Canadian Proposals for a Guaranteed Annual Income

by Nicole V. Martin
Professor, National School of Public Administration,
University of Quebec

and Pierre-Paul Bellerose
Research Assistant (Economics),
National School of Public Administration,
University of Quebec

The purpose of this appendix is to present a comparative analysis of various plans put forward recently in Canada for a guaranteed annual income.[1] A brief summary of these proposals will be followed by a discussion of their effects on poverty and on income deficiency.

The Plans

From 1965 to 1970, the guaranteed annual income was a popular subject for study in Canada. A number of organizations concerned with the lot of low-income families have recommended or encouraged the introduction of such a plan in Canada. At present, there are at least seven specific proposals for a guaranteed annual income. Two are contained in official reports, one of which was submitted to the Quebec government by the Commission of Inquiry on Health and Social Welfare[2] in the spring of 1971, and another to the federal government by the Senate's Special Committee on Poverty[3] in November, 1971. In addition, some academics formulated proposals

---

1. The results given here form part of a research project whose object is to compare and analyze over a period of time the development of these proposals and their effects on low-income groups. This research, of which the present analysis is only an initial step, was made possible by a grant from the Quebec Department of Social Affairs.
2. Quebec (Province) Commission of Inquiry on Health and Social Welfare, *Report,* V, *Income Security* (Quebec: Official Publisher, 1971).
3. Canada, Parliament, Senate, Special Committee on Poverty, *Poverty in Canada* (Ottawa: Information Canada, 1971).

for a guaranteed annual income,[4] some of them inspired by the federal government's white paper on income security. The tax credit proposal made by the Ontario government in 1971 is another element in the debate,[5] although it cannot be placed on the same footing as a guaranteed annual income proposal. Interest in this topic is also evident in United States writings.

1   The Smith formula[6]

In "A Simplified Approach to Social Welfare," a title that reveals the article's philosophy, D.B. Smith suggested in 1965 the concept of a *social dividend*. According to the Smith formula, the proceeds from a proportional tax of 40 per cent on all personal income could be devoted to redistribution[7] according to a per capita rate based on the ratio between personal income and population. Thus, in 1963, redistribution of 40 per cent of personal income would have made possible an annual grant of $1,000 to every adult and $200 to every child.[8]

According to Smith, such a plan would make it possible to eliminate a whole range of programs such as income maintenance programs, including unemployment insurance and agricultural grants.[9]

Transposed to 1961, the Smith formula provides for a guaranteed income of $870 per adult (22 years of age and over) and $195 per child (21 years of age and under).[10] Table 1 gives the principal coordinates for this formula, namely the guaranteed floor income as

---

4.   Antal Deutsch and Christopher Green, "Income Security for Canadians: A Review Article," *Canadian Tax Journal,* XIX, 1 (January–February, 1971), 8–18; D.B. Smith, "A Simplified Approach to Social Welfare," *Canadian Tax Journal,* XIII, 3 (May–June, 1965), 260–65; Ronald W. Crowley and David A. Dodge, "Cost of the Guaranteed Annual Income," *Canadian Tax Journal,* XVII, 6 (November–December, 1969), 395–408; James Cutt, "A Guaranteed Income–Next Step in the Evolution of Welfare Policy?" *Social Service Review* (Canada), XLII, 2 (June, 1966), 216–31; Colin J. Hindle, "Negative Income Taxes and the Poverty Problem in Ontario," *Canadian Tax Journal,* XIX, 2 (March–April, 1971), 116–23.

5.   W.D. McKeough, Ontario Minister of Economics, "Preliminary Outline of a System of Property and Sales Tax Credits for Ontario," presented at the federal-provincial meeting of finance ministers in Ottawa, November, 1971.

6.   Smith, "A Simplified Approach to Social Welfare."

7.   Smith points out that the amount now being redistributed is almost equal to the proceeds of the income tax.

8.   These payments would be made 24 times a year, with the payments for children added to the mother's payments. The tax would be deducted at source.

9.   Where a plan such as a medical care plan is in force, for example, Smith recommended deducting its average cost per adult from the amount of the social dividend, so that all the "social benefits" would be financed from the social dividend fund.

10.   This guaranteed income would be in addition to the health services provided at that time by the government. See addendum, D. B. Smith, p. 325.

Table 1

Basic Allowance, Break-Even Point and Rate of Taxation Proposed by Smith, according to Family Size and Transposed to 1961*

Family unit (number of persons)	Basic allowance	Basic allowance as % of poverty line	Break-even point	Rate of taxation on income other than benefits
1	$ 870	58.0%	$2,175	40%
2	1,740	69.6	4,350	40
3	1,935	64.5	4,837	40
4	2,130	60.9	5,325	40
5	2,325	58.1	5,812	40

*Transposition of this formula to 1961 may seem archaic. However, it enables us to make cross references with income, age of the family head and types of transfers received. Such comparisons are available only through the census. As the authors have based their proposals on data extending from 1963 to 1970, and as these proposals are to be compared among themselves, it does not matter much whether the base chosen is 1961 or 1969.

a percentage of the poverty line,[11] the break-even point and the rate of taxation on earned income.

2 The Cutt formula[12]

In an article published in 1966, James Cutt proposed that Canada adopt a guaranteed income plan of the negative income tax type. Unlike Smith, Cutt agrees in principle that certain complementary income maintenance plans are still necessary.[13] He explains his proposal as a progressive rate scale:

Initially, the tax exemptions could be raised to $1,500 for an individual, $2,500 for a couple and $500 for each child. A progressive scale of negative income tax rates based on the amount of exemptions not used could then be introduced. It would go from 50 per cent for exemptions of $4,000 and over, 45 per cent for $3,500 to $3,999, and so on, to 15 per cent for $500 to $999.[14]

The rate scale reproduced in table 2 would apply
in the case of a family of five whose earnings increase gradually up to $4,000, when their payment of negative income tax becomes nil. Beyond this point, the family would pay a (positive) tax on income at current rates.

Further on, he explains that:
Under the proposed scheme, an elderly couple with total exemptions of $2,500 would receive only 35 per cent of $2,500 or $875.

According to Cutt, this rate scale is preferable to a proportional rate because it contains a graduated incentive to earnings (the marginal rates of taxation decrease) and because it avoids the "notch problem."

a A second stage

The plan proposed by Cutt provides for what could be called a "second stage." It would permit elderly persons and others unable to work to claim, in addition to a first negative income tax payment, a supplement equal to the difference between this first payment and the minimum income stipulated by the basic exemption.[15]

---

11. Unless otherwise indicated, the poverty line is that adopted by the Economic Council of Canada. In 1961, this was $1,500 for a single person, $2,500 for two adults and $500 per child. This line is set at about 60 per cent of the average income.

12. Cutt, "Guaranteed Income."

13. In fact, Cutt eliminates all existing plans except unemployment insurance which he recommends increasing and incorporating in the negative income tax. Similarly, the amounts paid in assistance to persons unable to work would be incorporated in the negative income tax.

14. Cutt, "Guaranteed Income," p. 229. The two quotations immediately following are also from this source.

15. Chart 1, p. 304. By introducing this second stage, Cutt sees the possibility of combining an adequate minimum income for persons without income with a minimum of the disincentive effects and at a reasonable budget cost.

Table 2

Scale of Negative Income Tax Rates for a Family with a Total of $4,000 in Exemptions[a]

Negative income tax rate	Earnings from work	Payment of negative income tax[b]	Total income	Marginal rate of tax on earnings
50%	$ 0	$2,000	$2,000	85%
45	500	1,575	2,075	75
40	1,000	1,200	2,200	65
35	1,500	875	2,375	55
30	2,000	600	2,600	45
25	2,500	375	2,875	35
20	3,000	200	3,200	25
15	3,500	75	3,575	15
0	4,000	0	4,000	

a.   Cutt, "Guaranteed Income," Table 2, p. 222.

b.   The negative income tax payment is computed by applying the specified rate of negative income tax to the difference between earnings and $4,000. For example, the payment to a family earning $1,000 is 40 per cent of $3,000 or $1,200. For the first $500 earned, 85 per cent is disregarded. For each additional $500 earned, a smaller percentage is disregarded. For amounts between $2,000 and $2,500, only 45 per cent is disregarded. (Cutt, "Guaranteed Income," p. 222.)

Table 3 describes the guaranteed income as a percentage of the poverty line and the break-even point implicit in the Cutt formula transposed to 1961.

b *Financing*

The plan is financed from the increase in personal income tax receipts resulting from a broadening of the tax base and an increase in tax rates, if necessary. Income is defined so as to include all types of income, and the family is the basic unit. The amount of the benefits is revised annually according to a productivity index and the regional cost-of-living indexes.

3 *The Crowley-Dodge formulas*[16]

Ronald W. Crowley and Daniel A. Dodge estimate the cost of three guaranteed annual income programs in the form of a fixed amount paid monthly to every person residing in Canada.

a *A social dividend*

The authors say they prefer the social dividend to the negative income tax because of its administrative simplicity and because the absence of an eligibility test enables payments to be made as frequently as desired. The basic allowances considered vary between $750 and $1,250 per adult:

Program A $750 per adult, $300 per child;
Program B $1,000 per adult, $400 per child;
Program C $1,250 per adult, $500 per child.

b *Financing*

These benefits would be financed by a proportional tax levied on the gross income defined so as to include all income. Although a high degree of progression is implicit in this method of financing, the authors say that when the allowances are considered, the proportional rate could be replaced by a progressive rate scale. It is estimated that in 1968 Program A would have necessitated a proportional tax rate of 29.1 per cent,[17] Program B 37.7 per cent and Program C 46.3 per cent. In 1964, these rates would have had to be 33.6 per cent, 45.4 per cent and 56.6 per cent respectively.

c *Role of supplementary plans*

According to the authors, only Program C provides a sufficiently high benefit to permit elimination of the supplementary assistance plans. However, it would make hardly any improvement in the position of persons receiving assistance allowances who have no income potential. The introduction of this program favors primarily

16. Crowley and Dodge, "Cost of the Guaranteed Annual Income."
17. In addition to the social dividend payments ($13,182 million for Program A in 1968) and the administrative costs (estimated at $35 million), the revenues from this tax would have financed expenses (other than welfare expenses) assumed by personal income tax amounting to about $1,407 million in 1968.

Table 3

Basic Allowance and Break-Even Point Proposed by Cutt, according to Family Size and Transposed to 1961

Family unit (number of persons)	Basic allowance	Basic allowance as % of poverty line	Break-even point	Basic allowance Stage Two
1	$ 262	17.5%	$1,050	$1,050
2	612	24.5	1,750	1,750
3	840	28.0	2,100	2,100
4	1,102	31.5	2,450	2,450
5	1,400	35.0	2,800	2,800

families on low incomes who are not eligible for assistance, particularly those in the $3,000 to $8,000 income bracket.

In 1961, the application of Program A would have required a tax rate of 42 per cent.[18] It is this version of the program which is compared in this appendix to the other Canadian proposals. It would have enabled basic allowances to be paid to families, as shown in table 4.

4   *The Deutsch-Green formula*[19]
In the course of a critical analysis of the white paper on income security,[20] Professors Antal Deutsch and Christopher Green show that for the same budget cost, the family allowances and public assistance plans could have been replaced by a guaranteed income plan with allowances tied to income.[21] After setting the break-even points at $1,500 for a single person, $2,500 for a couple, $3,500, $4,500, $5,500, $6,000, $6,500, and $7,000 for families of 3, 4, 5, 6, 7 and 8 persons or more, the authors consider that in making up 50 per cent of the gap between earned income and these break-even points, it would still be possible to stay within the budget of the government's proposed program.[22] Compared to the federal proposal, the Deutsch-Green plan would provide increased benefits to persons with incomes below $3,750 and smaller benefits above that figure (table 5).

a   *Role of the supplementary plans*
The plan applies only to persons not receiving old age security.[23] The proposed plan does not eliminate the need for unemployment insurance, veterans' pensions and workmen's compensation. Furthermore, in cases where the guaranteed income floor is lower than the welfare benefits, the authors suggest that the provinces make up the minimum allowances by welfare payments.

---

18.   See Crowley-Dodge in the Addendum to this Appendix.

19.   Deutsch, and Green, "Income Security."

20.   Canada, Department of National Health and Welfare, *Income Security for Canadians* (Ottawa, 1970).

21.   The criticism of the government's proposal centres mainly on the following aspect: half the allowances paid under the proposed Family Income Security Plan (FISP) would go to families with incomes of between $5,000 and $10,000, whereas low-income families whose head is working remain excluded from these transfer plans.

22.   This limit is set as follows: the amounts estimated for FISP ($660 million) and 80 per cent of the sums allowed for the financial assistance programs ($891.2 million for 1969-70), for a total of $1,373 million. See: Canada, Department of National Health and Welfare, *Income Security for Canadians,* pp. 46, 63.

23.   The old age security plan is equivalent in its structure to a guaranteed income plan and pays slightly higher benefits than those proposed by the authors.

Table 4

Basic Allowances, Break-Even Point and Rate of Taxation according to Crowley and Dodge's Proposal A, by Family Size and Transposed to 1961

Family unit (number of persons)	Basic allowance	Basic allowance as % of poverty line	Break-even point	Rate of taxation on income other than benefits
1	$ 750	50%	$1,786	42%
2	1,500	60	3,571	42
3	1,800	60	4,286	42
4	2,100	60	5,000	42
5	2,400	60	5,714	42

Table 5

Basic Allowance, Break-Even Point and Rate of Implied Tax according to the Deutsch-Green Proposal, by Family Size and Transposed to 1961

Family unit (number of persons)	Basic allowance	Basic allowance as % of poverty line	Break-even point	Rate of implied taxation on income
1	$ 525	35.0%	$1,050	50%
2	875	35.0	1,750	50
3	1,225	40.8	2,450	50
4	1,575	45.0	3,150	50
5	1,925	48.1	3,850	50
6	2,100	46.7	4,200	50
7	2,275	45.5	4,550	50
8+	2,450	44.6	4,900	50

5   *Castonguay-Nepveu proposal*[24]

The Castonguay-Nepveu proposal recommends an overhaul of the whole income maintenance system. Within this umbrella proposal, financial assistance programs would be replaced by a guaranteed annual income plan.[25] The revised social insurance plans would continue to give basic protection to regular participants in the labor force. A system of uniform family allowances tied to income would serve as a point of contact between these two types of plans because it deals directly with the economic hardships created by dependents among low-income groups.

The general social allowances plan contains two formulas or two stages. For Stage One, the basic allowance is set at 60 per cent of the poverty line[26] for the first and second adult and 50 per cent for each child.[27] Each person living alone or each family is entitled to this basic allowance, reduced by one-third of earned or other income considered for the segment from $0 to $2,000 and 55.56 per cent for the portion above $2,000. For Stage Two, the basic allowance is set at 100 per cent of the poverty line per adult. The allowance for each child remains the same. The rate of implied income tax is set at 100 per cent. The Stage Two allowance is therefore advantageous for persons with very low or no incomes. Stage Two is designed for individuals or family heads who have no opportunity to work or are incapable of working. However, it is the established income figure and not employment status that determines the choice of formula. A recipient may pass from a Stage Two allowance to a Stage One allowance at any time. However, a three-month waiting period is required for any movement in the opposite direction, unless there is clear evidence of inability to work. Chart 2 illustrates the behavior of total incomes in relation to earned income according to the two formulas. We find that there is a basic earned income line above which the Stage One allowance is more advantageous than the Stage Two allowance.[28]

---

24. Quebec (Province) Commission of Inquiry on Health and Social Welfare, *Income Security*.

25. This plan, offering allowances tied to income, is called the General Social Allowances Plan.

26. The poverty lines used are those of the Economic Council of Canada, *Challenge of Growth and Change*, Fifth Annual Review (Ottawa: Queen's Printer, September, 1968).

27. The family or school allowance pays at least 30 per cent of the poverty line for each child under 18 years of age.

28. This line is called "the stage change line": whenever the values of the basic allowances are changed, the rates of implied taxation on income or the portions of income to which these rates apply must also be revised so that the stage change line will also be moved. Thus for 1971, the portion of income to which the rate applies would have been increased to $2,500 or 1/3 and the rate of the second portion would have been set at 61.21 per cent.

Table 6

Basic Allowance, Break-Even Point and Rate of Implied Income Tax according to the Castonguay-Nepveu Proposal, by Family Size, 1961

Family unit (number of persons)	Basic allowance				Break-even point Stage One	Rate of implied income tax Stage One
	Stage Two		Stage One			
	In dollars	In % of poverty line	In dollars	In % of poverty line		
1	$1,500	100.0%	$ 900	60.0%	$2,420	$0–2,000:33⅓%
2	2,500	100.0	1,500	60.0	3,500	
3	2,750	91.7	1,750	58.3	3,950	
4	3,000	85.7	2,000	57.1	4,400	
5	3,250	81.3	2,250	56.3	4,850	$2,000 and over:55.56%
6	3,500	77.8	2,500	55.6	5,300	
7	3,750	75.0	2,750	55.0	5,750	
8	4,000	72.7	3,000	54.6	6,200	

Chart 1

Income after Transfers and after Tax,* according to the Cutt Proposal, in Relation to Income Earned and according to Family Size, 1967

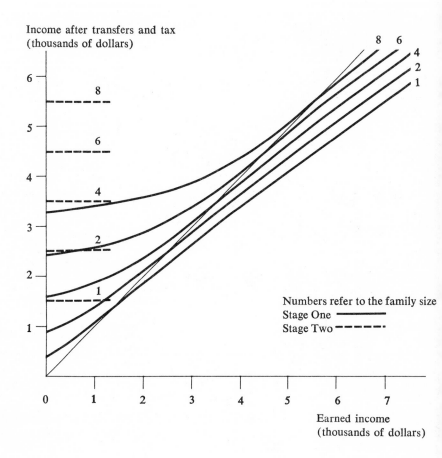

*Calculation of the positive income tax is made on the basis of the tax reform that came into effect in Canada in 1972.

Chart 2

**Total Incomes Including Personal Income and Social Allowance
(First and Second Stages) Paid by the General Social Allowances Plan
in Relation to the Personal Income Considered and according to
Family Size, 1961, the Castonguay-Nepveu Report**

Social allowance and
personal income considered
– total amount
(thousands of dollars)

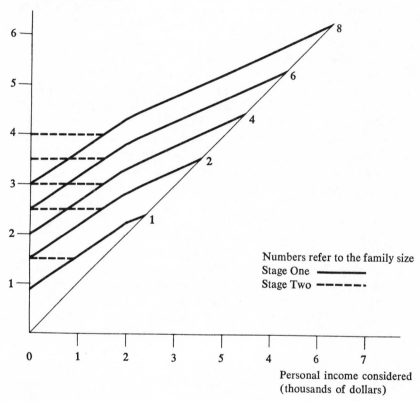

Numbers refer to the family size
Stage One ——————
Stage Two – – – – – ·

Personal income considered
(thousands of dollars)

Note: $900 = stage change line for single persons, $1,500 = stage change line
for families, and $2,000 = income level at which the 33 1/3 per cent rate applies.

When income declines and falls below the stage change line, it is to the recipient's advantage to pass over to the second stage. On the other hand, when income rises, there is a time lag near the stage change line, and the decision by the recipient to change to the other stage will depend on his subjective assessment of two factors: (1) what it will cost him to remain at the second stage; and (2) what it would cost him to change over in the event that his income should again fall below this line, when he would encounter the waiting period before having access to the second stage.[29]

The beneficiary unit of the General Social Allowance Plan is the family.[30] All the family's income is lumped together but, as for income tax, compulsory contributions are deducted. Table 6 gives the values of the basic allowances transposed to 1961.

a *Supplementary plans*

The guaranteed annual income benefits are supplemented by family allowances. These were increased to $130 annually per child under 12 years and $170 per child from 12 to 18 in 1961.[31] They are offered to all families but about 30 per cent is recovered by a special rate of taxation. Amendments are proposed to the unemployment insurance and pension plans. The old age security plan is maintained during a transition period and then incorporated in the general social allowances plan.

6 *Senate committee proposal*[32]

The main recommendation of the Senate's Special Committee on Poverty deals with recognition of the right of every citizen to an adequate minimum income. Implementation of a guaranteed annual income plan is a first step towards translating this right into reality. Table 7 summarizes the Senate committee's proposal for setting a basic allowance rate that is adequate and that can be adjusted annually in accordance with variations in the average standard of living. To be adequate, the basic allowance levels must be at least equivalent to 70 per cent of the poverty line. The poverty line fixed by the Senate committee is a compromise solution which takes the budgetary needs as a starting point and adjusts the resulting

---

29. The stage change line represents the minimum income level a job should have to encourage the recipient to move from the second to the first stage. In this respect, the mechanism of the General Social Allowance Plan complements the minimum wage law. A criterion of employment duration is added to that of remuneration rates. This line should be set at rates compatible with the minimum wage. This mechanism is likely to hasten the disappearance of marginal jobs.

30. It is emphasized, however, that starting at age 18, a person who is in the labor market and cannot be a dependent of his parents should be able to receive this allowance.

31. In 1971 these amounts were $150 and $200 respectively.

32. Special Committee on Poverty, *Poverty in Canada.*

Table 7

Basic Variables of the GAI Program Proposed by the Senate, for 1969

Family unit (number of persons)	Minimum cost of maintaining a family of 2 adults, 2 children	Family size equalizer points[b]	Basic allowance	Basic allowance as % of poverty line	Poverty line	Rate of diminution of basic allowance	Break-even point
1		3	$1,500	70%	$2,140	70%	$2,140
2		5	2,500	70	3,570	70	3,570
3		6	3,000	70	4,290	70	4,290
4	$3,500[a]	7	3,500	70	5,000	70	5,000
5		8	4,000	70	5,710	70	5,710
6		9	4,500	70	6,430	70	6,430
7		10	5,000	70	7,140	70	7,140
10		13	6,500	70	9,290	70	9,290

a. The amount in column two was set at $150 more than a family of 4 with no income received in the province giving the most generous welfare allowances.
b. The coefficients in column three, which are called Family Size Equalizer Points, were established by Jenny Podoluk, author of *Incomes of Canadians*, a 1961 census monograph. They were used in setting the poverty lines of the Economic Council of Canada. By dividing $3,500 by the appropriate coefficient (7), we obtain the allowance per "potential" person.

line to take account of the yearly increase in average income.[33]

According to the Senate committee's position, the 70 per cent rate of implied taxation still represents a reasonable compromise between the constraints of budget cost, incentive to work and the goal of an adequate income level.[34] The chief characteristic of its plan is that it pays no allowances over the poverty line.

The Senate committee's proposal would apply to all Canadians except citizens who are single, unattached individuals under 40 years of age.

The "reverse" adjustment of the poverty lines by the mechanisms suggested (table 7) would give the plan the basic variables for 1961 as shown in table 8.

a *Complementary plans*

The GAI proposed by the Senate committee would replace family allowances and old age security. The assistance plan would continue to pay benefits to persons under 40 years of age. The social insurance programs would be retained.[35]

Comparison between Proposals

A comparison can be made of the proposals we have enumerated with respect to their basic variables and the effect of the benefit on income after transfer. Table 9 lists each of these programs in ascending order of basic allowance. We add two variants to the Senate committee's proposal. Transposed to 1961, the committee's proposal gives a basic allowance of only 60 per cent of the poverty line set by the Economic Council of Canada. The first "adjusted" variant in the Senate plan consists in correcting the basic allowance so as to maintain it at 70 per cent of the council's poverty lines.[36] The second variant, that of the "modified" Senate committee plan, approaches the ideal guaranteed income (according to the Senate committee) by increasing the basic allowance to 100 per cent of the poverty line. The rate of income tax is maintained at 70 per

---

33. To make this adjustment, the allowance paid per "potential" person is varied in proportion to the average standard of living per potential person. This latter figure is equal to the total available income over the sum of the products of the number of families of each size by its family size equalizer point.

34. According to the Senate committee, an ideal guaranteed annual income plan would give a basic allowance equal to 100 per cent of the poverty line combined with a rate of implied taxation of 50 per cent on income.

35. The Senate committee also recommends that income tax exemptions be raised so that no Canadian whose income is below the poverty line would be subject to income tax.

36. The Senate committee's proposal is interpreted literally by using its own poverty line transposed to 1961. In the first variant, the spirit of the proposal is interpreted; according to this, the basic allowance should not be increased beyond 70 per cent of the poverty line.

Table 8

**Basic Allowance, Break-Even Point and Rate of Taxation
according to the Senate Committee Formula, by Family
Size and Transposed to 1961***

Family unit (number of persons)	Basic allowance	Basic allowance as % of poverty line	Break-even point	Rate of implied taxation
1	$ 903	60.2%	$1,290	70%
2	1,505	60.2	2,150	70
3	1,806	60.2	2,580	70
4	2,107	60.2	3,010	70
5	2,408	60.2	3,440	70

*See: The Senate, Cutt and Deutsch-Green proposals, in the Addendum to this Appendix.

cent, however, because a lower rate becomes distinctly prohibitive in relation to cost.[37]

In charts 3 and 4 the effect of these plans on each income category can be measured, but only in the case of a family of five.

Application of These Proposals to Quebec

Most of the authors have given an estimate of the total amount of social benefits that should be paid in the event that their formula is implemented. These estimates, just as relevant as ours, of the budget impact of a plan at a particular time are difficult to compare, however. They do not apply to the same population: the Castonguay-Nepveu proposal applies to Quebec and the others to Canada; the Deutsch-Green proposal does not apply to the elderly population, and the Senate committee proposal does not apply to single unattached individuals under 40 years of age. The calculations use different base years, and often the methods of estimating are not explained, so that we do not know to what extent the figures used are comparable. Finally, implementation of the plans implies a variety of adjustments to the existing plans which are not necessarily incorporated in the estimate of their cost. The first task was, therefore, to choose a base year and a population that would serve to compare the incidence of each of the proposals. From the statistics we were able to obtain, we could have chosen the Canadian population in 1967[38] or the Quebec population in 1961.[39] The circumstances favored 1961 because more complete information was available concerning the structure of the transfers and the population distribution according to the age of the family head and income; this information was desired in order to evaluate the effects of the proposals, according to certain characteristics of low-wage earners.

This choice, therefore, enabled a comparison of the plans to be made, although the estimates of cost are less up-to-date because income maintenance plans have changed greatly since 1961. In making the proposals more comparable rather than securing absolute

---

37. A rate of 50 per cent would have meant a break-even point in 1969 of $11,420 for a family of five.

38. Canada, Dominion Bureau of Statistics, *Statistics on Low Income in Canada, 1967*, D.B.S. Cat. No. 13-536 (Ottawa: Information Canada, 1971).

39. Statistics provided by the Dominion Bureau of Statistics in response to a special request from the Commission of Inquiry on Health and Social Welfare in Quebec. Gilles Desrochers, *L'insuffisance des revenus au Québec et le Coût d'un revenu minimum garanti*, Appendix 28 of *Report*, Quebec (Province) Commission of Inquiry on Health and Social Welfare (Quebec: Official Publisher, 1971). (Hereinafter referred to as *L'insuffisance des revenus au Québec*.)

Table 9

Values in 1961 of the Basic Variables according to the Various Guaranteed Annual Income Proposals

Plans	Basic allowances as % of poverty line					
	Family of 1	Family of 2	Family of 3	Family of 4	Family of 5	Rate of implied income tax (t)
Cutt	17.5%	24.5%	28.0%	31.5%	35.0%	*
Deutsch-Green	35.0	35.0	40.8	45.0	48.1	50%
Senate committee	60.2	60.2	60.2	60.2	60.2	70
Crowley-Dodge	50.0	60.0	60.0	60.0	60.0	42
Smith	58.0	69.6	64.5	60.9	58.1	40
"Adjusted" Senate	70.0	70.0	70.0	70.0	70.0	70
Castonguay-Nepveu						
Stage Two	100.0	100.0	91.7	85.7	81.3	100
Stage One	60.0	60.0	58.3	57.1	56.3	*
"Modified" Senate	86.0	86.0	86.0	86.0	86.0	70

*In the Cutt and Castonguay-Nepveu (Stage One) programs, the value of t is composed of a scale of marginal rates applying to the marginal portions of income deficiency to be made up.

Chart 3

**Income after Transfers
according to the Various Guaranteed Annual Income Plans Compared,
for Families of Five in 1961**

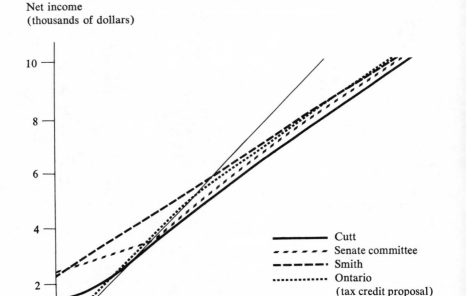

Net income
(thousands of dollars)

Income earned
(thousands of dollars)

Notes:
1. For the Castonguay-Nepveu proposal, the transfers are composed of the
General Social Allowance Plan payments (first and second stages) and $450
in family allowances.
2. The positive income tax is applied starting from the break-even points on
the basis of the tax reform that came into force in Canada in 1972, except
in the case of the social dividend proposals (Crowley-Dodge and Smith), in
which the proportional rates suggested by the authors are used (42 per cent
and 40 per cent), and the Castonguay-Nepveu proposal which does not
provide for integration into the positive income tax system.

Chart 4

**Income after Income Tax
according to the Various Guaranteed Annual Income Plans Compared,
for Families of Five in 1961**

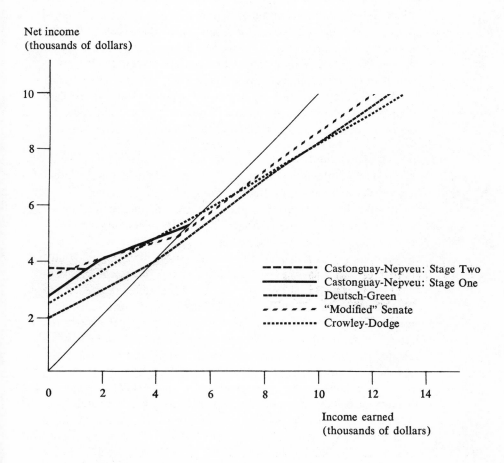

Net income
(thousands of dollars)

- - - - - - Castonguay-Nepveu: Stage Two
——————— Castonguay-Nepveu: Stage One
----------------- Deutsch-Green
- - - - - "Modified" Senate
················· Crowley-Dodge

Income earned
(thousands of dollars)

results in our estimates, we were able to formulate certain simplifying hypotheses. For example, we assumed that all economic families consisted of two adults and a number of dependent children equal to the family size minus two. Such an assumption, however, does not perfectly meet the eligibility conditions set out by the authors. Some of the proposals provide different basic allowances according to the age of the individuals; others, according to the number of persons in the family; and still others, according to the links between individuals in the same economic or census family. In comparing these eligibility conditions, we realize that most of the authors have adjusted them to the type of data either at their disposal or which they knew they could obtain. Hence the difficulty, when using common base data, of including all the relevant items in each of the proposals. To sum up, it can be concluded that in no case does our application of the proposals meet the strict conditions laid down by the authors, but in all cases they come as close as possible.

1 *Characteristics of low-wage earners*

In 1961, 83 per cent of inadequate incomes in Quebec were found among the non-agricultural population.[40]

The incidence of poverty among single unattached individuals was 43.7 per cent. Their income before transfers totalled $39.4 million, whereas the corresponding income at the poverty line is $144 million. To make up the income deficiency, it would have been necessary to pay $104.6 million to single unattached individuals (more than $1,000 per person, or 72.6 per cent of the income corresponding to the poverty line). Single unattached individuals form one-quarter of all poor families, but only 5.1 per cent of the poor population. Twenty-eight per cent of these persons were eligible for the old age security pension in 1961. In 1971, using the same poverty lines,[41] we can project an incidence of poverty of 42.7 per cent among single unattached individuals. However, the deficiency of income after transfers would have decreased from 58 to 52.6 per cent.[42] The plans now in force paid $30 million to single individuals, of which $20.6 million or 68.3 per cent helped to decrease the income deficiency. More than 50 per cent of these amounts came from the old age security plan and the rest from insurance benefits, social assistance or veterans' pensions or allowances.

Among non-agricultural economic families, the incidence of poverty before transfers is 38.5 per cent of all family units. There were 1,798,642 poor persons, or 42.7 per cent of the families. To

---

40. Desrochers, *L'insuffisance des revenus au Québec.*
41. Adjusted only to take into account the rise in the cost of living.
42. Desrochers, *L'insuffisance des revenus au Québec.*

eliminate poverty, it would have required $582.1 million or 39.6 per cent of the total income corresponding to the poverty line.[43] Under the 1961 system, $349.8 million was paid to families, of which $163.5 million or only 47 per cent went to poor families. These benefits therefore contributed to making up 28 per cent of income deficiencies.

2 *Effect of the proposed plans on income deficiency*
The immediate goal of the guaranteed annual income proposals is generally expressed in terms of making up income deficiency. Thus, the portion of income deficiency that is made up will be a yardstick for measuring the adequacy of a plan. The proposals mentioned here, with the exception of those put forward by Cutt and by Deutsch-Green, will reduce income deficiency before transfer by at least half. The distance between the two proposals mentioned and the others is not so great as it appears at first sight, since the authors were the only ones in the group to retain at least partially the financial assistance programs now in force. In fact, Cutt suggests that this assistance should be incorporated in the negative income tax plan. It would take the form of supplementary benefits for persons unable to work. If we adhere strictly to this eligibility requirement, these additional benefits might have represented at the most $40 million.[44] Deutsch and Green suggested that the provinces should pay supplementary benefits to make up the difference between the level of assistance allowances and the appropriate negative income tax payment; this could have represented from $25 million to $40 million. These correctives would imply that the income deficiency made up has increased from 14.5 to 20 per cent under the Cutt formula.[45] It would increase from 38.3 to 42 or 44 per cent under the Deutsch-Green plan (table 10).

A comparison of these various programs indicates that 70 to 75 per cent of income deficiency can be made up by providing for basic allowances equal to 50 per cent of the poverty line, provided that the rate of taxation is also around 50 per cent, or with a 60-40

43. In 1971, the incidence of poverty in families was estimated at 17.6 per cent, a result that is strongly influenced by the use of poverty lines whose real value has remained constant. On the other hand, income deficiency after transfer was 31.8 per cent, compared to 35.7 per cent of the income corresponding to the poverty line in 1961. Desrochers, *L'insuffisance des revenus au Québec*.
44. On the other hand, if we make all persons receiving assistance eligible for these benefits and if we assume that their incomes are negligible, these additional payments might go as high as $100 million.
45. At the maximum, in cases where the additional payment is extended to all persons receiving assistance, the income deficiency made up would be 28.5 per cent, that is to say the incidence of his plan is equivalent to that of the system in force.

combination of these variables (Crowley-Dodge and Smith). As table 12 indicates, the budget cost will be much higher than in the case where the 70-70 combination is used to obtain an equivalent effect (p. 320).

3 Reduction of poverty

A person is defined as poor when his income is below the poverty line. The number of individuals or families who have escaped from poverty is composed of those who, by any given plan, will receive an income at least equal to the poverty line. A formula whose basic allowance is equal to 100 per cent of the poverty line and whose rate of implied taxation is equal to 100 per cent will remove the entire population from the poor category. On the other hand, a formula whose basic allowance is below the poverty line will only make possible a reduction in the number of poor persons if the break-even point is higher than the poverty line. Because of the universal benefits,[46] the present system contains a break-even point above the poverty line. Its effect is to reduce the number of poor families by 16.8 per cent (table 11). The plans proposed by Cutt and the Senate committee contain break-even points which are respectively below and level with the poverty line. They have no effect on the number of poor families or individuals. On the other hand, income deficiency among unattached individuals is such that the Crowley-Dodge and Smith plans leave the number of poor unattached individuals unchanged, whereas they would enable about 50 per cent of the families to escape from poverty.

As for the combined advantage of making up income deficiency and reducing poverty, only the Castonguay-Nepveu proposal and the modified Senate committee plan could be termed really adequate. They would have required a doubling in 1961 of the amounts allocated to social transfers.

4 Net financial costs or budget costs

Table 12 gives the total of net benefits paid by each of the plans compared. For social dividends, the rate of income tax suggested to obtain the net benefits is applied. In the other plans, the benefits are a component of income before tax, and the total then coincides with the budget cost. But as we have seen, most of these proposals, except that of Smith, would complement the social insurance plans.[47] In the case of Deutsch-Green, the total budget cost includes negative income tax for the non-elderly and old age security which

---

46. Family allowances and old age security pensions.
47. Among the insurance plans, Cutt would retain only unemployment insurance.

Table 10

Incidence of the Plans under Comparison on Income Deficiency before Transfer, Quebec, 1961

	Deficiency made up						Column 3 as % of Column 5
	Unattached individuals		Families		Total units		
Plans	Millions of dollars	As % of income deficiency	Millions of dollars	As % of income deficiency	Millions of dollars	As % of income deficiency	
Present system	$ 20.6	19.7%	$163.5	28.1%	$184.1	26.8%	79.4%
Cutt	13.7	13.1	86.0	14.8	99.7	14.5	86.3
Deutsch-Green	35.2	33.6	227.5	39.1	262.7	38.3	86.6
Senate committee	59.1	56.5	282.1	48.5	341.2	49.7	82.7
"Adjusted" Senate	73.2	70.0	407.5	70.0	480.7	70.0	84.8
Crowley-Dodge	55.5	53.0	442.8	76.0	498.3	72.5	88.9
Smith	67.8	64.8	437.3	75.2	505.1	73.6	86.6
"Modified" Senate	94.1	89.9	551.1	94.7	645.2	93.9	85.4
Castonguay-Nepveu	104.6	100.0	555.6	95.5	660.3	96.1	84.5
Total income deficiency							
In millions	$104.6		$582.1		$686.7		
In % of income corresponding to poverty line		72.6%		39.6%		42.7%	
Income deficiency in families as % of total deficiency							84.8%

takes the place of guaranteed income for aged persons.[48] In the Castonguay-Nepveu proposal, there is added to old age security a system of family allowances which forms part of the guaranteed income. In so doing, however, an overestimate of $86 million for family allowances is obtained. This is due to two factors: on the one hand, family allowances are paid to about 300,000 members of economic families aged 18 and over. On the other hand, by recovery, repayment of 15 per cent of the gross cost is obtained instead of 30 per cent suggested by the report.[49] There is also an overestimate of the costs of the Senate committee proposal, since single unattached persons under 40 years of age are also included. Finally, in the Crowley-Dodge and Smith plans, persons belonging to a family who were over 20 and under 21 years of age received the dividend for persons under 20, whereas they were entitled to the amount prescribed for an adult.

These adjustments do not change the ranking of the various proposals as to the amount of benefits. Three groups of proposals can be distinguished: those with a cost similar to that of the existing programs – Cutt, Deutsch-Green and the Senate committee plan as originally interpreted; the "modified" Senate committee and Castonguay-Nepveu plans which represent a cost at least twice as high as that of the existing plan but whose effect on poverty and income deficiency is also at least twice as great; and the Crowley-Dodge and Smith formulas, which are very similar to one another and occupy an intermediate position.

5 Cost-benefit ratios

The proportion of benefits which serves to make up income deficiency (table 12) is the chief indicator of the effectiveness of the plan. It is because less than 50 per cent of the benefits paid out help to remove poverty that the present system is termed ineffective. With the proposed plans to replace it, the proportion of income deficiency that is absorbed rises from 72 per cent in the Castonguay-Nepveu to 100 per cent in the Cutt and Senate plans. However, to compare these plans – whose budget costs fluctuate greatly – it is preferable to rely on an assessment of the benefit represented by each additional dollar spent. Table 13 gives a few cost-benefit coefficients of our contemplated proposals on a comparative basis. The benefits are measured solely in relation to the criterion on income

---

48. According to the calculations made, whenever the benefit paid by the general guaranteed income plan to which the elderly person would have been entitled was higher than his pension, the difference was made up by a guaranteed income benefit as suggested by the authors.

49. This arises from the fact that a continuous scale of recovery is applied rather than a discontinuous scale.

Table 11

Incidence of the Plans Compared on the Number of Poor Families or Unattached Individuals, Quebec, 1961

Number of units escaped from poverty as percentage of the number of poor units

Plans	Unattached individuals	Families		Total units	
		Number of units	Total persons	Number of units	Total persons
Present system		16.8%	16.1%	13.4%	15.3%
Cutt					
Deutsch-Green		8.6	5.6	6.9	5.3
Senate committee					
"Adjusted" Senate					
Crowley-Dodge		47.6	47.7	38.0	45.3
Smith		47.7	44.7	38.1	42.4
"Modified" Senate	24.9%	63.7	67.3	55.9	65.2
Castonguay-Nepveu	100.0	69.7	61.4	75.8	63.3

Incidence of poverty before transfers

Number of poor units	96,097	380,905	1,798,642	477,002	1,894,739
As % of total number of units	43.7%	38.5%	42.7%	39.5%	42.7%

Table 12

Total of Benefits Paid and Income Deficiency Made Up as a Percentage of the Benefits Paid (Plans Compared), Quebec, 1961

Plans	Unattached individuals		Families		Total units	
	Benefits paid (Millions of $)	Deficiency made up as % of benefits	Benefits paid (Millions of $)	Deficiency made up as % of benefits	Benefits paid (Millions of $)	Deficiency made up as % of benefits
Present system	$ 30.2	68.3%	$347.8	47.0%	$378.0	48.7%
Cutt	13.7	100.0	60.7	100.0	99.7	100.0
Cutt^a					139.7	100.0
Deutsch-Green	39.2	89.6	86.0	82.7	314.4b	83.6
Deutsch-Green^c					339.4	84.8
Senate committee	59.1	100.0	275.1	100.0	341.2	100.0
"Adjusted" Senate	73.2	100.0	407.4	100.0	481.7	100.0
Crowley-Dodge	57.4	96.7	580.3	76.3	637.7	78.1
Smith	73.4	92.4	606.5	72.1	679.9	74.3
"Modified" Senate	100.3	93.8	676.1	81.5	776.4	83.1
Castonguay-Nepveu	120.2	87.0	794.9	69.9	915.1d	72.1
Castonguay-Nepveue	120.2	87.0	740.5	75.0	860.8	76.6
Castonguay-Nepveuf	120.2	87.0	705.0	76.3	825.3	77.8

a. Estimate revised to include $40 million in negative income tax payments to persons eligible for assistance by reason of inability to work.

b. Includes negative income tax payments of $205.6 million and $108.8 million in old age security benefits.

c. Estimate revised to include $25 million in supplementary assistance payments.

d. Includes $516.6 million in payments under the General Social Allowance Plan, $108.8 million in old age security benefits and $289.8 million in family allowances.

e. Estimate revised to raise the amount of recovery of family allowances to 30 per cent of the total. The net amount of family allowances drops from $289.8 million to $235.4 million.

f. Estimate revised to withdraw family allowances from dependents 18 years of age and over. The next amount drops from $235.4 million to $200 million. It is estimated that half of these amounts was paid out to offset income deficiency.

Table 13

**Additional Income Deficiency Made Up
in Relation to the Additional Cost of the Various Proposals**

Plans	Cutt	Present system	Deutsch-Green	Adjusted Senate	Crowley-Dodge	Smith	Modified Senate	Castonguay-Nepveu
Cutt								
Present system	0.19							
Deutsch-Green	0.74							
"Adjusted" Senate	1.00	2.89	1.37					
Crowley-Dodge	0.72	1.21	0.71	0.11	0.16			
Smith	0.68	1.06	0.64	0.12	1.06	1.45		
"Modified" Senate	0.79	1.16	0.82	0.56	1.06	0.86		
Castonguay-Nepveu	0.72	0.99	0.71	0.47	0.72	0.86	0.17	

deficiency made up. From this point of view, all the proposals are at least as profitable as the existing systems, if not much more so. Although under the formula suggested by Cutt, both the cost and the making up of income deficiency are lower than under the existing system, the present structure of transfer has no advantage over Cutt's plan; the additional gains represent only 18 per cent of the additional cost. Among the various options, the Senate committee plan seems the most attractive in relation to cost-benefits.[50] It is more advantageous than the Deutsch-Green plan. The "modified" Senate committee plan has little to offer which the Senate committee proposal has not; on the other hand, it becomes attractive compared to the Crowley-Dodge and Smith formulas. The Castonguay-Nepveu proposal also seems to offer no clear gain over the Senate committee plan. On the other hand, these relative judgments are valid only to the extent that we consider the removal of income deficiency a satisfactory criterion for assessing the advantages. It has already been emphasized that although the Senate committee's original proposal achieves a high degree of effectiveness, it has one major drawback: that of not bringing anyone out of poverty. Obviously, it is difficult to consider an anti-poverty measure as fully effective when it leaves all the beneficiaries below the income corresponding to the poverty line.

6 *Distribution by quintiles*
Finally, taking into account the general goal of the guaranteed annual income, it is advisable to include the redistribution effect among the relative advantages of the proposed plans. Chart 5 compares the incomes of each quintile before and after transfers.[51] Whereas it received 3.1 per cent of the total income before transfers, the first 20 per cent of the population would have received 5.5 per cent under the Deutsch-Green program and 8.6 per cent with the Castonguay-Nepveu plan. The upper income limit for the first quintile rose from $1,711 before transfers to $2,988 with the Castonguay-Nepveu program. As for the second and third quintiles, they would be favored more by the Crowley-Dodge, Smith and "modified" Senate committee formulas. With this last formula, the upper income limit of the second quintile increases from $2,455 to $3,782. For the third quintile, the Smith plan increases the upper income limit from $3,752 to $4,436.

---

50. The programs are discontinuous and the value of the coefficients indicates that there are intermediate solutions between some of the options expressed whose coefficients would be close to unity.
51. That is, income before tax.

Chart 5

Income of Families and Unattached Individuals before and after Transfer, 1961 (% of income)

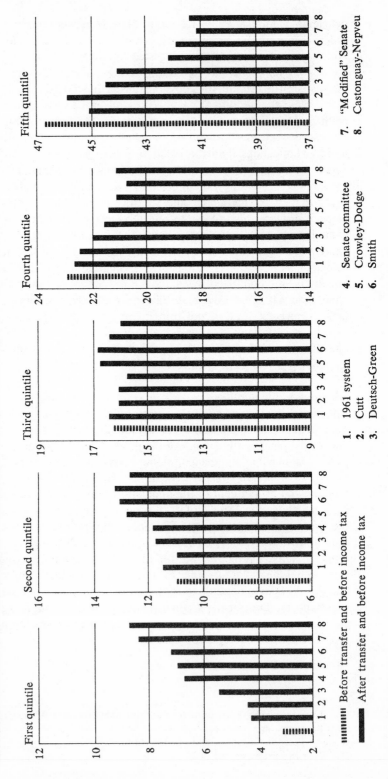

IIIIIII Before transfer and before income tax	1. 1961 system	4. Senate committee
▬▬ After transfer and before income tax	2. Cutt	5. Crowley-Dodge
	3. Deutsch-Green	6. Smith
	7. "Modified" Senate	
	8. Castonguay-Nepveu	

Addendum to Benefits and Costs of Canadian Proposals for a Guaranteed Annual Income

Transposition to 1961 of the values of the basic allowances provided by the plans compared.

1 *D.B. Smith*
Smith suggests redistributing 40 per cent of adjusted personal income in Canada. The health costs assumed by the government should be financed from these funds. The income figure used is 1961 personal income, 40 per cent of which would provide a social dividend of $971 per adult and $194 per person under age 21. ("National Accounts, Income and Expenditure, 1967," DBS Cat. No. 13–201 gives adjusted personal income total of $28,522 million.) The average health expenses per adult are deducted from his allowance, giving a net dividend of $870. (Public expenditures on health total $1 billion. Source: "A Consolidation of Public Finance Statistics, Municipalities, Provinces and the Government of Canada," 1961 fiscal year, DBS Cat. No. 68–202, Table 2.)

2 *Crowley-Dodge*
Program A proposed by Crowley-Dodge would have required in 1961 an income tax rate of 42 per cent if it had been implemented as a replacement for the welfare programs. Programs B and C would have required income tax rates of over 46 per cent. Since the authors consider, as a maximum, a plan which redistributes 46 per cent of income, we use Program A in 1961. The same procedure is followed as in the Smith plan for setting the basic allowance.

3 *The Senate committee, Cutt and Deutsch-Green proposals*
For the Senate committee proposal, the method used in transposing to 1961 the values of the basic allowances is the one suggested in the committee's report. The same method is used to determine the 1961 value of the tax exemptions according to the level suggested by Cutt in 1966, namely $500 for a child, three times $500 for a single, unattached individual, and five times $500 for a couple with no children. Their 1961 value is determined by the following formula:

$$\frac{\text{Average standard of living in 1961}}{\text{Average standard of living in 1967}} \times \$500 = \$350$$

The same method is used to transpose to 1961 the basic variables of the Deutsch-Green proposals.

Family unit	1967		1961
One-person family	$1,500 = $500 × 3 ×		$350 = $1,050
Two-person family	2,500 = 500 × 5 ×		350 = 1,750
Three-person family	3,500 = 500 × 7 ×		350 = 2,450
Four-person family	4,500 = 500 × 9 ×		350 = 3,150
Five-person family	5,500 = 500 × 11 ×		350 = 3,850
Six-person family	6,000 = 500 × 12 ×		350 = 4,200
Seven-person family	6,500 = 500 × 13 ×		350 = 4,550
Eight-person family	7,000 = 500 × 14 ×		350 = 4,900

The method takes into account the course of economic growth, the cost of living, and the average per capita income according to change in family size.

4 *Castonguay-Nepveu*

The proposal sets the values of the basic allowances in reference to the poverty lines determined by the Economic Council of Canada for 1961 and 1971.

Nuffield Seminar Planning Committee

Co-chairmen:

Dr. Gérald Fortin, *Quebec*
Director, Centre for Urban and Regional Research
National Institute for Scientific Research
University of Quebec

J.H. Perry, *Toronto*
Executive Director, The Canadian Bankers' Association

Members:

Marion H. Bryden, *Toronto*
Research Director, Ontario New Democratic Party Caucus

Jacques Larin, *Montreal*
Professor, School of Social Work
University of Montreal

Dr. David Woodsworth, *Montreal*
Director, School of Social Work
McGill University

Project Director:

Patricia Godfrey, *Ottawa*
Program Director, The Canadian Council on Social Development

(The Seminar Planning Committee is a sub-committee of The Canadian Council on Social Development's Task Force on Social Security, whose members are listed below.)

**Task Force on Social Security of
The Canadian Council on Social Development**

Co-chairmen:
Dr. Gérald Fortin, *Quebec*
John M. Godfrey, Q.C., *Toronto*

Members:
R. Max Beck, *Ottawa*
Marion H. Bryden, *Toronto*
Charles E. Hendry, *Toronto*
David Kirk, *Ottawa*
Jacques Larin, *Montreal*
F.R. MacKinnon, *Halifax*
Gower Markle, *Toronto*
Nicole V. Martin, *Quebec*
William F. Mitchell, *Toronto*
Rev. Clifton L. Monk, *Winnipeg*
Andrew Nicholas, *Fredericton*
J.H. Perry, *Toronto*
Rev. Edward W. Scott, *Toronto*
T.H.B. Symons, *Peterborough*
E.F. Watson, *Toronto*
Dr. David Woodsworth, *Montreal*

Ex-officio, The Canadian Council on Social Development:
President: Mrs. W.M. Benidickson, *Ottawa*
Chairman, Program Planning Committee: Dr. J.E.F. Hastings, *Toronto*
Chairman, Executive Committee: Jean Séguin, *Montreal*

Nuffield Canadian Seminar

Participants

Anthony B. Atkinson, *Essex, England*
Professor, Department of Economics
University of Essex

Reuben C. Baetz, *Ottawa*
Executive Director, The Canadian Council on Social Development

Dr. Jacques Brunet, *Quebec*
Deputy Minister of Social Affairs, Department of Social Affairs
Province of Quebec
– alternating with –
Dr. Aubert Ouellet, *Quebec*
Assistant Deputy Minister, Department of Social Affairs
Province of Quebec

R.I. Downing, *Victoria, Australia*
Professor, Faculty of Economics and Commerce
University of Melbourne

Dr. J.-J. Dupeyroux, *Paris, France*
Professor, University of Law, Economics and Social Science of Paris

Dr. Gérald Fortin*, *Quebec*
Director, Centre for Urban and Regional Research
National Institute for Scientific Research
University of Quebec

Per Holmberg, *Bromma, Sweden*
Consultant, Research and Statistics on Welfare
Government of Sweden

Dr. Colin J. Hindle, *Ottawa*
Senior Policy Analyst, Planning Branch
Treasury Board
Government of Canada

---

*Co-chairman of the Seminar.

Dr. Israel Katz, *Jerusalem, Israel*
Director General, National Insurance Institute

Dr. Elisabeth Liefmann-Keil, *Saarbrücken, West Germany*
Professor, Department of Economics
University of the Saar

Nicole V. Martin, *Quebec*
Professor, National School of Public Administration
University of Quebec

Dr. S.M. Miller, *New York, U.S.A.*
Director, Urban Center
New York University

Joseph Morris, *Ottawa*
Executive Vice-President, Canadian Labour Congress

C.A. Oram, *Wellington, New Zealand*
Assistant Director-General, Department of Social Welfare
Government of New Zealand

J.H. Perry*, *Toronto*
Executive Director, The Canadian Bankers' Association

Dr. Tom Philbrook, *Toronto*
Professor, Faculty of Environmental Studies
York University

Dr. Eugen Pusić, *Zagreb, Yugoslavia*
Dean, Advanced School of Public Administration
University of Zagreb

Dr. Martin Rein, *Cambridge, Massachusetts, U.S.A.*
Professor, Department of Urban Studies and Planning
Massachusetts Institute of Technology

J.A. Rhind, *Toronto*
President, National Life Assurance Company of Canada

R.S. Ritchie, *Toronto*
Senior Vice-President and Director, Imperial Oil Limited

---

*Co-chairman of the Seminar.

Barbara Rodgers, *Manchester, England*
Reader in Social Administration
Faculty of Economic and Social Studies
University of Manchester

Dr. Vladimir Rys, *Geneva, Switzerland*
International Social Security Association

Helen Salisbury, *Toronto*
Chief, Human Resources Section
Economic Planning Branch
Ministry of Treasury, Economics and Intergovernmental Affairs
Province of Ontario

Dr. Arthur J.R. Smith, *Ottawa*
President, The Conference Board in Canada

Dr. David C. Smith, *Kingston, Ontario*
Professor and Head, Department of Economics
Queen's University

Dr. John C. Spencer, *Edinburgh, Scotland*
Professor and Head, Department of Social Administration
Faculty of Social Sciences
University of Edinburgh

Dr. Gilbert Y. Steiner, *Washington, D.C., U.S.A.*
Director, Governmental Studies Program
The Brookings Institution

Richard M. Titmuss, *London, England*
Professor, Department of Social Science and Administration
London School of Economics and Political Science

Dr. Melville J. Ulmer, *Potomac, Maryland, U.S.A.*
Professor, College of Business and Public Administration
Department of Economics
University of Maryland

Kemal Wassef, *Montreal*
Director, Research Branch
Confederation of National Trade Unions

Dr. J.W. Willard, *Ottawa*
Deputy Minister (National Welfare)
Department of National Health and Welfare
Government of Canada

Dr. David E. Woodsworth, *Montreal*
Director, School of Social Work
McGill University

Dr. Nicolas Zay, *Quebec*
Director, School of Social Work
Laval University

Observers

H.R. Balls, *Ottawa*
Deputy Minister of Services and
Deputy Receiver General for Canada
Department of Supply and Services
Government of Canada

R. Max Beck, *Ottawa*
Director, Opportunities for Youth
Department of the Secretary of State
Government of Canada

Marion H. Bryden, *Toronto*
Research Director, Ontario New Democratic Party Caucus

J.I. Clark, *Ottawa*
Principal Research Officer, Social Security Research Division
Research, Planning and Evaluation (Welfare) Branch
Department of National Health and Welfare
Government of Canada

William Dyson, *Ottawa*
Executive Director, The Vanier Institute of the Family

Mrs. E.G. Etchen, *Toronto*
Director, Research and Planning Branch
Ministry of Community and Social Services
Province of Ontario

John M. Godfrey, Q.C., *Toronto*
Campbell, Godfrey and Lewtas
Barristers and Solicitors

Charles E. Hendry, *Toronto*
Past-President, The Canadian Council on Social Development

Jacques Larin, *Montreal*
Professor, School of Social Work
University of Montreal

F.R. MacKinnon, *Halifax*
Deputy Minister of Public Welfare, Department of Public Welfare
Province of Nova Scotia

Rev. Clifton L. Monk, *Winnipeg*
Executive Secretary, Social Services
Lutheran Council in Canada

Marvin Novick, *Toronto*
Senior Planner, Social Planning Council of Metropolitan Toronto

J.E.E. Osborne, *Ottawa*
Assistant Deputy Minister
Research, Planning and Evaluation (Welfare) Branch
Department of National Health and Welfare
Government of Canada

Dr. Aubert Ouellet, *Quebec*
Assistant Deputy Minister, Department of Social Affairs
Province of Quebec

Michael Wheeler, *Ottawa*
Social Policy Analyst